THE
POISED
CENTURY

THE
POISED
CENTURY

On Living Today As If Tomorrow Mattered

DAVID A. ROBINSON

TOWER
PRESS

THE POISED CENTURY
On Living Today As If Tomorrow Mattered

Published by Tower Press, St. Paul, Minnesota.
www.TowerPressStPaul.com

Printed on demand by CreateSpace. Available at Amazon.com,
TowerPressStPaul.com, and bookstores everywhere.

Cover and book design: Zan Ceeley, Trio Bookworks

Cover Image: *Queen Anne's Lace*, Tom Maakestad, ©2009. Courtesy of Groveland
Gallery, Minneapolis, Minnesota, www.grovelandgallery.com. Choosing a loca-
tion close to his birthplace in Northfield, Minnesota, Maakestad advocates for
the preservation of the undeveloped rural view. The high clouds and long, unclut-
tered horizon honor the natural beauty of the rural Midwestern landscape.

ISBN: 978-1466338838

LCCN: 2011916726

Manufactured in the U.S.A.
16   15   14   13   12   11   1   2   3   4   5   6   7   8   9   10

CONTENTS

PART 3 ✻ WORK AND TRUST

PART 4 ✻ WORK AND TASK

To the Reader

Poised systems need no massive mover to move massively.
—Stuart Kauffman

We have met the enemy and he is us.
—Walt Kelly's Pogo, Earth Day, 1971

This book is about choosing a future we can all live with. It is about daily decision making—decision making that ensures not only our own individual well-being but also the well-being of our communities. Animating such a future will require conscious living from each of us, a new way of life grounded in discernment and conscious decision making. On the far side of America's ever more frenetic, complex, and unsustainable economic and social order lies a conscious and abundant life for all Americans. In this book I offer maps and metaphors we can use to get there.

Stories provide a good way to understand the conscious work we must do to ensure America's future. I'll tell some stories of my own and of others, as well as a few gleaned from the daily news. The value of this book, however, resides not as much in the stories it tells as in the stories we each bring to it. It is our own stories, not those of others, that ground the new work.

Today, America's most pressing problems rise as much from the collective actions of an unconscious citizenry as from the policies of government or the economics of enterprise. Only by increasing our individual consciousness as citizens from whom much will be required can we ensure a sustainable future. My purpose is not to provide definitive solutions to today's problems, but to offer ideas that we may use to examine our own experiences. Thoughtful consideration of our own experiences, not reams of data from me or anyone else, is required of each of us to begin a new and conscious life.

The spirituality of the text reflects my Lutheran upbringing and present engagement with the United Methodist Church. Although today I am far removed from orthodox Christianity, I remain captivated more than ever by the wisdom tradition of Jesus. I speak from a progressive Christian perspective because that is what I know, not because I believe it is the best or only way to be soulful.

My wish has been to write in an invitational rather than an imperative voice. Yet, since passionate invitations may appear imperative, at times my efforts may be lost. I hope that you will not take me to task for this, but will join me in your own soulful search for personal and community transformation.

As you read, keep these matters in mind. Chapter 10 may be read either first or last, as an introduction or summary, as you wish. Endnotes matter and ought to be read along with the text. References and comments are shown by traditional superscripts, like this.[10] Sidebar comments are shown as numbers in parentheses, like this (10), and I particularly recommend that you take a look at them.

Importantly, this is not a self-help book. Although it may enhance our individual lives, I do not intend it to improve our individual ability to cope. Our ability to cope is so well evolved that today our adaptability threatens our very existence as a species. What is required of us today is a transformation of our current individual mindlessness into a new community consciousness from which a new world of abundance may emerge. *The Poised Century* is my offering to the bits and pieces out of which we may construct such a reimagined and mindful world.

Today the world is poised on the brink of a new age, and the quality of this age will be no better than the quality of the daily work we each bring to it. I invite each of you to bring your own bits and pieces to this confusion and to become agents of change in a world where hope is renewed and lives are transformed.

My best wishes go with us all as we get on with this work, the work of the poised century.

David A. Robinson
Saint Paul
October 2011

PART 1

WORK AND TIME

CHAPTER ONE

The Addiction to More

The Hard Work of Laziness

Without work all life goes rotten.
—Albert Camus

The avoiding tendency lies at the very root of American character.
—Philip Slater

Getting and spending, we lay waste our powers.
—William Wordsworth

The Inventor's Dream

Knowing more than anyone could have imagined from his simple manner and greasy overalls, Sumner Sommers visited our physics department on and off over several years, each time seeking assurance that his magic machine was worth betting the farm on. Neatly drawn on shirt cardboards from the local laundry, Mr. Sommers' plans of curved pipes and steam engines presented the inventor's dream—free energy.

With each visit, Mr. Sommers had further honed his idea in the hope that it would yield a more favorable response than "Don't bet on it." And with each visit, on being told that success was not possible, he would graciously accept our verdict and return home to reconsider.

Mr. Sommers' ideas were clever enough that simply trotting out "It won't work because it violates the second law of thermodynamics" seemed inadequate. It too easily dismissed his efforts and too easily provided us with a cover for explaining why it really wouldn't work. Self-taught, Mr. Sommers understood as much as any college physics major about the laws of thermodynamics, and while he accepted the first law that tells us energy is conserved, he had reservations about the second, which holds that energy cannot be got without messing up the order of the universe. And so he, like many others, proceeded undeterred in his dream.[1]

Such dreams are graphically illustrated by M. C. Escher's lithograph *Waterfall*. In this print, Escher shows water flowing continuously upward from the bottom of a waterfall to its top, from where it perpetually drops to power a water wheel.[2] Viewed separately, each straight portion of the water's path appears to flow downward, away from the bottom, but yet, viewed as a whole, the path appears to flow continuously upward, showing us that something is out of place. Escher demonstrates that by separating the parts from their whole, we can come to conclusions that, though we desire, nature denies. With such separation the impossibility of our devices is not always evident, and so we humans begin to bargain with nature herself. What if we reroute the water this way or that, or change the height of the waterfall, or reposition the water wheel? Engaging in such arguments can readily become work itself, and the effort required to make and dismiss them can quickly become as great as the effort that went into the idea in the first place. No matter how clever we are, or how hard we work, we need to accept the realities that the natural order brings to our lives. The inventor must accept that his or her machine, no matter how clever or well oiled, will in time run down and stop, and all of us must accept that, in time, so too shall we.

In her classic work on death and dying, Elisabeth Kübler-Ross identifies five steps that emerge as we deal with the losses of life.[3] Although Kübler-Ross examines the ultimate loss brought by death, her identified human responses to death apply to the lesser losses of life as well. Her responses of denial, anger, bargaining, depression, and acceptance are so well known today that they have become part of the received wisdom. In the case of lesser losses, such as facing the facts of thermodynamics, we move through denial and bargaining, until, after exhausting all possibilities, we go into a funk and finally accept the fact that no matter how clever we are, nothing in this life runs forever. The effort of avoiding our losses will always exceed the effort required to accept them. Avoiding unwanted work always leads to more of the same. This is the hard work of laziness.

Work, Friction, and the Nature of Nature—
A First Lesson from Physics

The desire to get something for nothing seems to be such a part of the human condition that the U.S. Patent Office continues yet today to receive applications for perpetual motion machines. In theory, machines of a certain type violate no known physical law and could actually be built. For example, given perfect bearings and a vacuum environment, a bicycle wheel could be made that, like a planet, would spin on indefinitely. The first law of thermodynamics, which says that energy is conserved, is not violated, since after its initial spin a perfect wheel neither gains nor loses energy. Unfortunately, we know from experience that real wheels eventually do stop because of friction. So while our bicycle wheel may spin for a very long time, eventually it slows and grows warmer through friction; its mechanical energy of spinning becoming the thermal energy of heat, an example of the first law in action. Absent perfection, the wheel simply runs down due to friction.[4]

Beyond the perfect wheel lies a spectrum of all sorts of less perfect inventions that hold the promise of free energy. On one end of this spectrum, the more mechanically minded violate the first law by building machines that convert mechanical or electrical energy to either heat or electricity, or to some other form of mechanical motion with the claim that more energy is got out of the machine than was originally put in. By using a variety of devices to convert input energy to heat, electricity, or motion, such devices at first blush seem to work just fine. Yet thanks to friction and the conservation of energy, they all produce no more energy than they consume.[5]

Such inventiveness appeared during the energy crisis of the 1970s in the form of a so-called hydraulic furnace. In this device, oil was heated by running it through a hydraulic pump driven by an electric motor, with the claim that the heat energy generated by the pump was greater than the electrical energy used by the motor. Yet thanks again to the conservation of energy, such a furnace produces no more or less heat than one would get from a simple electric space heater.

On the other end of the inventor's spectrum lie the more sophisti-
cated, but just as unworkable, inventions of the basement-laboratory scientist. Working from questionable understandings about the nature of
nature, they conjure up ways of extracting energy without consequence.
These inventions can't possibly work either, since such energy extraction
violates the second law of thermodynamics, as we will see in the next
chapter.

We humans find perpetual motion appealing because we all like to
get something for nothing, particularly if it gives us dreams of wealth
and fame for having found something as valuable as a source of unlimited energy. But beyond wealth and fame lies the further attraction that
natural law is not so much given as discovered, and the reason we can
speak of the unworkability of perpetual motion devices is not that we
have proved they cannot work, but that we have never observed one
that has. Such knowledge leads us to the optimistic conclusion that just
because something has never been observed by others does not mean
I may not discover it myself. Indeed, it is such optimistic curiosity that
drives our will to discover in the first place, and our lives, like those of
the scientist, are guided by how we explore and what we expect to find. It
is by being open to surprise that we discover. In the end we are all looking for "perpetual motion," whether as financial freedom in stocks and
bonds, longevity in nutrition and exercise, or life eternal in some better
place.

Finally, what we do know is that, whether they conserve, multiply, or
extract energy, perpetual motion devices produce no more energy than
they consume. They all dissipate energy, and none of them will ever run
perpetually or produce anything more useful than a lesson for us and
their inventors. The nature of nature is to run down, to go from organized motion to disorderly heat. Our challenge today is not to invent ever
more clever ways around what nature allows, but to discern that when the
demands of our dreams meet the reality of nature, nature always wins.
There is no free lunch.

Work, Discernment, and Addiction

Essential to all of human life is the work of discernment, the work of conscious decision making that tells us just what our work ought to be. It is
the effort that leads to meaningful living, and one that most of us would
rather avoid. Let's grab some chips, turn on the TV, and forget it!

Although the work of discernment is always easy enough to avoid, we, like the inventor, cannot avoid the consequences of our actions, whether they spring from intentional choice or not. Today, intentional or not, when we act we most frequently choose work that favors our immediate and personal rather than our future and communal lives. That is, we choose those actions that minimize our present and personal difficulties with scant regard for future consequences. As a simple economic example, our immediate time horizon so discounts future investments that few people will accept energy-saving investments that don't pay for themselves in three years or less. Such investing serves neither the long-term interest of the person spending the money nor the common good of saving fuel for future generations. The failure of the criteria "immediate" and "personal" to serve the common good is one of the central problems of our age (6).

The hard work of laziness, the work of avoiding the unavoidable, is at its worst when we thwart the common good through the assertion of our immediate and personal goals. From breakneck freeway driving to outrageous boardroom conniving, our unrelenting desire for instant gratification frustrates the common good and points to a culture deeply steeped in what can only be called addiction. More prevalent than an ordinary street-corner drug fix, our addiction to the personal and immediate permeates our country and diminishes the civility of our daily life. Worse yet, because it appears in the guise of daily work, we don't even see it as an addiction. Hidden in the very dailiness of our lives, our addiction to the personal and immediate quick fix is our national neurosis, and it is leaving both us and our communities physically, emotionally, and spiritually drained.

Addictions grow from the belief that suffering and pain are never legitimate and must be avoided at all costs. From the work perspectives of this book, addiction shows itself as the hard work of laziness, the neurotic work we do to avoid the existential work of suffering.[7] By defining addiction as work-avoiding behavior, most of us fall under its broad umbrella. As people given to the hard work of laziness, we all need to address the addictions in our own lives. But even with such attention, our lives remain difficult, since the existential or neurotic efforts of either accepting or avoiding life's challenges may at first blush appear to be the same.

For example, at one time in my life I lived along the route of the Twin Cities Marathon. Each October runners from around the world gathered for this highly competitive event, and although their differences in style and speed were obvious, the runners' motivations for being in the race were not. Were the runners, some of whom appeared as if they were punishing themselves, running to affirm life or to avoid it? A casual observer couldn't tell, and perhaps the runners themselves may not have known. The work of knowing the difference between the neurotic avoidance and the existential engagement of life becomes the runner's work of discernment.

For me, there is no easy way to discern the difference between behavior that either accepts or rejects my own life or anybody else's. But I offer here a simple idea from my understanding of the way the world works: sit and watch.[8] As we watch our lives, do the measures of life that we observe show a life in growth or decline? Are our lives moving toward healthy social and physical interdependence or toward physical dependence and social avoidance? In our living, do we postpone immediate and personal pleasure for a greater good, or do we enhance our immediate and personal pleasure without regard to the future? Sitting and watching can be painful as we examine our own values and motivations or as we resist the temptation to rush in with simple and ineffective solutions to the suffering of others. As observers, we need to do our own work of knowing when help for ourselves or others may be either life-affirming or life-rejecting. One very practical return for our own watchful waiting is that the immediate solution we might recommend for others may actually be a good sign of what we need for ourselves. Ouch!

Meaning and Suffering

My purpose here is not to glorify suffering, but to discuss some ways in which we can understand and bring meaning to the inevitable losses that we each experience. The reason for bringing meaning to our suffering is to transform our losses so that our ultimate suffering is reduced. Some losses come swiftly, such as losing our home to a tornado or a fire. Others come more slowly and painfully, such as losing a partner or friend to cancer. Although these losses are not unusual, for each of us they are unwelcome and unexpected. We have no choice about these losses other than how we choose to respond to them.

But in our life journeys, we also experience losses of another kind. These are the expected and necessary losses that come from just being alive. As participants in the natural world, we give through our work to a living system that in turn gives us the resources for our own living. In this way we plant a garden with the hope that it will provide us with food. This exchange between the individual and the living system is what it means to be alive. Because we are a conscious species, we have choices about how we make these necessary exchanges of work between ourselves and the larger natural and social systems of which we are a part. Our work is to select exchanges so that our necessary efforts, our necessary losses, are no greater than they need to be. By properly choosing our necessary and expected work today, we can reduce both our expected and our unexpected work tomorrow. Although our earlier examples of avoiding pain led to the hard work of laziness, our work in this case calls us to be lazy in the best sense of choosing only that work necessary for daily well-being. Given this we can begin to live lives that balance the give-and-take, the literal supply and demand, of our personal resources and lives. Choosing our work, discerning our lives' efforts, is a simple idea, but that does not mean it is easy, or that we do it particularly well. Although we may reduce our ultimate work through our choices, we cannot avoid altogether either our expected or our unexpected losses.

Whether expected or not, when suffering does come to our lives, we each have a choice about what we do with the pain we experience. In *Man's Search for Meaning*, Viktor Frankl described his own suffering as a prisoner in the concentration camp at Auschwitz. Externally reduced to an expendable number, Frankl survived the experience by visualizing himself "standing on the platform of a well-lit, warm and pleasant lecture room. . . . I was giving a lecture on the psychology of the concentration camp!" By choosing to see himself as a survivor, Frankl survived. This does not diminish the courage or character of the many who did perish, for no one's life was secure under the circumstances that Frankl experienced. But Frankl did maintain faith in his future, a faith that if lost would have led to his mental and physical deterioration. Frankl's life demonstrates that even under the most extraordinary and dehumanizing circumstances, one can still choose to act as a survivor. Frankl said of his experiences, "I succeeded somehow in rising above the situation, above the sufferings of the moment, and I observed them as if they were already of the past."[9]

By forming a picture of his future life based on his prisoner experience, Frankl brought meaning to the suffering of the concentration camp. Like Frankl, whatever our condition, we have the choice of either "rising above" our problems or being so captured by them that we remain unable to bring any meaning or goodness to our lives. Each day we encounter opportunities for the future that require sacrifices from the present. The daily decisions that value the future over the present are the single most important factor in shaping the lives we lead. By choosing the future and communal over the immediate and personal, we can all bring meaning to our daily work.

Suffering and Recovery

One of the best measures of the extent of personal suffering in America is the growing variety of personal recovery groups. A recent count in my local area shows thirty-seven different types of groups offering programs for what seems to be an ever-expanding list of addictions—drugs, food, spending, gambling, shoplifting, sex, and more. The recent growth in the number of recovery groups and the variety of afflictions represented is more than a sign of personal suffering in the lives of people. It is a sign that we live in a culture that not only accommodates addiction, but invites it.

Placed in the men's room of a tony suburban delicatessen was this advertisement for a swimming pool company: "Until there's a cure for bills, traffic, deadlines." In short, until there is a cure for life, calm your cares away with our pool. Offered here is a recreational reprieve from life, an invitation to sit poolside drinking margaritas while waiting for Godot. This wonderfully appealing image invites us into addiction by offering us a reprieve from the work of owning and solving our problems.

The pool ad becomes a metaphor for our lives in America when it calls for a "cure" to the dailiness of life. But there is no cure for our daily work, and since there is no cure, there can be no recovery either. The ad reflects a culture that fails to value or even tolerate the personal toil of daily living. By encouraging a low tolerance for the ordinary, the ads that surround us seduce us into believing that life is something to be recovered from. Yet the cure for the dailiness of life lies not in recovery, but in the social transformations that bring meaning to daily living.

The intrinsic value of all recovery programs is their potential for creating the social transformations that will make them unnecessary. My friend Jean sees people "getting honest" and "walking the talk and not just talking the talk" much more often in twelve-step groups than in other work or social groups, including many churches. For those who join and do the work of really "walking the talk," group programs offer a legitimization of the problems of daily living that is hard to find elsewhere. The potential for such group processes is that they can transform individuals who then can transform their larger communities.

Like the work of the runner, the work of recovery may be either life-affirming or life-avoiding. Required again is watchful waiting to see if our lives are growing toward owning or avoiding the dailiness of life. In his teachings on addiction and recovery, Earnie Larsen defines the work of discernment in the recovery process when he divides recovery work into two stages. Stage one of recovery is to give up the primary addictive substance or behavior. But with this done, Larsen contends, recovery has just begun. The next stage, stage two, is to reconnect to ourselves, to those around us, and to God. In short, Larsen identifies stage-two recovery as "learning to love."[10] Failure to move from stage one to stage two results in no recovery at all. If the work of stage-two recovery is not done, then the recovery program becomes nothing more than a holding pattern for life.

The holding pattern that Larsen identifies is the hard work of laziness. With this the recovery program becomes another quick fix, and the program itself a new addiction. The work of owning our suffering is replaced with the busyness of going to another meeting. And when the recovery program becomes an addiction, the recovery process itself becomes socially dangerous. Rather than turning us from our addictions, such recovery may make our problems so tolerable that we fail to confront them. The social danger arises when the avoidance of existential suffering offered by the group leads to ever-greater neurotic suffering by the individual and society at large.

The avoidance of suffering becomes further institutionalized when therapy or drugs are used to avoid stage-two recovery. In *Beyond Therapy, Beyond Science*, Anne Wilson Schaef charges that the helping professions are active in this process because they have become "systematic enablers to an addictive society."[11] Others are debating the value of using antidepressants for what Peter Kramer, in *Listening to Prozac*, calls "cosmetic psychopharmacology."[12] To these issues we again need to bring the work of discernment. For some people, therapy or medication might be an existential blessing that allows them to reconnect to the world. For others, they might be just another neurotic response to the unavoidable suffering and losses of life. The danger here is not so much to the individual as to society at large. Therapies or drugs that make our personal and social pain tolerable may so reduce our built-in biological survival response that they invite extinction. Whether we choose therapy or drugs for ourselves is not as important as learning to live with the pain of remaining a fully conscious member of a larger social order.

Meaning and the Material

Most of us believe that we do our daily work so well that we could not possibly be addicted to anything at all. We get up and go to work each morning, work hard enough to please the boss and the customers, and at the end of the day pay our bills and hang up our clothes. We obey the law, vote, and do good works. We eat the right kind of food, live in a decent place, and love our friends and families. As engaged people we wish for lives like those we see in the romantic, adventurous, or well-appointed images that beckon from our televisions or coffee-table magazines.

Yet when we examine our daily round, we find a different truth. We don't lead the soft-focus life of the latest home-and-garden magazine or television ad; instead, we find that our life has sharper edges and is more complex and messier. The images appeal to us because they show us what we wish our lives to be: attractive and problem-free. The slick images that surround our daily lives seduce us with the bargain that our lives could be something better, if only we could have what they show. We find these images appealing because they bring meaning to the dailiness of our lives by offering us relief from it.

The images, in short, offer us meaning in the material. And when the material fails to bring meaning to our lives, we are led to addiction, an addiction not to a substance or unworkable relationship, but to possessions themselves. We believe that as soon as we get a name-the-possession we will be okay. Here the hard work of laziness becomes the work of accumulating ever more of the material.

From the enormous amount of wealth that Americans accumulate and display today, I can only conclude that we are a people addicted to the accumulation of material possessions. This argument could be dismissed if there was some proportionality between what we possess and what we need for life. But families with houses so large that members need not see each other, children with more toys than they can play with in a year, and households with more vehicles than drivers convince me that something is wrong with the way we live in America. Isolated from each other and the natural order, we participate in a self-perpetuating cycle of getting and spending that seems to know no end. Rich in material things but poor in contentment, we accumulate ever more stuff, hoping to find meaning, if not in others, then at least in our possessions. Today, America is a nation addicted to the accumulation of more.

The Addiction to More

I once asked a colleague frustrated by his lot in life what he really wanted. The answer was swift and simple: "More." But the simple response of "more" raises two further questions: "More of what?" and "How much more do we need before it actually *feels* like more?"

For many of us today the answer to "More of what?" seems to be more of everything—money, power, sex, houses, cars, boats—the list goes on. I am not questioning the desire for such things as adequate food and clothing or a simple, decent place to live. But what we must question is the deep-seated American belief that more is always better and that our individual self-worth is measured by how much we accumulate. For Americans today, this attitude is captured by the bumper sticker: "He who dies with the most toys wins." Here life is defined as a competitive race to the end, an end that is measured only by what can be purchased and possessed. It is in this race that accumulation itself becomes addictive, since the more we compete, the more we want, and the more we want, the more we compete to acquire yet more. In the end, the answer to "More of what?" is less important than understanding our desire for ever more of the material in the first place.

Beyond our desire for more, the second question, "How much more actually feels like more?" can be answered somewhat generally. Most simply it depends on how much we already have. For example, if I own one pair of shoes and I buy another, I double, increase by 100 percent, the number of shoes I own. But if I already own ten pairs of shoes and I buy one more pair, the satisfaction is far less, since I have increased the number of shoes I own by only 10 percent. To feel like "more," a new possession needs to increase what we have not by a constant amount, but by a constant percent. The more we have, the more we need to feel satisfied. And, by always requiring a constant percent increase in whatever we are accumulating, we quickly compound our possessions in just the same way that a savings account compounds our money.

Our recent history of compounding wealth goes a long way toward explaining the current malaise in the United States. In 1946, just after World War II, my father bartered some batteries and got us our first second car. It made my mother happy, since it was her first car, and it made all of us feel better off, since we had just doubled the number of cars we owned. For the next fifteen years, many families purchased cars for the first time, and many others purchased their first second car. The relative growth in wealth that we experienced during that time was unprecedented. Automobiles, dishwashers, televisions, automatic clothes washers and dryers flooded the marketplace and flowed into the homes of America. The percent rate of increase of these goods reached an all-time high, and Americans reported the greatest happiness in their lives.[13] Our first cars created a great sense of well-being; second cars then shaped our expectations as they doubled the number of cars we owned. Today, because we are far wealthier than we were after World War II, we need to accumulate far more new possessions in order to have the same sense of well-being. With far more work required to compound our material wealth, the satisfaction of accumulating "more" just isn't what it used to be.[14]

Choice and Meaning

The ever-increasing work required to compound our material wealth has not diminished our addiction to "more." Rather than reducing our addiction to the material, we have turned to more of the same, except better, and if not better, at least different. In place of more of the material, we now seek greater quality or more choice. The qualities and choices offered vary widely. Some add to our lives, while others offer no more than gratuitous diversion. Needed again is the work of discernment to tell which "new and improved" product is really new or improved. For example, many of the advanced safety and performance features on today's automobiles are genuine technical improvements that make the autos of the 1950s seem primitive by comparison. But automakers also offer amenities that go far beyond what is required to simply get from A to B.

Other new products seem so meaningless that they appear to be designed only to provide an illusion of choice, an illusion that readily accommodates our addiction to more. A full-page ad in the *Wall Street Journal* for Nabisco Brands, Inc., illustrates the point. In a signed message, Nabisco's CEO announces that the company has just won a coveted marketing award for introducing one of the year's top new products, a graham cracker in the shape of a teddy bear. The message concludes, "At Nabisco we know that new product success comes from the astute marketing of deceptively simple ideas."[15] The purpose of this example is not to question Nabisco for wanting to make a dollar, but to ask why they were so successful at it.[16]

By offering a proliferation of superfluous choices, the Nabiscos of the world offer each of us a way to avoid making the more difficult yet more meaningful daily choices that we do have. Rather than accepting that our lives may be routine or even at times—God forbid—boring, today's merchants of more offer each of us the bargain of a more exciting life through an ever-increasing number of ever more unnecessary choices.[17] Here the hard work of being lazy is to keep busy with consumer market choices, hoping that tomorrow we will find meaning in whatever the market has to offer.

Today's proliferation of choices readily accommodates our reluctance to do the work of discernment. The neurotic work of being seduced and sold keeps us from the reality that all the products in the world will not make us what the advertisers would have us believe—thin, rich, and beautiful. But by suffering this, we each can come to the peace and understanding that we all have worth far beyond the hopes and dreams of those who seduce our souls with the myth of the material.

CHAPTER TWO

The Ultimate Limit to More

Time

What is time then?
As the future, it is possibility;
as the past, it is the bond of fidelity;
as the present, it is decision.
—Karl Jaspers

For everything there is a season,
and a time for every matter under heaven.
—Ecclesiastes 3:1

Live the questions now. Perhaps then, someday far in the future, you will
gradually, without even noticing it, live your way into the answer.
—Rainer Maria Rilke

Work and Discernment

"Bake on Saturday."

This homespun recommendation neatly embroidered on the corner of our kitchen towel speaks to a simpler time of hearth and home. We see the words but forget the wood chopped and hauled for the fire, the water pumped for the dough, and the sameness of each week. We dream of the good old days, forgetting what life would be like without gas and electricity, running water, and the convenience of the neighborhood bakery.

Today, "Bake on Saturday" has been replaced with a note to stop for bread on the way home from work. Yet more has been replaced than Saturday baking: we have replaced the work of household living with the work of earning and spending. We have traded our time for money, and like all trades, it may be either good or bad. Like all trades, whatever their nature, discernment is required to know the difference.

Since discernment takes time of its own, it is easy to put off the work of discovering just what our work ought to be. When brought up in group discussion, the very concept is often dismissed with comments such as, "If I spent my time doing the work of discernment, I wouldn't have any time left for life." Missing is the recognition that much of the work of life *is* discernment and that the lives we lead grow from the choices we make, whether they are discerning or not.

The value of discernment was made apparent to me when I began working in solar design. At that time, large, complex, and therefore costly systems were being used to heat ordinary houses. The question being asked then was, "How do you use solar energy to heat a house?" For me a more proper question was, "How do you use solar energy to heat a house for least cost?" The short answer turned out to be remarkably simple: spend as much money on saving energy as providing it. That is, over any given period of time, spend as much money on insulation as energy. Surprisingly, thanks to the cost effectiveness of insulation, when money is invested this way, a house requires so little energy to heat that the optimal solar system for a modest house consists of little more than a few south-facing patio doors.[1] Because of its simplicity and low cost, such superinsulated design has never been particularly well received by those building professionals whose livelihoods seem to favor the complex and costly over the simple and inexpensive.[2]

Asking the right questions requires discernment. For this book our central question is, "What must we do now so that we may have a desirable life in the future?" The quality of our lives can be no greater than the quality of the questions we bring to them.

Diversion and Dialogue

Finding a balance between time and money in today's economy results in more than just a trade-off between time and the amount of stuff we own. When we tire of working and spending, we trade what time and money we do have left for diversions offered by others. Rather than filling our space with more of the material, we fill our time with diversionary activity. With this choice we transform ourselves from participants in life to people who vicariously consume whatever the market supplies. Rather than cooking a meal or taking a walk, we go out for fast food or watch a game on TV. And rather than talking with one another, we remotely view our collective life by watching the ten o'clock news.

The social danger of passive participation is that it reduces our dialogue with others. Without conversation our common ground becomes less well known and our capacity for community problem solving is diminished. An important exception to this occurs when the diversionary activity becomes art that invites us to examine our lives so that both our work and that of the community are enhanced. In this case, art becomes socially transforming not by diverting us from the work of life, but by engaging us in it. The work of the writer, composer, painter, playwright, musician, or actor is to inform us about ourselves and our lives by keeping life itself before us. In this way artists and performers add immeasurably to the civility of our communities.

Since we may pass our time either mindfully or mindlessly, choosing our diversions becomes yet another exercise in discernment. Do we consciously choose mindless activity to enliven and refresh our lives between times of more mindful work? Or do we always pursue the mindless, ever hopeful that the harder work of life can be avoided indefinitely? For example, like the marathon of chapter 1, television can just as well provide existential engagement as neurotic avoidance, depending on why and how much we watch it. As one of today's most popular diversions, television may be our most popular drug. But whether television, or for that matter alcohol, shopping, or even running, is a drug or not depends on what we make of it.

As time goes by, we constantly choose how we will spend not only our next dollar, but also our next minute, hour, or day. The criteria we apply to make these choices about time are the same as those we apply to the material—we choose those pastimes that most increase our immediate and personal pleasure. Beyond grabbing some chips and turning on the TV, we also keep our problems at bay by keeping busy with a myriad of other activities. Activity in school sports, church, and social and political organizations can easily consume all our waking hours. And even though we are with people in all these activities, by their very busyness, they can diminish the sharing of significant ideas, beliefs, or feelings. In short, such activity may readily become more about doing than being.

One way to experience being is to be in dialogue. *Dialogue* comes from the Greek words *dia*, which means "through," and *logos*, which means "word" or "speech." Thus to be in dialogue is to connect with others through conversation. For example, as a personal reality check while writing this book, I participated in a variety of study groups to help keep me grounded. As a member of each group, I became a neuron in its collective brain, allowing it to form a mind of its own, one more capable of reflecting the group's thoughts than any individual. By engaging in dialogue, each group could form a conscious entity of its own, an entity that through its participants could then become a part of the larger social fabric.

Physicist David Bohm wrote on the force of dialogue in forming group consciousness this way.

> Some time ago there was an anthropologist who lived for a long while with a North American tribe, a small group of twenty to forty. Now, from time to time the tribe met in a circle. They just talked and talked, apparently to no purpose. They made no decisions. There was no leader. And everybody could participate. There may have been wise men or wise women who were listened to a bit more—the older ones—but everybody could talk. The meeting went on, until it finally seemed to stop for no reason at all and the group dispersed. Yet after that, everybody seemed to know what to do, because they understood each other so well. Then they could get together in smaller groups and do something or decide things.[3]

Bohm describes the power of dialogue in the conduct of collective life. The value of such dialogue is that it leads to a shared group consciousness that allows the group to act in new and unexpected ways. By enhancing the understanding between people, group dialogue enhances group consciousness, and through this it builds the problem-solving capacity of the community.

The difference between dialogue and diversion is that over a period of time, dialogue enhances our social order, while diversion, with the exception of art, at best leaves the social order unchanged. Our work is to carefully choose our diversions, whether mindless or not, so that they enhance not only our personal lives, but the civility of our communities as well.

Work, Disorder, and Time

In chapter 1, I told the story of Mr. Sommers and his perpetual motion machine. Ideally such a machine would spin a shaft while at the same time cooling the air around itself. At first glance the idea appears plausible, since energy is conserved and the first law of thermodynamics is not violated. That is, the machine is not producing something for nothing, since the energy made available in the spinning shaft has simply been extracted from the air around it. With such a machine Mr. Sommers could cool his house and use the spinning shaft to run an electrical generator that would, in exchange, heat the kitchen range. The energy would go from heat in the house, to a spinning shaft, to electricity, to cooking heat, and finally back to heat in the house to start the cycle all over again, just as desired for perpetual motion. However, as attractive as this prospect might be, the second law of thermodynamics tells us that it has never been observed and that the world does not work this way.

The reason such a machine does not work is that heat energy is of a lower quality than the mechanical energy of the spinning shaft. The heat energy in the house comes from the random, agitated motion of the air molecules in the house. The electrical energy from the generator comes from the mechanical energy of the spinning shaft of the machine. In the first case, the motion is disordered, random, and not useful for doing work; in the second case, the motion is orderly and can do work by turning an electrical generator. Unfortunately, the second law of thermodynamics states that the transformation of low-quality heat energy into nothing but high-quality mechanical energy has never been observed and that such a machine does not exist. Most simply, the second law says that it is impossible to build an engine that changes heat completely into work. That is, there is no machine that can change the low-temperature heat of the house into the high-temperature heat of the kitchen range. This confirms our everyday observation that, left to themselves, things go from hot to cold, not the reverse.

Practical engines like steam turbines that are used to generate electricity do convert heat into useful work, but they do this by lowering the temperature of steam and discharging unused heat at a lower temperature. Such engines have working efficiencies of 25 to 50 percent; that is, they convert 25 to 50 percent of the boiler fuel's energy into work and discharge the rest as heat into the environment. Because of this, your local power plant may keep the river next to it free of ice all winter.

The reason these practical engines work is that they create orderly energy (electricity) by discharging disorderly energy (heat) to the environment. The orderly energy of the spinning turbine can only be got through the destruction of the original order between the hot flame of the boiler fuel and cold water of the river. Yet, in time, even the orderly energy of the electricity becomes nothing but disorderly heat. Electricity first begins to degrade when it is sent out over power lines that act as low-temperature toaster elements, converting a little electricity to heat. The electrical energy may then go to a substation, where the voltage of the electricity is reduced and a little more energy is lost. Nearby you can hear the transformers hum as some electricity is converted to sound, and see radiator fins that dissipate the heat resulting from the inefficiency of the transformers. From here the electricity may go to a factory where bulbs are lit and motors are powered. Yet, even as they light the factory and move the production line, because of their own inefficiencies, the bulbs and motors of the factory produce heat of their own. In the end, even the light and motion of the factory degrades into thermal dust. The light bounces around the factory until it cannot be seen, and the energy of motion dissipates until all of the original electricity has been reduced to heat. In terms of the second law of thermodynamics, the energy degrades from being more useful to less useful, from being more ordered to less ordered. This is nature's most fundamental and inescapable law.

By talking about order and disorder in general without reference to any specific machine or process, we can begin to talk most basically about how nature works. Here scientists use a physical measure of order called entropy. Entropy is a measure of the number of ways that something can be arranged. A disorderly room can be arranged in more ways than an orderly room, as the parent of any teenager knows. Because of this, the disorder or entropy of a messy room is greater than the disorder or entropy of a tidy room.

As much as we might wish, messy rooms do not spontaneously organize themselves. Thanks to the second law, straightening up or reducing the entropy of messy rooms requires work. Given this, entropy becomes a useful measure for the effectiveness of our work. Genuine work brings order to our lives, while the hard work of laziness simply rearranges our messes and leaves our lives as disordered as when we started. We can now describe discernment as the work that allows us to tell the difference between work that actually brings order to our lives and that which merely rearranges our messes. For example, some people live hand-to-mouth disordered lives of constantly getting into and out of debt, while others, through experience, learn to manage their earning and spending in ways that enhance life's quality and order.

We now come up against the ultimate limit to more—the time required to organize all the stuff of our lives. In America today we have so much stuff that we are running out of time to store, maintain, repair, and use all the stuff that we own. When we have so much stuff that it detracts from our lives, we have met the entropy or clutter limit of accumulation. The work of keeping our clutter at bay consumes our lives as we rent space in the local mini-storage to supplement our basements and garages that have become full of material goods little used. With our cars parked in the driveway, we buy and save everything in sight, hoping that greater security or happiness will be ours. But happiness and security lie not in the material clutter of our lives, but in the human diversity of our communities.

To put your stuff on a time scale, try this experiment. Imagine moving everything in your home (including the clutter!) to someplace outside. With a few friends, you might be able to do the job in a day. Now imagine doing a similar exercise with a family living in a lower-income country of the world. Out would come a few pots and pans, a blanket or two, and maybe a small cooking stove. If the family were less poor, there might be some beds, a sewing machine, or a bicycle. The better-off might bring out a small refrigerator, a television set, or even a motorcycle or compact car. Most families in the world could move out everything they own in a matter of minutes, not hours.[4] Although beds or a refrigerator would improve the well-being of a poor family, can we honestly say there is anything that if added to our own hoard would truly add to our lives? The pile of stuff that each of us could put in front of our houses represents a gold mine of time, happiness, and serenity. All we have to do is let it go.[5]

Time, Consumption, and Meaning

The ultimate limit to more—time—is itself limited by the fact that there are only twenty-four hours in a day. Because a day is just a day long, only so much time is available for earning, consuming, and if you can afford it, sleeping. As people who economically optimize our personal use of resources, we balance our hours worked to earn money with our free time to spend it. Given this, we become economically optimum earners/ consumers when we work for one-half our waking hours and consume for the other half. Thus, with sixteen waking hours in a typical day, our eight-hour work day remains robust even though our industrial productivity continues to soar. Given the choice between time and money, we choose money.[6]

By choosing money over time, we maximize our ability to consume while reducing our leisure time to a minimum. This not only feeds our consumption habit but also makes the amount of time we have to think about it as small as possible, an ideal system for maintaining our consumerism. Changing our American work-and-spend habit will not be easy, because our choices are limited by the system we are trying to change. Yet, even though we may have limited choices about our work, we all have choices about how we spend. Whether we are poor or rich, basic foods cost less and are better for us, and living in a small house requires less work and expense than living in a large one.[7]

Reducing consumption requires new ways of doing our work and using our resources. It requires time, talent, tools, and most of all, interest. Tools may mean pots and pans or drills and screwdrivers, a cookbook or home repair manual, or helpful advice, all useful. For example, although today's cars have gotten too complex for easy repair, a shop manual to help me figure out what the problem might be makes it more likely that any problem will be fixed correctly the first time, and for a reasonable cost. Some things I still repair, such as the cord on our iron or the carburetor on our lawn mower. Still, time and tools are required for such work, and for the time spent, most savings are slim.

But if the dollar savings are scant, I am rewarded by the satisfaction of having an iron or lawn mower that should last many more years.[8] Not everybody can do this. Many don't have the skill, interest, and, yes, the time. But being informed about the ordinary can give each of us a sense of satisfaction and even that certain sense of control we need to keep our lives sane.

For example, I have known people who paid plumbers generously for simple repairs, repairs that with minimum skill and a few dollars in parts, they could have made themselves in only minutes. Although many people can afford such services, simple knowledge would have led them to a less expensive result. But more important than savings is that such knowledge keeps us grounded in the ordinary. I am not suggesting that everyone should plumb the depths of his or her soul through a properly performing faucet, but I do believe that by keeping ourselves grounded in the ordinary, we greatly enhance our ability to connect with the earth and one another. Some might plant a flower or vegetable garden, cook a fine meal, or play in a community band, while others might offer the gift of just being who they are. Today as we have turned more and more of our lives over to the experts—over to external authority—we have lost much of the grounding that is essential to our very survival. By not understanding where things come from or how they work, we set ourselves up for the rude awakenings of chapter 8.

Although we all must make choices about how we consume, those with the most money have the most choices. In 2008 the top 20 percent of U.S. households had a mean income of $171,000 a year and accrued 50 percent of all the income in the country.[9] But even with the opportunities for leisure-and-saving that come with outsized wealth, the top 20 percent are just as readily caught in the insidious cycle of work and spend. Rich Americans, like other consumers, have become "addicted to the accoutrements of affluence," and feel as financially strapped as the rest of us—the four out of five of us who earn the other half of America's income.[10] In the end, the wealth that provides choice leads to decisions that actually reduce choice. If you have a modest income, you spend the Fourth of July relaxing at a public park. If you're rich, you feel obligated to go to your mortgaged cabin, where you either mow the lawn or find someone to do it for you. Few, regardless of income, seem to choose the abundance of time and money that comes from simply living beneath one's means.

Time and Value

One of the reasons we accumulate things is that we believe that they will be of greater value in the future. Some might buy home furnishings, original art, or handwoven rugs with the anticipation of growing pleasure. Others might invest in stocks, bonds, or real estate in the hope that what they buy today will be worth more tomorrow. Still others—most of us, I suspect—accumulate stuff because we never know when we might need it.

The expectation of growth is a given of our culture, and is one supported by many economists who cannot imagine an economy that is not growing.[11] We invest with the expectation of growth, with the expectation that we will have more wealth tomorrow than today. The idea of growth, and in particular constant growth, becomes institutionalized when we expect investments such as stocks and bonds or certificates of deposit to offer investment growth sufficient to attract our money, sufficient to yield a real return beyond inflation.

Yet a culture that expects constant growth is fundamentally at odds with an equitable economy on a finite planet. Either the planet will be overrun with the accoutrements of wealth, or a few superwealthy will have all the money. Neither end serves the common good. Although today it seems we universally expect constant growth, the notion that our finite world can accommodate the unlimited growth of anything, material or not, is an idea that is no longer possible or even desirable (12). With the expectation of constant growth, time enhances inequality and reduces the social coherence that comes from a more uniform distribution of wealth.[13]

In his book *Bowling Alone*, Robert Putnam presents numerous examples showing that life is better in those states possessing a high degree of what is called social capital. States with high social capital, that is, states exhibiting high levels of trust and of civic and social engagement, are consistently the same states that have an enhanced environment for children, better public health, less violent crime, and, perhaps most important, greater income equality.[14] Putnam reports that America's social capital is on the decline and speculates on a variety of reasons for it: changes in work, housing sprawl, long-term generational change, and entertainment, particularly television. My belief is that much of today's social distress as measured by America's declining social capital is produced by our ever-widening income gap, a gap that both allows for and encourages the changes cited by Putnam.[15] I will return to this idea at the end of the chapter.

Although we expect to have more money in the future than now, we still value the present more than the future. For example, given two identical appliances, except that one costs a bit more and uses 30 percent less energy than the other, most people will buy the less expensive appliance, even though, thanks to energy savings, the more expensive one would cost less in the long run. Yet "the longer run" is not very long at all, since the payback period for savings from an efficient appliance can be as short as two years. Here the consumer is offered a no-risk investment that returns a 50 percent interest rate, and they refuse the deal. Similarly, given the choice between identical houses with the same price, except that one uses far less energy and the other has an upscale kitchen, most people will take the house with the upscale kitchen. Both examples demonstrate that given a choice, we prefer the personal and the immediate over the communal and the future.

Each of these examples is based on the application of a large discount rate to future events (16). When I have mentioned this phenomenon, particularly to those whose business is finance, it is commonly met with the reaction that "we'll cross that bridge when we come to it." Inherent in this response is the belief that material and financial resources will be available to solve whatever problems today's lack of foresight might bring to us tomorrow, that we will somehow recover tomorrow whatever we lay waste to today. Even though such wishful thinking is supported and shared by many people, it is one of our most dangerous assumptions about what will happen to value as time passes.

Beyond applying a large discount rate to things future, we apply a small discount rate to things past. Things past retain value because we believe that in the future they may be of use to us. So in our attics and garages we find the carpet we replaced fifteen years ago and the child-hood bicycle of the recent college graduate. Our irrational internal discount rates are a measure of our resistance to the passage of time. By valuing the past and discounting the future, we hope to stop time in its tracks and remain in a present that we want to believe we can understand and control.

Making Time

Time is of such value today that we will use any means to get more of it. The *Wall Street Journal* once described a number of one-handed devices as the newest gadgets to help make time. As one advocate said, devices such as a one-handed egg beater allow a person to "pack as much into the day" as possible.[17] Presumably while the right hand is busy with one task, the left may be kept busy with another, allowing us to, say, beat an egg while checking our email. Multiplying the user's effectiveness by a factor of two can thus double the number of working hours in the day. Today we can talk on the phone while we drive, place one telephone conversation on hold while we answer a second, watch two programs on the same TV screen, or jog while listening to a presentation on how to better make love or money. By shrinking and multiplying the devices that give us access to all of the information flying through our lives, we are led to believe that we have gained an advantage of actually adding time to our days.[18]

Today, because information is so readily available, we believe, as with much else in our lives, that more is better. By filling our lives with more and more information, we make ourselves feel better prepared for tomorrow, while what tomorrow requires is not more information, but more thought.

Keeping Time

Earlier I called for us to spend time "sitting and watching" to see what is going on. In order to make such observations, the observer's clock must tick along at the same rate as that of the activity observed, or else important information will be missed. If my house were on fire, I would call 911. Such fast oxidation occurs in minutes and is clearly visible: bright flames, smoke, and heat make it clear that my house is burning. Less apparent are the many houses falling apart due to corrosion or rot, slow oxidation or biological growth, processes so gradual that they go unnoticed until a pipe springs a leak or the piano falls through the living room floor.[19]

On a personal time scale, if we are open to being careful observers, we can watch changes in ourselves and others, since we all share the same clock. We can keep records and compare what we see this year with what we saw last year. This is the value of keeping medical reports, personal journals, or records of when plants bloom in the spring. But if things move too fast, they can only be seen using methods such as high-speed photography or fast electronic detection. These techniques allow us to see bullets going through apples or atoms "beating" as they absorb or radiate energy. Such technology has given us the lasers that check out our groceries and the computers that process our words.

However, when things move so slowly that changes are not readily apparent, the ability to get useful information requires more than technology. Is the temperature of the earth's biosphere increasing? Is the ozone layer that protects us from the ultraviolet radiation of the sun increasing or decreasing? These are difficult questions to answer, since over shorter periods of time such quantities may fluctuate irregularly, while over longer periods their average values may be either growing or declining. For example, much of today's global warming discussion hinges on whether or not our observations reflect either a natural fluctuation or a long-term trend in global temperature. In this case, we need to understand that the only way to tell the difference between a fluctuation and a trend is to sit and watch. Only time will tell.

Most people would agree with this idea. But how long must we wait and watch before we act? And when we do act, what and how large, should our response be? Most people today look at these problems and ask whether or not the quantity in question is increasing, and depending on how the data are used, people can get a variety of answers. Standard statistics does not serve us well here, since the experiments we are doing today cannot be repeated in the laboratory. For example, we cannot collect data for policy analysis and implementation by conducting repeated global warming experiments. Global warming is an example of a one-time experiment—a one-time experiment of large consequence. The longer we watch, the more data we have, and the more likely our observations will be true. But we cannot wait and watch forever. At some time, based on some criteria, we need to act.

The problem of when to stop looking and start acting was addressed in 1763 by the Reverend Thomas Bayes, an English clergyman and amateur mathematician. Bayes' work made the hidden subjectivity of when to stop taking data visible by allowing an experimenter to start with some subjective, guessed at, probability as to the truth of the matter under study. With Bayesian analysis the purpose of an experiment is to collect data that can be used to calculate whether the initial probability of truth is getting larger or smaller as the experiment proceeds. The Bayesian result of any experiment then depends not only on some subjective starting probability as to what the truth is, but also on how long one spends seeking it. Although the Bayesian method is taught as a part of advanced statistics courses, its acknowledgment that statistical inference is subjective has not made it popular.

If we are going to act on issues such as global warming, it will be essential to acknowledge the subjectivity of our science and the need to act on incomplete data. The value of Bayes' a priori subjectivity is that the results of any ongoing experiment may be observed as time goes by to see if something, for example global warming, is getting better or worse. In contrast to standard statistics, in which the investigator decides when to stop taking data and report a result, Bayesian statistics yields an ongoing result that can be used at any time as a reason to act.[20] By keeping the possibility of global warming rather than a yes-or-no conclusion in the public discourse, we would all be in a better position to affect policy.[21]

Time, Discernment, and Consciousness

Meaningful living requires that we bring meaning to the passage of time. Each moment in time invites us into a decision that either affirms or denies our life, and with each decision, intentional or not, we act in ways that carry our life from the present into the future. The quality of the discernment that we bring to these daily decisions is the single greatest determinant in the quality of life we lead.

Times goes by. Things change. This happens without any work on our part, and although we may resist the flow of time, we cannot avoid its consequences. How we discern the consequences of the flow of time lies at the core of the survivability of our species. Today our survival is at risk because we remain much as we were when our ancestors walked out of Africa fifty thousand years ago. Our survival response today is the same as it was then. We respond to the danger of the moment, to the leap of the tiger, all the while expecting the larger world to be the same year after year.[22]

Out of this evolved sense of time comes a false security about the nature of nature that is leading us to extinction.[23] For example, primed for the tiger, we survive in a jungle of competitive driving, all the while keeping our cars filled with fuel, never thinking that today's fuel is finite and that tomorrow's is yet to be developed. We continue to believe as we did millennia ago that the world is a place uniform in time, and that our work is not to worry about tomorrow, but to remain primed for the tiger today.

Our species has been enormously successful in its domination of the planet. So successful that today we believe the planet will continue to be good to us no matter what we do to it. But like bugs in a petri dish that evolve and then pass from the scene, we too could also evolve and pass from this place. In fact, for a remote observer of planet Earth, there would be little reason to expect a species primed for the tiger to have much else happen to it. Mindless of the disorder required to create our wealth, we live in ways that threaten our very existence. With our ever-growing and interconnected population, we could deforest the planet, reduce our soil to inert minerals, alter the way ocean or air currents carry energy around the earth, or act as a host for some smart bug that might make our petri dish his.

The fact that I can write these things and that you can read them is of course cause for hope. This book and many similar efforts today show that as a species we have a great resource that the bugs in the petri dish do not have—consciousness. Given consciousness, we have the capacity for conscious evolution, the ability to look at our own actions, see their effect on ourselves and the world, and then act in new ways that will change our course from extinction to sustainability. As a reader of this book, you are a participant in this learning process. So am I. I can write this book today because of the material and cultural wealth of our country, and while I could just as well say the hell with it, I have chosen to write about what I think needs to be said. Surrounded with material things—a house, a home office, a word processor, a fine neighborhood library, and nine colleges and universities—I have resources made abundant by the very system I question. The irony of our common lot today is that the wealth and technology that threatens our very survival may, with conscious living, redeem us all.

Time to Live

Saving ourselves and the world from mindless extinction will be no simple trick, since it will require a growing consciousness not only within each of us, but within our communities as well. Earlier I told of belonging to a number of loosely organized study groups. They were mostly an opportunity to read something, to participate in group dialogue, and to have some coffee. Beyond this there was no agenda other than to grow in understanding of one another and of the idea of the day. Members often cited the pleasure of attending a meeting where no agenda was followed, no notes were kept, and no decisions were made. For many, these gatherings were a time of being and not doing. It was never particularly evident if anything ever resulted from our conversations, yet we always left refreshed, informed, and encouraged in our ways. But, given these, we left better prepared for those meetings where agendas *were* followed, notes *were* kept, and decisions *were* made. As David Bohm wrote earlier, such dialogue can make a world of difference in the lives of those who participate and in the work of discernment that each person brings to the life and consciousness of the community. By enhancing the consciousness of our communities through dialogue, we can all create communities that honor the common good.

Because dialogue takes time, and often much time, the principal resource required to create communities is citizen commitment. I suspect my business roundtable foundered after a few years because most members found it to be a poor use of their time. Members were tied to the immediate and personal challenges of their jobs and families, so group commitment to the future and the communal became a low priority in a world of multiple demands. In today's ever more frenetic world, finding time to honor the common good becomes ever more difficult.

One of the most time-consuming tasks of honoring the common good is the rearing of children. Rearing children is more than a full-time job whether parents work outside the home or not. When parents work outside the home, exhaustion comes easily, since they are working two full-time jobs, one to put bread on the table and the other to be present at

it. This work is time consuming because the primary work of child rearing is the work of being rather than doing. Although meals need to be
prepared, laundry washed, and transportation provided, attending to a
child requires more than cooking, washing, and what at times may seem
like unending "windshield time." What we need is the time to be, to be
present, to be in relationship. Although today this may be called "quality time," what is required at heart is quantity time. Time that flows like
a river as children learn the simple and necessary lessons that come, not
from the quality of life, but from its very dailiness as it is lived with parents, siblings, and members of the larger community. Our failing with
children today is not that we have failed to achieve greatness, but that we
have failed to value the ordinary. We live harried, uncivil lives from work-
place to homeplace, caught in a web of wires and roads that provides little
respite from lives of unending competition and drive for the ever-elusive
"more." Such lessons are not lost on our children as they too become consumers ever more needful of the material.

One measure of our failure to nurture children into adults is America's ever-growing incarceration rate. Today the U.S. incarceration rate of
over 750 inmates per 100,000 population is the highest in the world.[24]
With more than five times the incarceration rate of other industrialized
countries, America's rising inmate population points to a growing disconnect between social and criminal justice in America.

Relating social condition to crime is a complex problem, because multiple correlations between bad behavior and social circumstance are easy
to find. Given this fact, statistics become messy since an unrelated "cause"
may be correlated with an actual cause. Unrelated causes are the bane
of statisticians, but nevertheless extensive studies leave little doubt that
some things do matter. As mentioned earlier, Robert Putnam in *Bowling
Alone* presents numerous examples that show life is better in states that
possess a high degree of social capital. With regard to crime in particular,
Putnam shows that states with greater social capital have less pugnacious
populations and lower murder rates.

Although it is commonly believed that poverty and access to guns
are precursors to violent crime, emergent thought suggests that income
inequality over the larger population may be equally important.[25] My deep
belief is that America's decline in social capital as reported by Putman is
largely driven by our ever-increasing wealth and the income disparities it
creates. With more than enough money for our daily needs, many of us
can now afford the personal privilege of leaving the social and economic

system that has made us wealthy. From cable TV and Internet access in children's personal bedrooms, to private schools, to gated communities, to autos that wrap us in the manufacturer's identity, to remote vacations to get away from it all, we are spending our money in ways that serve more to compromise than enhance our social capital. Our social capital is decreasing because we believe we can afford to live without it.

Yet this is a false hope for our children. The frequently cited African proverb, "It takes a village to raise a child," succinctly describes the social capital required for successful child rearing. A study of mostly Midwestern youths conducted by the Search Institute discovered that only 10 percent of the nearly fifty thousand youth surveyed led lives that included a minimal number of social assets, such as parental discipline, adult support, or community involvement. The vast majority of the students had too few assets and too many deficits, such as parental abuse, hedonistic values, or negative peer pressure.[26] Not all students classified as at-risk fail to become productive members of the larger community, but with such a large number of at-risk youth, we should not be surprised that we have the highest incarceration rate of any country in the world.

Much of our decrease in social capital is driven by a culture that does not value the relationships that come from simply taking time to live. For example, a study cited in the *Wall Street Journal* showed that men treated fairly on the job were more likely to treat their children more fairly at home. Stressful workplaces, it was found, create stressful homes. One father reported that after he told his coworkers he had not seen his family for three days, his supervisor told him in front of his colleagues, "You can always get another family, but you can't get another job like this one."[27]

Similar examples abound in the advertising media. An ad for bond paper explained that midnight oil, weekends, and even your anniversary were well worth every minute put into a proposal if it were just proffered on the proper paper. And an advertisement for a newsletter on how to achieve balance in life showed a group of achievers walking a tightrope one after the other, all on the same perilous path, all precariously balanced. No room for error, exploration, or others in this setting. The lonely people walking the high wire or writing the winning proposal are held up as examples of what you and I can be if we just subscribe to the newsletter or put our proposal on the proper paper. Our ever-growing preference for the work of doing business over the venture of being people strains America's social capital still more.

Finally, we value speed, efficiency, and choice far beyond their usefulness. We have replaced *being* alive with *acting* alive. And we act alive by keeping ever busier with useless work, things, and activities. If we keep doing enough, we will be successful. We will get the corner office, the raise, the plaque on the wall, and the Rolodex worth of acquaintances whose secretaries send us cards on our birthdays. Overrun by options, we believe that we can make time for everything. Yet, in the end, we cannot make time, but only choices. Our need for constant discernment cannot be avoided.

CHAPTER THREE

The New Work

Consciousness and Evolution

Consciousness precedes Being.
—Václav Havel

*The real voyage of discovery consists not in seeking new landscapes
but in having new eyes.*
—Marcel Proust

*The main test before us involves our will to change
rather than our ability to change.*
—Norman Cousins

The New Work

Show up! Pay attention!

These charges describe much of life's work. For many they mean coming to work on time, seeing what needs to be done, and then getting on with it. Although such directives may bring much to successful living, they do not answer the questions "Show up where?" and "Pay attention to what?" The questions "Where?" and "What?" are not simple to answer and once again require the work of discernment. But discernment is an empty concept without the availability of choice, and choice itself is limited for each of us by circumstance and imagination.

The circumstances of the concentration camp at Auschwitz clearly reduced the choices available to Viktor Frankl. Yet even in his deprivation as a prisoner, Frankl made a choice to rise above the situation by imagining his experience to be in the distant past even as it occurred. Limited in choice by extraordinary circumstances, Frankl used his imagination to do the work required for personal survival. Although he was given no choice about where to show up, he did retain the option of choosing what he would pay attention to, and for Frankl this made all the difference. Although his circumstances and the imagination he brought to them were both extraordinary, Frankl's story remains a powerful example for each of us as we show up and pay attention to the difficulties of our own lives.

Today we need new ways to show up and pay attention. Although our present criteria of selecting our work to meet our personal and immediate needs has served us well in the past, a new work is required of us today, one that will bring a new imagination to our abundant circumstances and enlarge our worldview beyond the personal and immediate to that of the communal and future. Establishing criteria for our new work will not be easy, because the personal and immediate *are* important, and few of us are willing to give up individual security for the security of the group. Our individual disregard of the communal and future is based on the belief that, even if the group does not endure, we will. The impossibility of this is kept at bay through our belief that even though others may perish economically, socially, or even physically, we can through our own work avoid these experiences. The first step of the new work is to acknowledge that we are as vulnerable to the vicissitudes of this world as those around us.

To begin the new work, "Show up! Pay attention!" means to show up to ourselves through our own consciousness and to pay attention not only to our own life, but to our neighbor's as well. It is by doing this that we each bring order and civility not only to our own lives, but also to our communities. Such work is required of us to reduce the messiness, or the entropy, of our personal and communal lives. And, like it or not, it is work immutably mandated by the second law of thermodynamics.

Worse yet, thermodynamics tells us even more we would rather not hear: that no matter how hard we work, we cannot reduce the entropy of any system, including the messiness of our own lives and communities, to zero. It tells us that perfect order is impossible. Most practically this final or third law of thermodynamics tells us that it is impossible to build a refrigerator that will make something perfectly cold.

A substance is perfectly cold when all heat has been removed from it and its atoms sit as still as they can get.[1] When something is this cold, about minus 460 degrees Fahrenheit, it is said to be at absolute zero. Through the use of very clever kinds of refrigerators, physicists have got matter to within a fraction of a millionth of a degree of absolute zero. Yet from these laboratory observations it has been learned that, no matter how clever the refrigerator, the achievement of absolute zero is not possible. Observed in each case is that an infinite number of processes, each removing a yet smaller amount of heat, is required. Since life is short, absolute zero can only be approached but never achieved. This is the third law. Even physicists have to accept some disorder in their lives.

All together thermodynamics' three laws tell us that energy is conserved, that work is required to increase the order of a system, and that no amount of work can create perfect order. From these come three analogous laws of life. The first law of life is: "Life is work." This existential reality tells us that without proper work now we may experience needless, and often more difficult, work later. We may put off such work, but in the end it cannot be avoided, and in this sense it is conserved. Given the reality that life is work, the second law is: "Work is required to reduce the difficulties of life." By properly choosing our work, we can increase the order and reduce the messiness and therefore the difficulties of our lives. But even the most careful choice of our work cannot take all our woes from us. This leads to the final law of life: "No amount of work can reduce our difficulties to zero." Knowledge of this third law directs us to accept our losses and to get on with our lives, both personal and communal.

Today we need citizen leaders whose lives and global understanding are deeply directed by the laws of nature and the laws of life and what those laws require of each of us. Such citizens become servant leaders, truth-tellers, when they show us what our work ought to be. We rarely elect them to public office, because they offer not simple solutions, but rather difficult processes that challenge and change us. Today the single greatest threat to democracy in America is our desire for leaders who promise us the personal and immediate without obligation to the communal and future.[2]

Consciousness and Evolution

As time passes, our choices determine the quality of life we lead. Do we mindlessly dismiss the problems and opportunities that cross our paths each day, or do we consciously engage them in ways that improve our fortunes? To see possibility where others see futility determines the path that becomes our life. Our answers to "Show up where?" and "Pay attention to what?" become our life, and the quality of that life is no better than the personal consciousness that we bring to the work of finding our answers.

As measured by Americans' personal wealth, the "where" and "what" of our work have been well served by the criteria of choosing our work based on the personal and immediate satisfaction of our needs. Driven largely by the accumulation of personal wealth, America's economy has been so successful that few question its ultimate virtue. Central to our never-ending accumulation of more is our unexamined belief that constant growth is not only good for the economy, but also essential for happiness. Yet as long as we believe in the myth of the material, we will continue to find our lives wanting. Developing new criteria for living our lives will be America's most important task of the twenty-first century.

Our entire cultural history, from simple cultivation and cave paintings to today's bioengineered crops and multimedia presentations, has occurred over a period of forty thousand years or less. In *The Evolution of Consciousness*, Robert Ornstein argues that although such a period is two thousand generations, it is but a blink of the eye in evolutionary time, and that our minds today are much the same as they were generations ago. He asserts that our biological evolution has left us ill prepared with little more than cave-age minds, minds prepared for the leap of the tiger, and that without "conscious evolution" there will be no further evolution.[3] Depending on the consciousness we bring to it, our cultural evolution over the next century will likely follow one of two paths. The first and least-conscious will be marked by an ever-growing reliance on technology that separates us from our environment and each other as we try with increased effort to bring order and security to our personal lives. Believing that through the use of ever more clever technology we can solve technology's problems, we will be led into a cyberspace life increasingly removed from one another and our natural environment.

The second more conscious path will be based on an intentional change in our thinking, one that will fundamentally transform our consciousness and lead us to mindfully and spiritually connect with one another and our environment in new and unexplored ways. We need today a new consciousness that we are part of a larger and inseparable whole, and that separating ourselves from the disorder of the whole through yet more technology and individual effort is to invite disaster.

The extent to which we reconnect with ourselves, each other, and our planet will be a measure of our success as we move from biological to conscious evolution. In the end, we will each need to grow in appreciation of ourselves, each another, and the earth as we discover our proper place on a small blue planet going around an ordinary star on the edge of an ordinary galaxy in an ever-expanding and unknown universe. In this grand scheme of things, whether we reconnect with one another and our planet or go extinct is small potatoes, but as people endowed with consciousness, we have the choice of moving into the future either mindlessly or mindfully. Given such a great adventure, it seems best that we stick together, get along, and proceed thoughtfully.

Evolution and Wealth

We did not get into our mindless collection of wealth accidentally. The social and economic structures we have today have evolved to meet our most basic needs. To continue our evolution is not to deny those needs, but to meet them in ways that are less destructive to our social and environmental fabric. The purpose of the new and conscious work I suggest is not to change the human condition, but to acknowledge and accommodate it in ways that enhance rather than compromise the survivability of our species. After all, if the human condition were as readily mutable as the advocates of the human potential movement would have us believe, the value of Greek tragedy would have disappeared long ago.

The transformation of our current work-and-spend culture into one of sustainable abundance will succeed only if it addresses our deepest human needs. Psychologist Abraham Maslow proposed that the needs for security, belonging, and self-actualization lie at the core of our being, and that the source of human destructiveness is not that we are inherently evil, but that we are frustrated by unmet core needs.[4] Today, with most of us working for others rather than ourselves, our security, belonging, and self-actualization frequently come not from who we are, but from what we do and who we do it with.

A frequent first question at social gatherings is, "And what do you do?" When asked this question, there was a noticeable difference in response when I was working for others and answered, "I'm a senior scientist with . . . ," and my present answer, "I'm a consultant." The first solicited a visceral response of approval, and the more prestigious the company the greater the approval; the second a look of, "Oh, so you're unemployed too." A primary marker of the new consciousness will be work lives that provide security, belonging, and self-actualization in ways that go beyond material accumulation, corporate identity, and ever-increasing income.

Before the Industrial Revolution, life in self-supporting communities provided a variety of daily work that met our most basic needs.[5] Until the turn of the nineteenth century, security and belonging were provided by communities where most all worked for basic survival in an environment made uncertain and dangerous by accident, disease, and natural disaster. Providing for our own daily needs and those of our family and community were all the self-actualization we needed as simple survival and community connections marked the successful life. Daily work was the work of feeding, clothing, and housing ourselves, with any extra time devoted to simple arts, education, religion, and self-governance.

All this changed with the advent of industrial specialization. Driven by Frederick Taylor's scientific management stopwatch, the varied work required to produce for one's own use was transformed into a specialized and compartmentalized job of producing for others.[6] But more was lost than the rewards of diversified work; we stopped talking to one another, teaching our children, and governing ourselves. More insidious than the specialization of production was the specialization of living that gave rise to the professional adviser, educator, and bureaucrat(7). We have been made materially rich by jobs that have left us disconnected from ourselves and our communities.

Although industrialization has vastly improved our material lives, it has at the same time fundamentally altered the ways in which we meet our most basic human needs for security, belonging, and self-actualization. Central to conscious evolution will be new and diverse patterns of working that will meet our fundamental needs in new and sustainable ways, ways that will mark the beginning of a transformation as significant as that of the Industrial Revolution.

Economics and the New Work

We will be led to the new work as we each answer the questions "Show up where?" and "Pay attention to what?" Depending on our individual circumstances and imaginations, each of us will bring different answers to the "where" and "what" questions of our own lives. At the root of our work will be the reexamination of our shared economic beliefs—of what John Kenneth Galbraith called the "conventional wisdom."[8]

Central to America's conventional wisdom is the belief that the best economic system is the one created when we each act out of our own best self-interest. That is, an economic system created by what Adam Smith described in 1776 as the "invisible hand"—a self-interest that not only directs our own lives, but also promotes the interests of society more effectively than even our best intentions.[9]

Adam Smith's invisible hand, a part of the conventional wisdom for more than two hundred years, has without doubt guided, if not driven, American self-interest toward the accumulation of enormous personal wealth, and free-enterprise advocates can justly claim that huge public benefits have resulted from its unfettered application. The wealth created by capitalism and free markets has given us the surplus to provide to virtually all Americans such worldwide rarities as potable water, sanitary sewers, and telephone and electric services that work twenty-four hours a day. Although most of us take these services for granted, it is the wealth of such universals that provides the basis for much of the life we enjoy. From a country free of plagues and epidemics to the unprecedented middle-class wealth of single-family houses and personal automobiles, most of us in the United States live lives of absolute privilege.

As a privileged American, I freely echo the message of America's free-market advocates. The unfettered invisible hand has contributed mightily to our prosperity by directing our work as individuals. But today, even as the invisible hand continues to generate an ever-increasing quantity of national wealth, the origins and distribution of that wealth are becoming ever more suspect. By serving our personal and immediate needs, the invisible hand creates unintended consequences that, contrary to Adam Smith, do not always serve the common good.

Today millions of Americans work for less than a living wage on poultry production lines or in electronic sweatshops where they eviscerate chickens or enter characters at speeds that leave them mind-numb and aching from fatigue and repetitive stress injuries.[10] With demanding speeds and few or no breaks, these unattractive jobs produce worker turnover rates of more than 100 percent a year. Although there is no way that I could take the rigors of such work, I benefit greatly from it when I thaw a skinned and boned chicken breast for dinner. By compromising the physical and economic health of a poultry worker, I add to mine by having a stir-fried chicken breast at the end of the day. And so I live a life made richer by the efforts of the working poor, my consumption enhanced by the subsidy of the nonliving wage.[11] By reducing the cost of what I need, the low-wage worker allows me the privilege to buy what I want.

As we approach the natural endpoints of human consumption, time, and rational need, the economic growth required to meet our ever-increasing wants makes distortions in the creation and distribution of our wealth ever more apparent. Today wealth is being created by the so-called working poor, those Americans who work full-time but still don't earn enough money to function independently in the economy, or by the extraction of natural wealth without regard to the effects of pollution or the depletion of resources. Little of this is new, since from sweatshops to strip mining, the exploitation of people and resources has long been a part of the American economy. What is new is that we now have sufficient wealth to extend a decent standard of living to every worker in the United States.[12] Although today we are wealthier than ever, our very success at producing wealth has made visible the problems of its inequitable distribution.

Few expect an equal distribution of wealth. Entrepreneurs who take risks with their career or capital that might result in the accumulation of personal wealth should not be denied that possibility, since the actions of such people have generated much of the general wealth we all enjoy today. Most Americans today accept that such risk takers earn the personal financial well-being that might come to them. For many this acceptance is based on the belief that the opportunity to accumulate such wealth is open to them also.

No one can expect equality from a social contract that favors the entrepreneur, but each of us can expect to be treated equitably. That is, each of us should expect a social contract that provides just, impartial, and fair opportunities. Two growing signs of inequity in our economy are the growing number of working poor and the ever-increasing divide between the household incomes of the low-wage worker and the top-tier professional.[13] Made visible by today's extraordinary wealth, the growing gap between the very poor and very rich shows that something is wrong with America's social contract.

In the United States we believe in opportunity for all, and that with the proper initiative and hard work, we can all become members of the middle class. The message to poor people is that all that is required is motivation, education, and hard work. This advice may work for some but fails for those whose circumstances do not allow for such choices. Many poor people *have* moved into the middle class, and others who

could have done so have remained poor because they *are* lazy and indifferent. But upward mobility requires more than hard work. It requires
economic niches that allow people to move from minimum-wage jobs to
work that pays a living wage. If the skill gaps between niches become too
large, upward mobility slows or stops altogether.

Beyond considering the availability of living-wage jobs, we need to
examine the belief that we all have the ability and interest to become computer whizzes making middle-class incomes. Our Declaration of Independence tells us that all people are created equal, and although we may
all be equal under the law and before God, we are not equal in ability. For
example, although I have a graduate degree in physics and am thus considered educated, the range of abilities both greater and lesser than mine
remains enormous. I consider myself a fairly handy problem solver; others avoid even the simplest problems. Still others can do quantum electro-
dynamics on the back of an envelope; I can't. With so little equality in skill
or in the ability to acquire one, how then can we bring equity to income?

Agreeing on what is equitable, that is, on what is a just and fair distribution of income, is not a simple matter. Since the current U.S. minimum wage
is not a living wage, entry-level jobs can only be considered as temporary
by anyone who wants to live above the poverty level in America. Our economic system can be viewed as equitable only if for each minimum-wage
job created there is another job created above it. The number of middle-
income jobs needs to grow as fast as the number of people who desire to
leave entry-level jobs if all people are to be upwardly mobile (14).

But beyond the belief in upward mobility lies the further belief that all
people have the ability for constant skill growth. It is economic hubris to
believe that everyone can, should, or must rise above the so-called entry-
level job in the United States. The hotel housekeeper who takes care of
the guests, the fast-food worker who greets the regulars, and the sales
clerk who meets the customers' needs are worth gold to any enterprise.
Because they perform the most valuable services of all—welcoming and
serving the customers, accepting their money, and keeping the place
tidy and clean—America's lowest-paid workers have economic value far
beyond their current nonliving wages.

Lack of a living wage for the lowest-paid workers in America is just
one part of an unworkable combination of beliefs that unless reexam-
ined will lead to the overall social decline of our country. Our unworkable combination is that we believe in compassion, law and order, and
the nonliving wage. Today these three work together to create a variety

of ineffective, costly, and socially destructive economic niches for many in America. Driven by compassion and the desire for law and order, we have today created a welfare and prison system that is growing and out of control.

A system of welfare and prisons will always be needed to care for those who can't care for themselves and to care for those who care for no one. Today, however, our care for the poor, driven by our dual passions for welfare and incarceration, has so distorted the economy of the low-wage worker that programs and institutions to meet basic needs are impossible to implement or evaluate. The nonliving wage has created a system of social and economic dependence in which it is impossible to distinguish between people who want to work and those who can't or won't.

Today welfare and incarceration have become economic niches of their own. We frequently hear stories of people who have worked to acquire office skills and then found office work not outside of the welfare system, but within it. And to accommodate the world's highest incarceration rate, small American towns are now building prison facilities to be operated under contract for any state that needs them. Lacking accessible niches for the poor in a living-wage economy, we have created an alternative economy of welfare and incarceration that serves neither the poor nor the rest of the country.

Although many will find the idea unworkable, the implementation of a living minimum wage needs to be given serious consideration. If as compassionate and orderly people we are going to support a complex system of welfare and incarceration, then it is reasonable to ask if our money is being well spent. Might it be cheaper and better for everyone if those who fry our fast food, make up our hotel rooms, and keep our workplaces clean were paid enough money so they too could participate in the economy? Including social costs, might the total cost of my hamburger and fries be less if the cook were paid a living wage? And if the cook could afford to go out to eat, would that be so damn bad for the economy?

To pay the low-income worker a living wage would require that today's minimum wage be more than doubled. This would not be an easy thing to accomplish, since raises of a few percent have generated great debate in the past. For many, doubling the minimum wage would seem plain crazy, yet we have in the United States a profoundly successful example of just such an idea. In this case, the craziness belonged to Henry Ford when in 1913 he doubled his workers' wages to $5 a day. Although the *Wall Street Journal* called it an "economic crime," Ford regarded it as one of the best business decisions of his life. Worker turnover of nearly 400 percent tumbled, quality improved, costs decreased, and profits grew.[15] But Ford did more than merely stabilize his workforce into a profit-making machine. By paying his workers enough money to buy the autos they were making, he created his own market niche and made the U.S. auto worker the foundation of an emerging middle class. Lost to us in today's low-cost labor market is what Henry Ford knew instinctively—that every worker is somebody's customer. Paid a living wage, Ford's workers joined the middle class, and the entire country prospered from it.[16]

With the inducement of the $5-a-day wage, workers left increasingly efficient farms to build automobiles in the city. Today as our increasingly efficient manufacturing sector requires fewer workers, and as the service sector grows ever larger, a second revolution in compensation is due. When Ford raised his workers' pay to $5 a day, he effectively invented the middle-class economy. Today by making the minimum wage a living wage, America's service companies could invent a new living-wage economy within our most socially and economically distressed communities.

Ford's middle class is not the only invented economy we have in the United States. Others include the Internal Revenue Service and the military-industrial complex. For example, during the twenty-one-year period from 1986 through 2006, regardless of the tax rules or rates, U.S. citizens paid an average of about 14 percent of their income in taxes, an amount seemingly regulated by an "invisible hand" of lawyers, lobbyists, and loopholes.[17] The existence of such a de facto constant tax rate in America indicates that much of the work of the lawyers and lobbyists that set our taxes and of the IRS employees and accountants that collect them is plain unnecessary. With an estimated cost of tax compliance of $250 billion annually, the efficacy and clarity of a much simplified flat-tax system become attractive if not compelling.[18] As an invented economy, the U.S. tax code is a major industry of its own and, for most taxpayers, an expensive and monumental aggravation.

While knowledge workers create complex tax codes known only to themselves or perhaps no one at all, and the military-industrial complex continues to develop weapon systems of dubious need or effectiveness,[19] the low-wage service workers of America continue to do work that if stopped tomorrow would compromise the work of everyone. Gone would be clean offices in the morning, fast food for lunch, and frozen chicken breasts for dinner. By mistaking added complexity for added value and simple order for simplistic order, we overvalue the complexity created by the knowledge worker while seriously undervaluing the order maintained by the service worker. Based on the value their work brings to the economy, the present wage gap between service workers and knowledge workers cannot be justified.

Finally, if all workers were allowed to earn a living wage, the distinction between those who want to work and those who can't, or won't, would become clearer. The provision of assistance to those who need it, and the natural consequences of the slacker life to those who don't, would bring a new clarity to the balance of charity and justice that seems central to our social and economic life in America.

The invisible hand has guided us so well in the production of wealth that today most Americans have more than enough food, clothing, and housing. Our wealth has carried us to a rational limit of material well-being and produced such a material surplus that we are running out of time to use it all. Yet, while the invisible hand has superbly directed many Americans in the accumulation of personal wealth, it has failed miserably at its equitable distribution.

Today we are at a fundamental turning point in our collective economic life. Central to our work of conscious evolution will be making Adam Smith's economic hand visible. Without conscious economic evolution within the next century, it is all too possible that we will begin a descent into a social hell of privately protected gated communities where an elite and dwindling middle class near the gates serves an even smaller number of the wealthy within, and where, far removed from the gates of the wealthy, the majority live in poverty.[20]

Toward a Conscious Future

Personal success in America today seems to revolve largely around the material and measurable: the size of our portfolios, incomes, or houses, or the number of cars we own, people who report to us, or awards won. We value what we can see and count, and for most Americans, compare. If we aren't comparing ourselves with our neighbors—keeping up with the Joneses—we're comparing ourselves with how much we had a year ago. We're driven in our comparisons by the cultural norm that each generation should be better off than the one before it.

Yet to be "better off" begs the question, "Better off than what?" Since the end of World War II Americans have answered this question through the accumulation of consumer goods. After World War II some of the people in my neighborhood still had houses without electric appliances or running water. They kept their food cool in an insulated icebox and cooked it on a wood-burning stove. They pumped their kitchen water from a cistern, and their commode was an outhouse in the backyard. It seemed clear then that to be better off meant having a house where the water ran, the toilet flushed, and the kitchen had a modern refrigerator and range. Considered luxuries only a generation or two ago, such material things are today's basics, and most of us have them all.

Since World War II, the accumulation of material wealth has met many of our needs for security, belonging, and self-actualization. We have the security of home ownership, we belong to the middle class, and we demonstrate self-actualization through the work we do and the way we live.[21] As we approach the rational limit of time to get and use material goods, we need new ways to live that provide the security, belonging, and self-actualization that in the past we have got from the accumulation of the material.

Our life of material accumulation is limited because the fundamental measures of human life are limited. We each have twenty-four hours a day to live, require about the same amount of food and nutrition, need one bed to sleep and a room or two for living. Our needs are finite, and to use more than we need takes resources from others, either through the labor of the poor or the exploitation of the natural environment. With material accumulation now exceeding finite human need, a life of ever more of the material no longer serves the common good.

We need today a new notion of prosperity, one based not on the personal belief that better off means having more of what we want, but on the communal belief that better off means doing more within the rational limits of what we need. The new prosperity will emerge as we learn that doing more with less can enhance both our lives and our communities.

Doing more with less is hardly a part of the American dream, and many would be repelled by the very idea of limits on personal consumption. Yet consumption itself is work, and today as we run up against the natural limits of time to get and use material things, it seems reasonable to ask the question: is there a better way to be better off?

For me the answer is an unequivocal "yes" based on a new economics that values who we are over what we have, that values living over accumulation and being over doing. Most important we must establish a new prosperity in America that meets the needs of all our citizens, and central to this is not the work of accumulation, but of transformation. Our new work is not to acquire more of the material for ourselves, but to use our wealth to change ourselves and the lives of those in our communities.

Such work of transformation will move us beyond our current material prosperity to a new economic order of abundance. The difference between prosperity and abundance is that while prosperity is measured by the quantity of our material things, abundance is measured by the equity of our income distribution and the quality of our relationships. Most important to this economic transformation is the creation of an economy that provides the basics of life for all.

The New Paradigm

In the parable of heaven and hell, banquet tables overflow with food and wine, yet some go hungry. In hell, tortured souls struggle to feed themselves with hands bound by chains. With full plates teasingly close, all go hungry even in the midst of plenty. In heaven, unbound by the chains of hell, all celebrate and are satisfied. But this heaven and hell are the same place, and those in heaven are unbound, not because they are without hell's chains, but because they have chosen to feed not themselves but one another. In the festive banquet of heaven and hell, it is the paradigm of the guest that makes all the difference.

A paradigm is an example on which we can model beliefs and behavior. The parable of heaven and hell illustrates the power of such examples by showing us the difference between cooperative and noncooperative behavior. Also illustrated is the power of transformation that one person may possess. In the above parable, the feast of heaven could just as well have started and remained the same as that of hell. But in heaven just one person modeling cooperative behavior by feeding their neighbor could have prompted all the others to do the same. The paradigms that direct our lives today have no less impact on our living than that illustrated by the banquet of heaven and hell. The lives we lead today emerge from our most basic beliefs about how life works.

As typical Americans, most of us live lives based on a personal and immediate criterion that more, and in particular, more *now*, is better. Yet our modern life of valuing the personal over the communal has made us slaves to the measurable and driven us to lives hell-bent on the accumulation of more. But a life based on the material is limited by the finiteness of our physical being and the world around us. Lives saturated with the material have left us anxious and asking, "Is this all there is?"

If the primary question of the personal life is "How much is enough?" the primary question of the communal life is "Can we all do it?" Central to both is the ability for all to participate in life, for all to have enough of the material to fully participate in the communal. This is the life that marks the beginning of conscious evolution, the beginning of an abundant life for all.

The new work of conscious evolution is to show up to our communities and to pay attention to others. With this we will transform our present criteria of work based on the personal and immediate to that based on the communal and yet-to-be—to work that moves us beyond the accumulation of material wealth to a social contract in which all may participate. And, in the end, we will know we have arrived at that place when our social contract provides an unequivocal "yes" to the question "Can we all do it?"

PART 2

WORK AND TRANSFORMATION

CHAPTER FOUR

❖

The New Liturgy

Returning the Work of the People to the People

All professions are conspiracies against the laity.
—George Bernard Shaw

The time has come to take the syringe out of the hand of the doctor,
as the pen was taken out of the hand of the scribe
during the Reformation in Europe.
—Ivan Illich

One of the principal problems in the modern world is that
we have delegated our survival instinct to the state.
—Norman Cousins

Problems, Problems, Problems

Everybody loves a dead battery.

It was a do-it-yourself crowd. We stood six deep at the auto parts counter at Sears, all asking for the same thing: "Give me the biggest battery you've got for a Belchfire 8." A cart full of dead batteries next to the counter gave witness to what had brought us there and made "Cold enough for you?" the conversation of the day.

A dead car battery, like a broken leg, is not something you wish for. But when you've got a problem, it's the kind you want. We value these problems because they are clear—my car engine won't turn over, or my leg has left me immobilized. Equal in value to their clear definition is that such problems also have clear solutions: get in line at Sears for a new battery, or call 911 and get carted to the hospital. Our problem is then quickly solved by the person behind the counter who provides a new battery or the emergency room physician who sets our leg. With a new battery our car will run again, and after a period of time to heal, so will we.

We like these kinds of problems not only because they are easy to identify and solve, but also because we need to do little more than show up and play a passive role while the problem is solved by someone else. But not all problems are so nice. Some, such as type 2 diabetes, cannot be readily solved by medical intervention but must be actively managed by the affected person. Here medical intervention fails, and the work of coping with impaired sugar metabolism belongs not only to the physician, but to the individual as well.

By looking at who needs to do the work, we can divide problems into two broad categories. E. F. Schumacher, in his book *A Guide for the Perplexed*, describes these as convergent and divergent problems.[1] Convergent problems are those problems we prefer, those best solved by someone else, like a dead car battery or broken leg. More onerous are Schumacher's divergent problems. Such problems lie beyond the work of the expert and require the work of all who are affected. The principal difference between convergent and divergent problems is that while convergent problems can be solved using the consensus-based solutions of experts, divergent problems may only be ameliorated—made better, not solved—through the cooperative work of those affected.

Most problems in technology are convergent. For example, the first commercially successful airplane, the Douglas DC-3, is an example of a convergent solution to the problem of building an airplane that could both fly and make money. Five critical design elements were required for its success: a variable-pitch propeller, a retracting landing gear, a method of lightweight construction, a radial air-cooled engine, and wing flaps. The convergence of these five technologies in the DC-3 caused commercial aviation literally to take off.[2] The great attractiveness of solving such convergent problems comes from the creative pleasure and commercial success that issue from such technology.

But life is not always so nice. When our problems become organic and alive, they become complex and messy, and finding consensus-based solutions becomes difficult if not impossible. These complex and messy problems of life that have no simple solutions are what Schumacher calls divergent problems. For example, there is no simple consensus on what constitutes a good education. Some will say education involves authority, discipline, and obedience. Others will claim that we learn best when we are set free and allowed to test or even break the rules. When it comes to education, well-meaning and reasonable people can differ sharply on what is proper or good. In this case, the problem of education is divergent, and reaching a consensus is not possible or even desirable, since different students learn differently.

Problems, such as abortion, are difficult and divisive because well-meaning people can hold opposite points of view. My own view is that I am both pro-life and pro-choice. It is my desire that all children be wanted children and that both fathers and mothers, when presented a choice, choose life. For me, the recommendation that abortion be legal, safe, available, and rare presents enough work for the advocates of either position. While taken together these goals might not be considered an ideal solution by either pro-life or pro-choice advocates, they can, in whole, serve as a remedy (3). Rather than presenting a singular solution, the recommendation that abortion be legal, safe, available, and rare becomes a remedy that allows a variety of people of differing views to work toward a common goal of few or no abortions. Although such work may leave advocates on either side less than satisfied, it is likely to be the best action that can be taken for the good of all.

A large part of living is the work of discerning between the convergent and divergent problems that we encounter in life. Most important is our need to accept the reality that divergent problems, unlike convergent problems, cannot be solved, but only be made better through the application of remedies. Remedies require the cooperation of many people and lead not to the solution of the problem, but only to its amelioration. While convergent problems may be solved by the work of the expert, divergent problems can be ameliorated only by the work of those affected.

The importance of separating the problems of our lives into convergent and divergent types cannot be overstressed. Conscious evolution mandates we recognize that our future survival cannot be guaranteed by ever-more clever solutions to convergent problems. The vast majority of our most serious problems—wage equity, housing availability, health care, transportation access, unemployment, poverty, drugs, and violence, along with worldwide resource issues such as water, food, energy, sanitation, and environmental degradation—have no single or simple solution.

As divergent problems, they lie beyond the convergent responses of either the technology of science or the programs of government. They require the work of everyone.

The central characteristic that makes divergent problems so onerous is that they require us to show up, pay attention, *and* get to work. They are the problems that we would rather have someone else solve for us. We would all rather pay our taxes and have the government feed the poor, educate our children, keep our streets safe, and provide for us ready transportation and low-cost energy. But all of these are divergent problems— problems over which reasonable people can hold widely divergent views and for which there are no single or simple answers. They are problems that deal with the complexity of life itself, and as much as we wish they would go away, they won't. Wishing becomes the hard work of laziness as we work to avoid the reality that these problems belong to us and no one else.

The work of reducing the difficulties caused by the divergent problems that surround us today is the work of the new liturgy. The word *liturgy* has its origins in two Greek roots meaning "work" and "people," and it literally means "the work of the people." *Liturgy* is most often used to describe the order of worship in Christian ritual, but I now wish to extend its meaning to include all the work that life requires of us. The new liturgy describes the ordinary work that brings meaning to our daily lives. Discovering what this work is and getting on with it is fundamental to the work of conscious evolution. The new liturgy tells us that divergent problems return our work to us no matter what.

The New Liturgy versus the New Alchemy

Today's institutions have grown from the belief that, given enough resources and experts, the solution to any divergent problem may be found. This belief is based on an unwritten theory of work that any large and complex divergent problem may be solved by dividing it into a number of smaller and simpler convergent problems, each of which may be solved by the appropriate expert. At the heart of this unwritten theory is our overwhelming desire to believe that we can transform complex problems that can only be ameliorated in cooperation with others into simpler ones that can be solved by someone else.

Our desire to convert divergent problems into convergent ones is the primary reason for the hard work of laziness that fills our lives. The work we do today to shift the burden of our work from ourselves to someone else constitutes a new alchemy that is as unworkable today as was the conversion of lead into gold during the Middle Ages. Just as it was impossible to convert lead into gold, the new alchemy fails because no matter how much we wish it were so, no amount of work will convert the divergent problems of the community into the convergent problems of the expert.

Our resistance to do the work required of us has given rise to a large and profitable "rent-seeking" class in the United States.[4] Members of the rent-seeking class are those who move around the resources we give them in order to solve the divergent problems we would rather not solve ourselves. While most workers in our culture contribute to the common good, the workers of the rent-seeking class profit whether they improve our common lot or not.

Who are the rent seekers, and what do they do? It is useful here to divide workers into two large groups: entrepreneurs and rent seekers. The entrepreneur is the inventor, the worker on the auto production line, the hotel housekeeper, the fast-food fry cook, the nonprofit worker, the civil servant, the attorney, and the physician who through their daily work improve the well-being of people. Members of the rent-seeking class are those whose work could be much like those just listed, but who work more to cash in on the human condition than to ameliorate it. Any work can be either rent-seeking or entrepreneurial, depending on its intent.

For example, consider the work of a plastic surgeon. While restoring the face of an accident victim would clearly ameliorate the effects of a devastating human experience, conducting a third or fourth cosmetic procedure on an attractive forty-year-old is more likely to be cashing in on, than ameliorating, the human condition. While the first restores dignity, the second may do little more than accommodate neurosis. And while one life is restored, the other may just go on to further discontent. In this case, the challenge of the surgeon and his or her community is to bring dignity to both, whether surgery is performed or not. The work of the entrepreneur is to maximize effectiveness over personal income. While such vocational discernment is not easy, I would hope that those who practice any vocation and have the privilege to make such decisions will make them as entrepreneurs rather than rent seekers. Similar examples could be made for attorneys to use alternative dispute resolution and for financial planners to work on a fee-only basis.[5]

Other rent seekers are those legislators, lobbyists, and bureaucrats who make money by distributing the wealth of others according to the wishes of special interest groups regardless of the common good. The peculiar atmosphere that permeates the DC Beltway comes largely from the exhaust fumes of the numerous rent-seeking engines that put the very life of our democracy at risk. As entropy workers, entrepreneurs create wealth and order, while rent seekers redistribute the wealth of others and at best leave the order unchanged, if not in disarray. The rent seeker's redistribution of the entrepreneur's wealth lies at the heart of today's rent-seeking culture and serves as a good measure of our resistance to accepting the work of the new liturgy.

The work of the rent-seeking class is particularly inefficient when it creates work for others. Earlier I cited the example of the work required to create and conform to the tax codes of the United States. Complying with America's complex tax code costs American corporations and individuals hundreds of billions of dollars a year, making the work of tax compliance one of the nation's biggest businesses.[6] The tax system becomes even more inefficient and expensive when the entrepreneur's work is required to clean up the rent seeker's mess. Although the money I spend each year to have my taxes prepared may keep my entrepreneurial accountant busy, I wonder whether the money I spend best serves the common good of creating an economy in which all may participate. Or, more directly, would it be better for me to pay my accountant less so that I could buy a ticket that would pay an actor more?

The worst part of the new alchemy is that it gets quantified in terms of the gross domestic product (GDP), the sum value of all finished goods and services produced in the United States. As a measure of U.S. economic performance, the GDP makes no distinction between the work of the rent seeker and that of the entrepreneur. By valuing the work of the rent seeker and the entrepreneur only in terms of their dollar contributions to the economy, the GDP produces a grossly misleading measure of America's economic well-being.

The GDP fails as a meaningful economic measure because it is a measure of activity maintained rather than order created. As measured by the GDP, building a jail cell adds as much to the economy as building a classroom and incarcerating a prisoner as much as educating a child. Beyond this, the GDP fails completely to include the degradation of the natural environment from which we have extracted much of our wealth. By failing to include either the social efficacy of our work or the depletion of our resources, the GDP is a specious and dangerous measure of our economic well-being.

No amount of work or wishful thinking can transform problems that belong only to us into problems that belong to someone else. No amount of work can convert the divergent problems of the citizen into the convergent problems of the expert. Central to the work of the poised century is the recognition that our most pressing problems belong to all of us.

The Tyranny of Time and the Low, Flat Curve:
How Time Challenges the New Liturgy

The low, flat curve presents an example of a simple problem made difficult by the passage of time. It frequently arises in the application of energy-conservation technology, and I will use such an example to illustrate my point. Imagine that you would like to build a house that not only would be energy efficient but also have the lowest possible total cost. Most people think of just one cost—the cost to build. But if total cost is to be considered, then the operating cost of the house needs to be included as well. For example, the least expensive way to build a house is to construct it using low-grade windows, little insulation, and an inefficient furnace. Although its initial cost would be low, the cost of keeping such a house warm in Minnesota would give most people the shivers. Wrapping the house with three feet of insulation would keep you warm even without a furnace, but in this case, the mortgage payment would leave you cold. Between these extremes lies a least-cost solution to the problem: insulate the house so that the total cost to heat the house (the cost of energy plus insulation) is the lowest possible.

One can solve this problem by making a graph that shows the total cost to heat the house versus the amount of money spent to insulate it. The curve is somewhat U-shaped and looks like this:

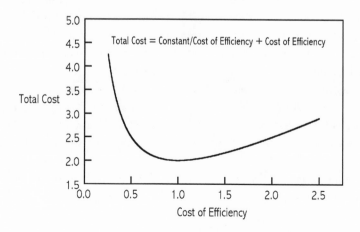

Total Cost = Constant/Cost of Efficiency + Cost of Efficiency

This is the low, flat curve.[7] It is the sum of two curves: (1) a decreasing curve for the cost of energy (shown as Constant/Cost of Efficiency in the graph) and (2) an increasing curve for the cost of energy efficiency (shown as the Cost of Efficiency in the graph). The cost-of-energy curve goes as the inverse of the cost of efficiency, because spending more on efficiency means that less is spent on energy. In contrast, the cost of efficiency is just a rising straight line. The sum of these two curves is the U-shaped curve shown in the graph. If the amount spent on efficiency is too little, the total cost goes up because too much money is spent on energy, but if too much is spent on efficiency, the total cost goes up again. The best amount to spend on efficiency is given by the cost of efficiency that provides the smallest total cost. A marble placed on the curve would roll to rest at this optimum point.

This all looks innocent and simple enough until something actually gets calculated, and therein lies the tyranny. Because we are not going to use any actual costs, the most we can do is say something about the shape of the curve. For example, at the bottom of the curve a 15 percent change either greater or less in the cost of efficiency produces a change of 1.5 percent or less in total cost. In other words, around the bottom of the curve a dollar spent on efficiency saves, within pennies, a dollar on energy. Near its minimum point the curve is nearly flat. Because of the flatness of this curve, what first appears to be a solution to a problem becomes an invitation for tinkering. And with this the problem becomes more divergent than convergent. What first appears as a *solution* now requires a *remedy*, as we bring our own economic values to the calculation. And the principal value we bring is how long we wish to invest in such energy savings.

Because the curve contains no units, but only relations between numbers, more information is required if the investment time is to be included. This requires a detailed calculation, so I will just give two general results from my work on this problem.[8] The first, which I mentioned in chapter 2, tells us that for any given time period, the total cost to heat a house is the least when the amount of money spent on energy and efficiency are equal. The second result allows us to find out what happens to the cost of efficiency when the investment time period changes. While the first result requires a detailed calculation involving weather data and the unit costs of energy and insulation, the second can be applied more broadly. To find out what happens to the cost of efficiency when the time period changes, all that is required is for the cost to be scaled by the square root of the period.

For example, consider investment horizons of 7, 28, and 112 years. The first is about the number of years many Americans stay in any one home; the second, the number of years people who move less often might be in same home; and the third, 112 years, the number of years a house is expected to be serviceable. Since the ratios of 28 to 7 and 112 to 28 are both 4, as we move from 7- to 28- to 112-year investment periods, the optimum amount of insulation increases by a factor of 2 (square root of 4) each time. This means that the optimum house insulation in a cold climate would increase from roughly four inches for a 7-year investment period to eight and sixteen inches for investment periods of 28 and 112 years respectively.

The problem becomes divergent when we make an investment that requires us to consider not only the personal costs of our project but the community costs as well. While a less-well-insulated house may cost the least for a short period of ownership, the long-term interests of future owners are compromised by having to heat an inefficient house for decades.

When guided by the tyranny of time and the low, flat curve, Adam Smith's invisible hand may readily produce social, economic, and environmental results far removed from those that best serve the common good. Housing sales show that, when given a choice, buyers are more attracted to personal amenities than invisible savings. While the home buyer receives the immediate and personal benefits of added amenities, his or her choice of a less efficient house compromises the economic and environmental order for decades (9). The tyranny of time and the low, flat curve tell us that any final answers can only be found by considering communal benefit as much as personal desire.[10]

Why the New Alchemy Fails

The new alchemy is based on the idea that a complex and difficult problem may be solved by breaking it down into a number of simpler and more easily solved problems. Applied to convergent technical problems, for example, putting a man on the moon, such problem solving is gratifyingly effective. The gratifying success of such problem solving leads us to believe that it should be applied to most of our problems, including those that do not have convergent solutions.

The reason we believe that the new alchemy works is that by dividing large problems into small ones, we transform problems with large boundaries into smaller problems with smaller boundaries. By containing and defining each part of a large problem, we believe that we can transform complexity into simplicity. What is forgotten in this process is that dividing up problems introduces a complexity of its own. What might appear to be true in principle fails in practice, since such divide-and-conquer problem solving depends on a critical, hidden factor: proper communication among the problem solvers.

The reason the new alchemy fails is that, as a physicist once said, "Everything happens at the boundary." As any problem is divided into more and more parts, more and more boundaries are created, and more and more communication is needed. If the solution to each sub-problem is to contribute to the solution of the whole problem in an effective manner, the communication across each boundary must be effective. It is at these boundaries that the new alchemy fails. For example, in the telephone game in which a message is passed from person to person in a circle, the message "Let's all have lunch on Thursday" might return as "All bets are on a Thursday launch." If a problem is divided into small enough pieces, even a minor communication failure across each boundary can result in large overall misunderstandings.

There are other reasons why the divide-and-conquer mentality of problem solving fails, even for convergent problems. First, diversity and dialogue are reduced or made difficult. By understanding only a small part of the problem and working with like minds, those who solve sub-problems are less likely to provide solutions that optimize the whole. By talking only among themselves, each group of specialists can easily forget the overall purpose of the work or who the customer is. Rather than producing for the customer, each worker ends up producing for the organization.

Second, a great deal of trust is required for such problem solving to work. Many organizations have such low levels of trust that each work group becomes its own territory as the workers defend their actions to others. In such organizations, a blizzard of defensive memos and papers becomes the problem-solving norm as the diversity and creativity of the group deteriorates or disappears altogether. Finally, such problem solving brings out the invisible hand at its worst as entrepreneurial workers become little more than rent seekers consuming resources without effect.[11] The new alchemy fails because diversity within and dialogue across problem boundaries are simply insufficient when the problem is divided into smaller parts.

Today's linear and hierarchal methods of problem solving break down because there can be huge differences of opinion between those doing the work and those managing it. Such discrepancies occur even in cases of highly technical problem solving. Physicist Richard Feynman discovered this when he was invited to join the Rogers Commission to investigate the explosion of the space shuttle *Challenger*.[12]

Against his better judgment, Feynman decided to accept the commission's invitation ("commit suicide," in his words) and travel to Washington, DC, a place he had successfully avoided most of his life. Feynman quickly tired of the official protocol of the investigation and appointed himself as an unofficial gumshoe, talking to all the technical people about the *Challenger* and all its parts. By asking all the right questions of all the right people, Feynman just as quickly made himself a pain in the neck to commission chair William P. Rogers.

As part of his process, Feynman conducted a blank-paper test that went to the heart of the issue of complex problem solving. During a review set up to find out how the main engines worked, he handed a blank piece of paper to each of three engineers and one manager. He then asked them to write down the probability that the main shuttle engine might fail on any flight. The manager reported the chance of failure was 1 in 100,000. The engineers responded that chance of engine failure was about 1 in 200. While the manager believed that flying the shuttle was as safe as flying your own plane to the lake, the engineers believed that the risk was five hundred times greater.[13]

Feynman's observations on the reliability of the shuttle were published as an appendix to the commission's report only after he told Chairman Rogers to either publish his findings or remove his name from the report. There Feynman reported his discovery that the overall opinions of the failure rate of the shuttle ranged from about 1 in 100 for the people building it to about 1 in 100,000 for the people launching it. Feynman speculated that these great differences were driven by management's desire to present the shuttle as a developed and safe technology worthy of ongoing government support. He concluded his appendix with these words: "For a successful technology, reality must take precedence over public relations, for Nature cannot be fooled."

The technical hubris Feynman discovered in his investigation of the *Challenger* explosion arose from more than simple perversity within the National Aeronautics and Space Administration (NASA). NASA may have been little more than a victim of its own success in sending men to the moon and back. This dramatic success has become an American expectation when we ask, "If we can put a man on the moon, then surely we can ... ?" Fill in the blank. Although such dramatic and public technological success gives each of us a justified pride in our institutions, it also gives us an unjustified confidence in the ability of technology to solve our problems. As complex as it is, the problem of space travel pales in comparison to the terrestrial problems we have today. The hubris of NASA or any other government agency may be as much a result of our own unrealistic expectations as theirs.[14]

Our great success at technical problem solving has led us to expect similar success with all our problems, including even our most divergent and divisive ones. But for these problems communication across boundaries becomes even more difficult, since the values communicated are no longer just numeric and programmatic, but social and psychological as well. We want to believe in the new alchemy because we want to believe that our problems can be solved by someone else. But what we discover is that failure of communication at the boundary always returns the work to us.

The Cost of Boundaries

The belief that we can simplify complex problems by ever dividing them into smaller problems creates a new complexity of its own that adds to the social and economic cost of our problem solving. We like to think we can make the new alchemy work by doing clever things at the new boundaries we have created. Like the enterprising inventor in the first chapter, we believe we can innovate our way out of the problem. As our example from chapter 1 showed, inventors will frequently divide their perpetual motion devices into several distinct systems where energy is converted from, say, electrical energy to hydraulic energy, and finally to heat, with the claim that their devices produce more heat than could be created by the electricity alone. Enthused by their discoveries, the inventors then proceed to make biased measurements to prove their point. But their alchemy to create energy out of nothing fails, because at each boundary energy is lost, not created.

In the case of the inventor's alchemy, the loss, beyond personal disappointment, is one of thermal energy to the environment. In other cases, the losses are tragic, such as the lives lost in the explosion of the *Challenger*. In the end, we cannot avoid life's losses through the ever more clever division of our work. The work we hope to avoid will always show up at the new boundary, and at these boundaries we will always pay the costs of work avoided. We may shift or transform our losses, but inevitably they will reappear. The work of avoiding our losses by shifting our problems to others is so deeply ingrained in our social fabric that I offer a few more stories to illustrate the point.

A number of years ago, my wife, Janet, and I were invited to a friend's cabin on the North Shore of Lake Superior. As an inducement to plunge into the lake's icy waters after the evening sauna, our hosts offered us some large stones smoothed by the ages and engraved with the name of the place—House on the Rock. Cleaved from the lake's rocky shore by the annual freeze-thaw cycle, such stones have razor-sharp edges when they first split free.

In taking her plunge, Janet stepped on one such razor edge and cut her toe to the extent that we all voted it needed stitches. After a short drive to the local community hospital, we were led into the emergency room, where a nurse was preparing for the arrival of the on-call physician. For a small community hospital, much elaborate equipment surrounded us. They were clearly ready for trauma greater than a cut toe.

The nurse gave the toe a cursory examination and did little else until the physician arrived. Janet was then instructed to lie facedown on the table while the physician hung a sterile blue cloth over her legs, thus separating the patient from the physician. With the appropriate boundary established, the physician began to sew up the wound, which had yet to be properly cleaned. Perhaps the physician thought the nurse had cleaned it, and the nurse, thinking the physician would clean it, said nothing. I assumed the nurse must have judged it to be clean by her inspection and said nothing myself. In any case, no one said anything about scrubbing the wound.

While I watched him sew up the toe, the physician, somewhat full of himself, spoke nonstop about his service as team physician with this or that outfit. To my chagrin, it then occurred to me that I ought to be more present to Janet than watching her toe get stitched, so I crossed the blue barrier to hold her hand. At that point, the physician stopped speaking to me and said nothing for the rest of his work.

As we were leaving, the physician shook my hand but extended no acknowledgment whatsoever to Janet. Here the sterile blue boundary became a metaphor for the lack of communication between the nurse and the physician, and between the physician and the patient. The cost of this boundary was assumed by Janet in the form of an infected toe that needed further medical care.

The care Janet received stands in sharp contrast to the care I received in the Kingdom of Tonga on my way home from teaching in the South Pacific. While wading in the murky waters off the shore of the place where I was staying, I, too, got a bad cut on the bottom of my big toe. From the gasps of the crowd that gathered, I gathered that stitches were going to be needed. Someone found a cab and kindly gave me a newspaper to bleed on as I got hauled to the island's hospital.

There I was led, shuffling and bleeding on my paper, down bare cement floors to what seemed to be the emergency room. A single light hung from the ceiling. Under it rested a bare gurney. A simple wood table in the corner held an autoclave and a two-pound coffee can of presumably sterile needles for sewing up people. No room for trauma here.

The physician came to the door, removed his flip-flops, and entered to do his work barefoot. After numbing up my toe with Novocain, he proceeded to scrub my wound as if he were removing barnacles from a boat. "A lot of horse manure in that water," he said as he proceeded. A few stitches later, his work was done and he sent me on my way. He said I owed nothing for the care he gave me, but if I wished, I could make a contribution to the hospital. A week later, the itching in my toe told me that I was healing without infection.

From these stories, it is clear that I received better care in the "primitive" island hospital than Janet received in the far better equipped, small-town-America emergency room. What separated the care we received was not technology, but rather the sterile blue boundary. Here the sterile blue boundary becomes a metaphor for the entire U.S. healthcare system, an illustration of the boundaries that separate the nurse from the physician, the physician from the patient, and the patient from the responsibility for his or her own care. The sterile blue boundary is one of the primary reasons for the ever-increasing cost of health care in the United States.

As a final example, consider the building boundaries that surround our daily living. Walls and windows separate outside from inside, floors separate above from below, a foundation separates the building from the earth, and a roof separates it from the sky. And within these boundaries are yet more: boundaries between the materials used to construct the building and between the systems that provide heating and cooling, electricity, light, and water.

A particular trade is responsible for each material or system in a building. Masons lay the bricks, steamfitters install the boiler, and electricians wire the lights. These workers are all directed by a general contractor following plans prepared by architects and engineers. Together, all work to meet the needs of the final owner—the one who is going to pay for it all.

With so many boundaries between workers, contractors, designers, and owners, conflicts are not only unavoidable, but expected. Conflicts are so common that the head of construction litigation for a local law office simply asserts, "There is no construction without construction litigation." The lawyer's assertion is well grounded in practice, where conflicts arise not only from the personal boundaries between the workers, but from the large variety of physical boundaries between various parts of the building. Again, everything happens at the boundary as workers share responsibility for whether a project performs as expected and gets completed on time and within budget.

Conflicts arise when projects take too long to build, go over budget, or fail to perform. Left to litigation, conflicts become huge resource sinks as more time, money, and personal energy are used to assign blame than to solve problems. Such costs have so challenged the construction industry that, today, those affected have invented their own new liturgy—partnering.

Partnering in the construction business does just what the new liturgy should: it literally returns the work to the workers. As described by the Associated General Contractors of America, "Partnering is not a contract, but a recognition that every contract includes an implied covenant of good faith."[15] Recognized is that, while a contract is a legal obligation to perform, partnering is a process that establishes the working relationships among all stakeholders in the process.

What happens when the work of solving construction problems gets done in partnership? Projects become far more likely to be completed on time and within budget, and to perform as expected. Trust and cooperation are enhanced, contractors gain improved reputations for timely work well done, paperwork is vastly reduced, profits grow, and everybody involved has more fun.

And what about all those unemployed lawyers? With partnering the work of the lawyer is to transform himself or herself from a rent seeker to an entrepreneur, from a litigator to a mediator—from someone who profits from the human condition to someone who ameliorates it. Entrepreneurial lawyers, by returning the work of the people to the people, can become leaders in the new liturgy. As for the ambulance chasers and other recalcitrant rent seekers of the profession, the hard work of laziness will, I fear, continue to serve them all too well.

No matter how many boundaries we put between ourselves and our problems, each boundary incurs a cost that returns our work to us. Whether personal or communal, we can only do our own work and remedy our own problems. This is the work of the new liturgy—the work of the people.

Leading the New Liturgy

It seems to be a measure of the American character that we are both rugged individualists as well as people who form associations for cooperative work. The dissonance between our "cowboy" and "cooperator" behaviors produces a creativity that is the envy of the world and a chaos that is not. Bringing order out of this dissonance are institutions unique to the American enterprise. The primary work of these American institutions is to lead the new liturgy, as we shall see next.

CHAPTER FIVE

The New Work

Servant Leadership and the Third Sector

A leader is at his best when people barely know he exists.
When his work is done, his aim fulfilled, they will say,
"We did it ourselves."
—Lao-Tzu

Non-profit institutions are central to American society
and are indeed its most distinguishing feature.
—Peter F. Drucker

The hope of the world lies in the rehabilitation
of the living human being.
—Václav Havel

The New Work and the Third Sector

Only in America.

Janet and I were just moving into our remodeled house when three girls from a nearby Jewish congregation came to the door. They were collecting household goods for recent Soviet immigrants and asked if we had anything to contribute. Although Janet and I had just combined households and had much to share, we had given our small items to the local Goodwill store and committed our unneeded furniture to a recently arrived Hmong family in our own church. Only in America would such a variety of volunteer not-for-profit associations be ready to serve immigrants, and only in America would such immigration be so accommodated.

The tendency of Americans to form associations for a common purpose is not new; indeed it was one of the primary observations of the young aristocrat Alexis de Tocqueville when he visited the United States in 1831. Tocqueville spent only nine months in the country but made observations about America and its associations that ring true yet today.[1] That many of his observations remain relevant shows the ongoing propensity for Americans to join together in associations that serve our political, economic, social, and religious aspirations.

Today over one-quarter of the adult population of the United States volunteers in what is called the independent or third sector. This work is done through more than a million nonprofit organizations, in which volunteers work the equivalent of three full weeks a year bringing a variety of services to their communities.[2] In my town, for example, Catholic Charities organizes nearly forty thousand volunteers a year, providing a workforce equivalent of nearly one hundred full-time positions. Each day through its Dorothy Day Center the hungry are fed, the homeless receive basic medical care, and school dropouts are tutored in preparation for high school equivalency examinations.[3]

The third sector is the country's largest employer and constitutes an economy of its own, one that provides substantial services through music, art, education, health care, child care, drug rehabilitation, recycling, food shelves, homeless services, activities for youth—the list goes on. Beyond these are advocacy and action groups that promote a vast array of agendas ranging from environmental conservation to natural resource development, gun ownership to gun control, nuclear energy to renewable energy, restricted abortion to full reproductive freedom, individual rights to individual responsibility. Moreover, central to much of this work are the moral principles and ethical teachings of the churches, synagogues, and mosques of America. Only in America do we have such a diverse and productive nonprofit sector, and only in America is so much of this work supported and carried out by religious institutions.

The importance of the nonprofit or third sector in the civil life of America cannot be overestimated. Today 10 percent of the gross domestic product of the United States flows through the institutions of the third sector, where it supports over 8 percent of all wages and salaries paid in the United States. As a result of the direct corporate and individual support of the third sector, Americans enjoy some of the lowest taxes and finest services in the world.[4]

The third or nonprofit sector is made up of those organizations that are neither business nor government. If the business sector provides products and services while the government maintains infrastructure and public order, what is the work of the third sector? It is the work of the new liturgy—the work of social transformation that builds secure communities through the nurturing and renewing of people. Most needed today are people of character who have the knowledge and self-control to cooperate in ways that enhance our communal life. Our challenge today is not to produce more things, but to transform people and build communities.

Toward a New Economy

At the end of the nineteenth century, over 40 percent of Americans worked on farms. Today our farm population stands at less than 2 percent of the total labor force and produces more food than we can eat. This enormous increase in farm productivity has occurred even though growing crops is an energy- and area-intensive business that depends on the weather to produce perishable products—products that need to be stored and brought to distant markets, some around the world, without spoilage. Rural electrification, refrigeration, farm mechanization, hybrid seeds, fertilizers, herbicides, pesticides, roads and railroads, all along with abundant water and oil, have combined to produce increases in farm productivity that have reduced the need for farm labor by more than a factor of twenty. If such large increases in farm productivity are possible—productivity that requires covering large areas of land and that depends on cooperative weather to produce a perishable commodity—then it seems reasonable that similar productive gains are possible in the manufacturing sector, since making nonperishable, nonliving things in a controlled environment is an intrinsically simpler problem.

For example, consider the production of glass fiber, a basic building material. Like farming, the production of glass fiber is an area- and energy-intensive process that uses ovens the size of football fields to transform bulk glass into hair-thin fibers. When it closed in 1987, the Jackson, Tennessee, plant of Owens Corning annually produced 130 million pounds of glass fiber with a workforce of 540 people. Refurbished and reopened seven years later, the renewed plant still produces the same 130 million pounds of glass fiber, but now produces it with just 80 employees, plus 20 contract workers. This more than fivefold increase in productivity resulted from a new glassmaking formula, plus automation and the creation of a core group of technical workers, each trained in every skill required to operate the plant. In addition, by assigning more routine work, such as security, general maintenance, and material handling to 20 contingency workers, full-time employees can continue to work during slowdowns in the building business by taking on these tasks while the contract workers are laid off. Thus, one of the less visible results of this refurbished operation is that the problem of keeping workers busy during business downturns has been transferred from the company to the contingency worker.

The Jackson glass-fiber factory captures well the transformation of a dirty old-line business into a cleaner and more streamlined operation. The new glass formula brought the plant into compliance with environmental regulations, eliminating the need for labor and equipment to clean up the air coming out of the plant. Along with cleaner air, the new technology allowed waste material to be recycled, further reducing the environmental impact of the plant while lowering the cost of production.[5]

In the 1950s, U.S. manufacturing employment peaked at about 30 percent of the workforce; today it stands at less than 9 percent. With additional efficiencies, such as the recent gains at the Jackson plant, along with the country's current agricultural productivity, it seems more likely than ever that America will be able to meet all of its manufacturing and agricultural labor needs with less than 10 percent of its workforce.[6]

For the individual laborer, such increases in productivity are unwelcome news, since fewer and fewer people are required to produce the food and goods we each need. For our collective economy, however, such increases in productivity do improve the lot of all. With fewer workers required to produce goods for our material well-being, we can begin to reduce our material consumption without risking the whole of our economy. Such reductions in material consumption will allow us to redirect our wealth toward a greater investment in people and the future of the country, including those workers displaced by the compound forces of increased productivity and reduced consumption. Today, beyond America's enormous gains in material productivity and personal wealth lies the capacity for a new economy, one marked by abundance for all.[7]

Creating a new economy will require the work of the new liturgy. It will require the daily attention and discipline of each citizen and will be directed by the institutions of the third sector. This new work will require new leadership—leadership that transforms by giving away its power.

Servant Leadership and the New Liturgy

In the previous chapter, I talked about our human inclination to avoid the work of solving our own problems. We do this based on the conviction that if we are just clever enough, we can convert problems that require our personal cooperation into problems that can be solved by someone else. We believe that if we are clever enough in the division of our work, we can always convert divergent problems into convergent ones. This is the work of the new alchemy.

Today such new-alchemy problem solving is miserably and tragically failing to resolve our most pressing problems of mindless wealth, senseless poverty, and the disintegration of community life. The divide-and-conquer problem-solving method of the new alchemy will always fail, since our work will always be returned to us no matter how hard we try to give our problems to someone else. This work that leads to more work is the hard work of laziness.

The failure of new-alchemy problem solving requires us to reexamine the efforts we bring to the problems of our lives and to acknowledge that for most of our difficulties we cannot give our work to anyone else but ourselves. This is the work of the people—the work of the new liturgy. Required today is leadership that redirects our efforts from that of the new alchemy to that of the new liturgy. This is the work of the servant leader.

Today we elect public officials with the expectation that they will take our tax money and solve our problems. We elect our leaders to get tough on drugs, crime, or terrorism, and to improve our health, education, or welfare, and when these efforts fail, we assume that the failure is theirs, not ours. By cleverly creating and moving around boundaries of authority and responsibility, we expect our elected leaders to make our problems disappear. But each new boundary creates more problems than it solves, and far from disappearing, our problems grow worse.

We elect such alchemists to public office because they promise what we all want to hear: that our problems are beyond us and only solvable by some higher authority. Rich or poor, we expect our public officials to propose programs that will bring us personal security without social obligation. But this is not the way life works, and our public problem solving fails because the work of solving our problems is ours and not theirs. Our present form of public problem solving—party politics—is popular because it simultaneously gives an illusion of power to our elected officials and an unfounded confidence in the political process to us. Yet personal security without social obligation is a political chimera. We cannot escape the work of the new liturgy.

For example, today we elect without blinking people who promise to maintain services, decrease taxes, *and* balance the budget. By clever manipulation, such an illusion can be maintained for a long period of time, and because of this, it is particularly dangerous, since in the end the system will always go broke. Two popular ways to create such budget illusions are deferred maintenance and debt. These mechanisms are everybody's favorites, since maintenance is easy to postpone and debt can be constantly shifted so nothing ever needs to be added up all at once. Families do this by using a home equity loan on an old house that needs a new roof to buy a new car instead. And Washington lets lapse our public infrastructure while using our Social Security payments to help balance the budget.

Much of the fiscal fantasy described above is driven by our belief that the best resource for improving anything is more money. For example, although there are inequalities in educational funding that need redress, one of the best assurances of educational success is not more money, but rather a school filled with students who come from homes where learning is valued. It is unlikely that much can be done to improve our children's education until we improve the learning capacity of the communities in which they live. The difference between a good and a bad school is not the presence of a critical amount of money, but the presence of a critical number of students prepared to learn. Similarly, while a living wage is necessary, it is not sufficient to end poverty, since ending poverty turns as much on community assets as it does on individual income. Like education, the problem of poverty has no single or simple solution but can only be addressed through the application of remedies based on the capacities of the community.[8]

Bringing truth to these matters is the work of the servant leader. Servant leaders do not do our work for us, but rather join us in getting it done. Rather than directing our work, the servant leader directs us to self-organize around the capacities of the group by allowing each of us to bring to the task those skills that best match what needs to be done. Such leadership is not easy; most of us would rather be directed than left to our own devices. After all, leaders are paid to lead, and so that is what we expect of them. The value of letting workers self-organize around the task at hand is well illustrated by the late Garland Wright's leadership of Minneapolis's Guthrie Theater.

When Garland Wright was appointed as artistic director of the Guthrie Theater in 1986, the theater's central goal became the cultivation of "America's finest acting ensemble."[9] During Wright's tenure, the change from a theater of stars to a company of actors was most palpable in his direction of Shakespeare's history plays. During the process of producing these plays as a single historical sweep, Wright took on the role of servant leader as he returned the work of the theater to the actors.

Beyond accepting ownership for their individual characters, actors were required to take ownership of the larger character of the production as well. This challenged the members of the acting company to the core as they began to examine their own beliefs, abilities, and reasons for being on stage in the first place. Encouraged to use their own devices to present what the plays were about, the company was forced to confront thirty opinions rather than accepting that of a single director. Actors reported that such work was "scary," made them feel "naked out there," and caused them to question whether they even "wanted to be an actor."[10]

Such nondirective directing and self-directed acting requires conviction, courage, and integrity and presents a demanding test of both the director's and actor's craft. The risk is that no matter how skillful the company, the resulting work is unknown until it emerges from the collective capacity of the acting company. Accepting an unknown outcome is a central part of the servant leader's work.

But the success of the work does not belong entirely to the actors or the director, for the theater under Wright's leadership described its mission as "the shared act of imagining."[11] In this act, actors and audience become engaged in a dance of laughter, passion, truth, and tears as they enter into the playwright's world. And with this, the boundary between the actor and audience wanes as one enters into the other's presence, and they become a seamless whole called theater.

Still success does not always emerge, nor can it be expected, since the whole is alive and living things are unpredictable and messy. Thus, in his principles of leadership for the theater, Wright asserted, "We reserve the right to fail." Leadership requires the understanding that success is achievable only by accepting the possibility of failure. A simplistic understanding of what is alive leads to expectations of perfection that are unachievable by any living system and is one of the reasons why criticism needs to be critically viewed itself.[12]

Theater shows us that what is required of us is not perfection, but participation. It is out of such participation that new life can emerge. The success of the company-building effort at the Guthrie Theater was that, by returning the work to the actors, the director as servant leader allowed the company to emerge as a whole.[13] And with this the audience became a part of that whole as well.

The metaphor of the theater is captured by Czech Republic president and playwright Václav Havel when he says, "Theater is a place for human encounter, a space for authentic human existence, above all the kind of existence that transcends itself in order to give an account of the world and itself. It is a means of giving a concrete shape to our hope. A hope which is the rebirth of a living humanity."[14] The work of the theater becomes a metaphor for the vocation of the servant leader, one who calls us to task and demands our participation in an emergent life.

The living work of the theater engages the audience in an experience that may or may not succeed in creating a seamless whole between actor and audience. But even if a theater's results are not perfect, it can still be effective. Some work, however, does require near perfection to be effective. For example, a theater's ticket-printing system must have bug-free software, a nonjamming printer, and a competent operator if tickets are to be properly prepared. But this sort of perfection is also well served by the new liturgy.

One example of such perfection is Reell Precision Manufacturing, a small company that makes critical mechanical and electromechanical parts for the computer and copier industry. Based on the simple idea that a coil spring tightens when wound one way but not the other, Reell Precision Manufacturing makes clutches that are as ubiquitous as the *whup, whup, whup* sound of the copy machines they help drive. Clutches are assembled by small groups of workers who assume responsibility for their own work, including setup and quality control, and who in the end produce boxes of clutches that without further inspection will be installed in their customers' products.

Reell Precision Manufacturing prepares its workers through a simple three-step program to teach, equip, and then trust those who join the company. At Reell each production line is an acting company that shares a commitment to the whole process. And out of this commitment to the whole emerges the quality demanded by the customer. In the process, lives are changed as group expectations to show up prepared to work replace showing up late or not showing up at all, and individual problems that affect work quality are addressed, for example, providing rides when a car breaks down.

The teach, equip, and trust work process at Reell Precision Manufacturing stands in sharp contrast to the usual plan, direct, control method practiced by most American businesses today. Like the organic farmer who raises soil and produces food as a by-product, Reell Precision Manufacturing develops workers who as a by-product produce high-quality manufactured goods. Flowing out of the high trust, low hierarchy of the company's teach, equip, and trust management paradigm is a stream of transformed workers, quality products, living wages, and sustainable earnings.[15]

Whether producing plays or products, the task of the servant leader is to trust the worker with the work. By replacing direction and control with responsibility and trust, the servant leader in each case enhances the quality of both the work experience and the product.[16] But beyond this work in the arts and manufacturing lies the servant leader's even greater challenge: leading the work of the third sector.

Leadership and the Shadow

Above the sideboard in my dining room is a pastel drawing of wildflowers and grasses on the near shore of a sunlit lake. Because the artist's preliminary sketch somehow seemed incomplete, I asked him to include the lake's far shore in the drawing. Shortly after I had hung the completed drawing, I realized that behind the beauty of the wildflowers on the near shore lurked the darkness of the far one. Behind the beauty lurked the beast, the drawing incomplete one without the other. Today, with each look the artist reminds me of my dark side, my shadow on that far shore, and with each look he invites me to cross the lake (17).

Like the artist, the servant leader invites us across the lake to own our shadow selves, to own the worst and the best of who we are. At first glance the lake appears serene enough, but we are unsure of ourselves and frightened by what we may encounter on the far shore. Such journeys are frightening enough to keep most of us on the safe side, warm and in the light.

But the servant leader will not let us get away with this. Thus, the heart of the invitational work of the servant leader is to guide our journey to the far shore of the lake. It is at the far shore that the task of telling the difference between the neurotic and existential gets done. As much as we would like the servant leader to do this for us, it is something that only we can do. Thus the first step in our work as followers is to accept that the work belongs to us and no one else.

But if the servant leader is to take us to the far side, to the boundary where the work of life gets done, then he or she must take the trip first. At this point the servant leader must confront his or her own insecurities, become empty of ambition, and accept the uncertainty that leadership brings.

Thus it takes courage to be a servant leader. It is the courage to be vulnerable to those who follow. Such leadership requires a commitment of personal understanding that few have the courage to undertake. Although owning one's shadow or worst self is a part of both the leader's and the follower's work, the leader must travel farther and deeper than the follower to be effective. Those who have not suffered at the boundaries of their own existence have little hope of leading others. The ultimate task of the servant leader is to own his or her own shadow and to encourage those who follow to do the same.[18]

Servant leadership remains a far cry from what many people experience today. Rather than calling on followers to own their shadows, today's leaders act more to facilitate than ameliorate their projection onto others. By exploiting rather than challenging the follower's shadow, the leader promotes the follower's projection by identifying a common opposition around whom everyone can rally for whatever purpose.[19] Given this, everyone outside the circle of those being led or governed is then labeled as the other, as someone to be outmaneuvered, compromised, or destroyed in effectiveness. Whether business, politics, or war, naming the other as beyond the pale becomes the principal role of leadership as leaders rally those around them to project their shadow on the other. Today's partisan politics, endless wars, and ruthless business competition are good measures of how present the shadow is in today's leadership.

Followership and the Shadow

As leaders or followers, we all drag behind us what poet Robert Bly calls our "long bag," which contains all the admonitions and pains of our lives.[20] It is into the long bag that we stuff all the things we aren't supposed to be. It's that place where we stuff ourselves away from ourselves and each other. It contains our shadow, and to dump it out for a good look requires more than most of us can bear. Still, although we might find the contents of our own bag frightening, the daily litany of physical violence and political hubris prepared for our consumption on the evening news clearly shows our interest in the long bags of others.

Bly's metaphor of the long bag takes on practical significance when it is used to describe the shadow work required of the servant leader and his or her followers. Here the effectiveness of the servant leader and the resulting problem-solving capacity of the followers can be described by how well they all cope not only with their own long bags, but with the long bags of one another.

Most of us have one of three general reactions to the contents of the long bag we each drag. The most common is simply to deny that the bag exists. This is clearly the easiest, since without a bag we never have to consider its contents. The first step beyond denial of the shadow is simply to acknowledge its existence. For many of us this is the most we can do, since to do more is just too painful. But beyond denial and acknowledgment lies the greatest challenge, which is to understand and own the contents of our own long bags.

Carl Jung in his founding work on the shadow offered that there exists little technique for doing such work other than having the proper attitude. He explains, "First of all one has to accept and to take seriously into account the existence of the shadow. Secondly, it is necessary to be informed about its qualities and intentions. Thirdly, long and difficult negotiations will be unavoidable." Jung claims that nobody can know the outcome of such work and that in the end conflicts are not changed as much by clever invention as they are by enduring them.[21]

The process of owning who we are requires a lifetime of work and commitment. But if we are going to begin solving our most pressing problems today, we each need to begin with incomplete knowledge of both ourselves and those around us. In any problem-solving situation, we must act on incomplete knowledge, but what most compromises our collective problem-solving capacity is imperfect knowledge of self.

Nevertheless, through collective work we can come to new understandings of ourselves and each other and from these understandings find remedies that simply could not have emerged from our individual efforts. Although we will never find perfect solutions within our communities, we can find remedies that invite our participation.

Servant Leadership and
Community Problem Solving

The work of a community and its leaders is to bring remedies to the community's problems. Most people and organizations find community problem solving to be imposing, if not overwhelming. It is inefficient and messy, and like the classic home-remodeling project, it frequently takes more time, money, and energy than expected. We expect our processes to be efficient and productive and to demonstrate that we are actually getting things done. Both those doing the work and those watching it can become anxious because "progress" is not being made. This drive for efficiency can readily cause the work to focus more on doing rather than being, and when this happens, the long-term problem-solving capacity of the group is diminished. The principal work of the servant leader is to enhance the problem-solving capacity of the group by directing its work from anxious doing to creative being.

Community problem solving is not easy. It requires each person to transcend his or her worst self and to reach out with understanding and trust. Working in a group means participating in dialogue and becoming tolerant of the anxiety produced by the passage of time—the time it takes to get things done. Community problem solving requires people to make a significant commitment to an uncertain process that calls for large amounts of personal time and emotional energy. Participation in such a process is not for the fainthearted, and few individuals or institutions readily enter into it.

Yet, however daunting, the success of any community problem-solving enterprise rests on the participation of each member of the community. It cannot be done by an individual leader, a committee, or some task force, but only by the daily direct civil activity of each citizen. For a community to be civil, the majority of its citizens must be civil. Individual civility begets corporate civility.

The social wealth created by individual civility stands in sharp contrast to the material wealth created by the unending production and use of consumer goods. Unlike the consumerism of material wealth, civility enhances our individual and community social wealth without compromising the social wealth of others. In answer to the question of chapter 3, "Can we all do it?," civility offers a unequivocal "yes" that affirms both the power of the individual and that of the community.

The idea of power is frequently a negative one based on the belief that power invariably means "power over." But when power becomes the power to transform a social situation through cooperative action between leaders and followers, then the leader's source of power is derived not from power over, but from "power with," the followers. Far from being powerless, the servant leader, by participating in the work of the community, has the power to effect lasting change within the community of followers. This is the power of the servant leader, and it can be got only by giving it away.

Need for an Improved Problem-Solving Model

A common problem-solving model is the well-known four-stage process of "Forming, Storming, Norming, and Performing."[22] Even though this model is used for much of our public problem solving, my experience tells me it is inadequate for many problems that matter. The norming-performing problem-solving process begins when we meet one another and form into a group that is supposed to get something done. During this time, we become socially acquainted and select those who will guide the process, take minutes, bring coffee. But if work is going to get done and some cooperative goal achieved, our social conversation must inevitably turn to intentional discussion. With this shift, forming ends and storming begins as we each state our personal positions and try to convince those around us to agree. At this stage, the contents of our long bags become important, for whether or not we are conscious of it, our storming is likely to be informed by what's in our bag. Finally, since most meetings are driven by an agenda to "do something" or even to "do anything," storming ends, and by necessity the group moves on to norming.

With norming the problem-solving capacity of the group becomes sorely compromised. Rather than venturing to the boundaries where the required work must be done, the group, consciously or not, now establishes new and uncrossable boundaries within which it decides to act. Rather than owning their individual shadows, the group has formed a long bag of its own, one newly filled with the undiscussables of storming. Thus prepared, the group begins to perform.

For simple, convergent problem solving, such performing is probably good enough. After all, life is short and practical stuff needs to get done. If we spent all our lives rummaging through our long bags, our routine work would certainly suffer. Sometimes it *is* best just to grab some chips, turn on the TV, and forget it!

But for complex divergent problems, for problems that are alive and messy, such norming and performing produces solutions that are temporarily effective at best. That most politically elected bodies produce Band-Aid solutions is a sure sign that they are performing without the benefit of moving beyond the undiscussables of the group's own long bag. The problem with the norming-performing model is that it fails to acknowledge the long bags that we each drag. By failing to acknowledge our shadow sides, this popular problem-solving model actually adds to the mess by creating a new long bag of its own.

The Work of the Servant Leader

For a group process to move beyond the chaos of storming, each member needs to stop converting others and to acknowledge and own his or her own shadow. Because of the sheer difficulty of this work, most of us, given the chance, would rather move on to the safety of norming. It is here that the servant leader by owning his or her own shadow becomes vulnerable and leads the group with the invitation that they too join in crossing to the dark side of the lake. It is here that our long bags, if not dumped out, are at least acknowledged. And it is here that the formation of a community built on trust and mutual respect begins.

The work of the servant leader is not easy. Today followership is a little-known concept, and left untempered by wisdom, the vulnerable servant leader is all too easily rendered ineffective. Unlike the realm of physics, there are few, if any, rules for leadership. If there is any single rule, it would be that the work of the servant leader is to develop the problem-solving capacity of the group.

Signs that a group has begun to do its work are that dialogue replaces argumentation, being replaces doing, and periods of silence are more frequent and comfortable. Still, as important as they are, dialogue and silence mark only the beginning of the group's work, since many individual agendas as well as the collective bag of the group remain (23).

At this juncture the servant leader begins his or her most difficult work by becoming an exemplar for the work of the group. Such work can be painful as the leader encourages others to follow and as hidden agendas necessarily become unhidden and truths are revealed. The servant leader needs to exercise discernment, since too much truth-telling may be a bad thing. Confessions as either a leader or a follower should not be made gratuitously, and knowing when to speak becomes as important as knowing when not to speak.

One approach for such conversations is to consider the required dialogue to be a form of negotiation. Successful negotiation may take place without needing to have all of one's cards on the table. Similarly, group dialogue may be successful in finding remedies to problems without everyone needing to know, heaven forbid, the contents of all the long bags in the room.

For such negotiation, it is useful to distinguish between what Roger Fisher and William Ury of the Harvard Negotiation Project call positions and interests.[24] A simple example was my observation of two colleagues tugging back and forth over a video disk. In this case, each held the position that they wanted the DVD *now*. What was missing from the tussle were their personal interests, that one needed it on Tuesday and the other on Thursday. If each had relinquished the position of "I want it now" for the interest of "I need it on Tuesday (or Thursday)," the problem could have been readily resolved to the advantage of both. Another example is the proverbial tale of the mother who always cut the Christmas ham in two because that was the way her mother had always done it. Held in the family tradition was the position that cut hams baked better. Long lost from the occasion was the knowledge that the ritual was simply based on Grandma's interest of fitting the Christmas ham into a smaller pan.

The value of distinguishing positions from interests is that by casting our dialogues in terms of interests, each person can examine his or her own personal position without revealing more than they wish. For example, the people tussling over the DVD might have had personal agendas of mistrust. The person who wants the DVD on Thursday needs to trust the Tuesday person to have the disk available as promised, and the Tuesday person needs to take on that responsibility. With this the DVD transaction can be completed without the Thursday person needing to share past grievances about all the times he or she has been hurt by trusting all the wrong people. And the Tuesday person doesn't need to recite a litany of failures to deliver on things promised. By focusing on interests rather than positions, we can legitimately address all the stuff in our long bags without the need for unnecessarily painful revelations. Knowing and owning what's in our bag may also tell us that there are some people with whom we should not negotiate or that with whom negotiation will be difficult at best. In these cases, our shadows become golden as they inform us not to be naive about the motivations of others.

Practical leadership is dicey at best. Most all who have participated in or led meetings have experienced "meetings from hell" where all sorts of unacknowledged agendas have come out of the bag. At times like this, previously unnecessary revelations may become necessary if the group is to continue to grow in respect, trust, vulnerability, and effectiveness. This is difficult for both leaders and followers. Yet without such efforts, our relationships may easily become defensive and without meaning. And with this, dialogue dries up and community vanishes.

By returning the work of the people to the people, the servant leader works toward the ultimate goal of making his or her efforts unnecessary. Leadership thus requires a special wholeness that allows the leader to identify with values and aspirations beyond those of the group. Such wholeness allows the leader to transcend the group and to make his or her leadership unnecessary. The leader in effect dies to the group so that the group may have a life of its own. Although followers must be functional and alive to accept the work of the leader, it requires a transcendent leader to return the work to the followers.

The Work of the Third Sector

Transforming people is the work of the nonprofit organizations of the third sector. From a hot lunch delivered by Meals on Wheels to hope renewed by the Salvation Army, to sensibilities civilized by Mozart in the Park, the organizations of the third sector bring dignity to life. A hot meal, a helping hand, a well-turned serenade—each adds to the wholeness of the individual and in turn to the wholeness, well-being, and civility of the community.

Far from being a mere benevolent adjunct to our material economy, the work of the third sector is essential to its success. It is the work of the third sector that directs us from the hard work of laziness, the work of the new alchemy, to the sustaining work of the new liturgy. In my town, for example, Freedom Place, Inc., turns problem properties into neighborhood assets by renovating neglected houses. Purchased or donated problem houses are renovated by poor and homeless people who simultaneously build skills and a place to live. Freedom Place offers people who are ready to make a commitment to sobriety and work a chance to live lives of dignity and self-sufficiency. Empowering the powerless to reclaim their lives is central to the work of the third sector and the new economy.

Third-sector organizations provide remedies to our public problems by returning the work of the community to the citizen, and with this both the community and the citizen are transformed. A transformed citizen produces a civil society by turning off the TV and reading to his or her children, participating at his or her place of worship, leading a scout troop—knowing his or her neighbors. That this community work fails to get done by so many regardless of economic or social class is a measure of our increasing lack of civility in America.

The principal work of the nonprofit third sector is the creation of social wealth. If the for-profit sector increases our material wealth through a new and improved product or service, the third sector enhances our social wealth through a transformed person or an ameliorated social condition. And where the for-profit economy measures its success by the volume of goods and services profitably sold, the nonprofit third sector measures its success by the number of citizens effectively engaged in the life of the community.[25]

The driving mission of the for-profit organization is to stay in business. This is achieved by competing in the marketplace to gain market share and to enhance profits. In contrast, the mission of the nonprofit social service organization is to go out of business. Like the work of the servant leader, the mission of the nonprofit organization is to so transform the community that the organization's work becomes unnecessary. In the same way that the servant leader's mission is to die to the organization, the nonprofit organization's mission is to die to the community so that the community itself may have life.

Most important, while the for-profit sector builds on our needs or deficiencies by supplying both essential and nonessential material goods, the nonprofit sector builds on our capacity to govern ourselves and to remedy our own problems. And while the for-profit sector is built on dominance by providing solutions in an ever more competitive market, the nonprofit sector is built on partners cooperatively bringing remedies to their communities. Our American government most frequently follows the for-profit model when it dominates communities with burdensome and overregulated programs designed to solve the problems of the community, often without the consensus or cooperation of the community it is supposed to be serving. By designing programs based more on a community's deficiencies than on its assets, government-mandated programs become not only expensive, but ineffective.

Programs designed to meet the perceived deficiencies of others more often than not end up serving the provider's needs more than the community's. Citizens end up dependent on the provider, and the provider ends up dependent on the largess of the state. With two-thirds of program money going to providers, it's hard to know just who is being served. In terms of the work metaphors of this book, the work of the people—the work of the new liturgy—is replaced by the work of the professional provider, and everyone in the community suffers for it.[26]

Whatever work we do—whether producing products or plays or, more importantly, bringing abundant life to ourselves and others—we must accept the personal responsibility for what happens at the boundaries of our lives. The worker on the production line produces with others to please the customer, and out of this a quality product emerges. The actor assumes responsibility for his or her own work with a company of actors, and from this emerges their shared act of imagining. And when the citizen assumes personal responsibility for his or her own community, dialogue, civility, and sane living emerge. Whether producing a product, presenting a play, or redeeming a social condition, these efforts require workers, actors, and citizens alike to go to the boundaries of their experience and encounter the work of being human.[27]

The ultimate purpose of the new liturgy is to enforce the unenforceable. For this, leadership must necessarily become transcendent as each person in the community assumes responsibility for his or her own behavior. By setting an example for each child and one another, the adults of the community become the bearers of civility for the community. And with this, neighbor knows neighbor, dialogue is maintained, civility emerges, and the unenforceable is enforced.

CHAPTER SIX

From the Apple to the Cross

Reimagining the Christian Message

Redemption occurs in communities where truth can be told.
—Rita Nakashima Brock

The genuine and simple religion of Jesus will one day be restored: such as it was preached and practised by himself.
—Thomas Jefferson

Every genuine religious person is a heretic and therefore a revolutionist.
—George Bernard Shaw

Hearing Things

Voices, voices, voices.

We met each Wednesday after school in the old parsonage a few doors down from the church where we sat on folding chairs meant more for keeping our attention than providing comfort. For two years, twenty-one of us spent restless afternoons in our hair-shirt seats studying what has been known since 1531 as Luther's Small Catechism.

I was twelve, and when you're a Lutheran and twelve years old, you start confirmation class. And with this I began to hear voices, voices that have remained with me to this day. The voices came not from my head, but from religious instruction that remains as incongruous for me today as it was over fifty years ago.

The language of Luther's catechism was new to me, and throughout confirmation my perennial but unasked question was, "Where did the foreign expressions that we were required to memorize, if not understand, actually come from?" The language did not reflect the stories of my Sunday school or my early understanding of Jesus and the Bible.

Most troubling of all were the creeds. With the tortuous language of the Nicene Creed, Jesus, my kindly shepherd, suddenly became "God from God, Light from Light, true God from true God, begotten, not made, of one Being with the Father." Already pimply, pubescent, and having little self-esteem, I now felt caught in the crossfire of some theological food fight. But my greatest trouble of all was that within the creeds the life of Jesus disappeared altogether. The Apostles' Creed told me he was "born of the Virgin Mary; suffered under Pontius Pilate, was crucified, dead, and buried." My Sunday school Jesus had become a semicolon in a confession of faith that I find as implausible now as I did then.

Clearly something had happened. Yet what happened to me in that class was not new; it had occurred once before, between the time of Jesus' death and the rise of the Christian church we know today. In a fleeting two years, my confirmation class had recapitulated centuries of church evolution, and by age fourteen, without knowing it, I had been theologically catapulted into Christian adulthood.

What did happen after Jesus' death was that his revolutionary and transforming ministry soon began evolving into an institutional church, a church designed more to preserve the world than to transform it. During the first century, the voice of Jesus became the voice of the early Christian movement, a voice that over the next four centuries became the voice of the established Christian church that we see today. From what started as a movement to empower the laity grew a powerful organization of clergy governing a hierarchical church that Jesus would not recognize today. During the church's first five hundred years, the three-year ministry of Jesus was transformed from a radical living example of what life could be like into a deadly theology of sex, sin, and salvation.

My reason for speaking about the church at this point is my belief that of all the third-sector nonprofit organizations in America, it is those that bring spiritual consciousness to our communities that are of the most importance. I believe that by returning to the radical teachings of Jesus the Christian churches of America can be powerful organizations for social transformation. The power of the church will come not only from a transformation of its own religious and social practices, but from a fundamental rethinking of its own self-invented, yet now ever more questionable, teachings and theology.

Three Voices and the Scholar's Work

The three voices of my confirmation class, those of Jesus, the early Christian movement, and the organized church, were not unique to me but have been examined throughout the ages by kings, clergy, and laity alike. Although histories of the early church have been available to laity for some time, it is only recently that accessible writing has become available on the history of God, the life of Jesus, and the origin of Christian myth. Although the information in such writings appears new to novices such as me and those in my church study group, the fact is that much of the information now being made available to the laity has been the scholar's currency for decades, if not longer.

We are fortunate that today there are men and women of faith who have begun to speak out publicly on the origins and nature of Christian belief and practice. One such group is the Jesus Seminar, a group of biblical scholars who had the audacity to ask the question, "What did Jesus really say?" Motivated by the observation that most critical biblical analysis remained buried in obscure journals while the biblical illiteracy of the general public went unaddressed, they decided to "quit the library and speak up" (1).

Over a period of ten years, dozens of biblical scholars joined in on the work of the Jesus Seminar. The seminar met twice a year to talk about position papers that members had prepared for discussion, and to vote, sometimes almost word by word, as to just what words were most likely to have actually been spoken by Jesus. The seminar set up a four-point scale so that the Jesus sayings could be ranked from "yes," Jesus said it, to "no," Jesus did not say it. Two intermediate levels identified those sayings that Jesus may have said and those that he could have said but probably didn't.[2]

As one might expect, the work of the Jesus Seminar has proved controversial, and public ridicule of the work has been generous. Some members lost academic positions, while others were forced to withdraw from the work due to institutional pressure. The greatest controversy has centered on the seminar's claim that of the words traditionally assigned to the historical Jesus, only about one in five were actually spoken by him.

Although there has been great objection to the assignment of 80 percent of Jesus' sayings to others, there has been scant mention of the remaining words, many of which we wish Jesus had not spoken in the first place. One wonders what the biblical literalist does with the seminar's assignment to Jesus of the words, "It is easier for a camel to go through the eye of a needle than for someone who is rich to enter the kingdom of God," or "Love your enemies."[3]

Primary to the work of the Jesus Seminar, as in any study, is the application of consistent rules of evidence for looking at the data, in this case the words of Jesus. Rules of evidence are used in any work where the data are particularly incomplete or messy. Still such data selection is at best a dicey business, since what we seek might be in the aberration we discard. Thus, if one were to criticize the Jesus Seminar in a meaningful way, a good place to start is with the seminar's rules of evidence.

The seminar adopted a range of rules of evidence and assumed as fundamental that only those sayings and parables that could be traced back to the oral period, from 30 to 50 CE, could have come from Jesus. Of the many other rules adopted by the seminar, those that provided a particularly good window into Jesus claimed that his words would "call for a reversal of roles or frustrate ordinary, everyday expectations," result in "surprise and shock," or express "exaggeration, humor, and paradox."[4] With these and other rules of evidence in hand, the Jesus Seminar found what they were looking for: a Jesus who fit their criteria.

Although it is easy to criticize the study's details, placing it in a broader context makes the study far more resistant to challenge. The larger context is the one I sensed as a youngster: the voices of my confirmation class. Although one may argue with the rules and results of the seminar, what one cannot dispute is that, using their rules of evidence, the seminar identified what they believed to be an authentic voice of Jesus. What substantiates the study is that not only did this voice emerge, but also a second, the voice of Jesus saying things that were not of Jesus. For me the contrast between these two voices is so sharp that to claim they belong to the same person strains belief. Regardless of the rules of evidence used by the scholars, there emerges a second Jesus who just doesn't seem to fit.

The second Jesus breaks the seminar's rules of evidence by speaking in the first person while claiming or giving authority. Jesus' words in Matthew illustrate this as he asks the disciples, "But who do you say I am?" Simon Peter answers, "You are the Messiah, the Son of the living God." To this Jesus responds:

> Blessed are you, Simon son of Jonah! For flesh and blood has not revealed this to you, but my Father in heaven. And I tell you, you are Peter, and on this rock I will build my church, and the gates of Hades will not prevail against it. I will give you the keys of the kingdom of heaven, and whatever you bind on earth will be bound in heaven, and whatever you loose on earth will be loosed in heaven.[5]

I still remember my college history teacher using these words of Matthew as an example of the power of historical authority. This authority remains with us today in the Roman Catholic Church when it claims that the pope follows in direct apostolic succession from Peter and brings to today's Catholics the very same spiritual authority that Jesus had given to Peter. The assignment of authority to others was a common practice during the time when the oral tradition of the early Christian movement was finding its way into the written scripture. For the evangelist in Matthew, what better way to establish the authority of the church than to have such authority come from the voice of Jesus himself?

The voice of the social radical identified by the Jesus Seminar stands in sharp contrast to the voice of Jesus giving authority to the church. While the first Jesus is giving power to the poor, the second is establishing a new and hierarchical authority. For me the incongruence is so great that no theological argument can be brought to bear that would reconcile these two characters of Jesus.

Still there is a third voice that appears from the work of the Jesus Seminar: the voice of the early Christian movement. These are the words that reflect Jesus' ways but according to the seminar were not spoken by him. The evangelist in Matthew informs me of the ways of Jesus when Jesus says, "Truly I tell you, just as you did it to one of the least of these who are members of my family, you did it to me."[6] Here Jesus identifies with the poor to the extent that serving the poor becomes the same as serving Jesus. Although one can debate whether or not Jesus said these things, the truth about who said it is not as important as the recognition that within the early Christian movement there were evangelists who understood just what work had been given to the people by the radical egalitarian Jesus.

Although this discussion of the work of the Jesus Seminar has been all too brief, for me it is hard to overstate the importance of the seminar's work as a useful starting point for illuminating the words of Jesus. A significant practical result of the seminar's work is that we can begin to examine the three voices identified here: the voice of Jesus, the voice of the early Christian movement, and the voice of the early Christian church. Central to renewing the church today is the work of renewing the voice of Jesus and that of the early Christian movement among the people of the church.

Jesus, Christ, and the Church

It is not often that we see Jesus and Christ separated as they are in the above title. The significant difference between *Jesus Christ and the Church* and *Jesus, Christ, and the Church* is that the commas allow the character of Jesus to reenter the dialogue. With this we can begin to discern between the work of Jesus and the character of Christ given to him by the Christian church. However, putting Jesus back into the dialogue creates more than a simple distinction between the historical Jesus and the theological character of Christ; it requires us to reexamine what Jesus' life means to us now.

At the time of Jesus' death, it was widely held that his second coming was imminent. Because his followers were dismayed over his death, Jesus' death and resurrection in the character of Christ became event markers that would hold his presence before believers until his return to the earth. Because of this, many find that further study of the historical Jesus is unwarranted or even threatening, because any reexamination of the work of the historical Jesus will alter how we look at what his work means to us now and in the future.

Thus, to reconsider the historic life of Jesus is to threaten those who remain in waiting for the second coming. Because such reconsideration confines the life of Jesus to historic time, the believer's task is no longer to wait for the rapture, to be literally abducted by God, but to work now for the world that Jesus indicated was possible then. Without an expected last day's miracle to end humanity's mess on earth, the work of earthly deliverance no longer belongs to Jesus, but to us.[7]

Jesus, Christ, and the Christian's Work

Essential to understanding the life and teachings of Jesus is the need to bring meaning to his crucifixion and death. There are three fundamental ways that the human spirit reacts to the death of Jesus on the cross, and a great deal of theology revolves around these reactions.

The first and simplest reaction to Jesus' death on the cross is that he did not suffer at all, so that his crucifixion requires little other than to believe it. With this belief, Jesus didn't suffer any more on the cross than a Saturday morning TV cartoon character when hit by a speeding locomotive. In both cases, Jesus and the cartoon character only seem to be alive and only seem to have suffered. Such denial of humanity, or Docetism, appeared early in Christian history and appears early in many of our lives as well.

I believe that most people start out as Docetists, trusting in the cartoon nature of life, and although some may carry this painless reality throughout their lives, for most of us the innocent life is over all too soon. Christian innocence ends when one begins to realize that Jesus really did suffer on the cross. And with this realization, theology gets messy in a hurry.

A second way to bring meaning to the death of Jesus is to believe that, even though Jesus' suffering on the cross was real, his suffering was a part of God's larger plan for his life. As I said earlier, Jesus' death left his followers dismayed, and bringing meaning to his death became the work of those left behind. Although the second coming was thought to be imminent, the return of Jesus could not explain his suffering and death in the first place.

Jesus' death on the cross had to have meaning in and of itself. Such meaning was given to the early Christian movement when Luke quotes the risen Jesus as saying to his disciples, "Thus it is written, that the Messiah is to suffer and to rise from the dead on the third day, and that repentance and forgiveness of sins is to be proclaimed in his name to all nations."[8] Because scholars believe these post-resurrection words are those of Luke and not Jesus, they represent one of the first statements of the gospel by the early Christian community.[9] Several decades earlier the saving action of Jesus on the cross had been announced to the church at Corinth by Paul when he wrote telling them that "Christ died for our sins."[10]

These early voices of the Christian movement brought meaning to the suffering of Jesus by telling his believers that he suffered to obtain their salvation. In the crucifixion, Jesus' singular act of suffering was substituted for the sins and suffering of many.

Yet beyond the claims of personal salvation brought by his death on the cross, whether Docetic or not, lies a third way of bringing meaning to the suffering and death of Jesus, and that is to bring meaning to his life and teachings. The claim here is that, far more than being sent by God to die on a cross, Jesus came to show us what God and God's world is like. In this case, the life and death of Jesus become more than a substitutionary act for our sins; they become an example of the servant leader's work.

Primary to Jesus' ministry were these teachings on servant leadership: "The greatest among you must become like the youngest, and the leader like one who serves."[11] Jesus tells his followers that letting go of position is vital to the servant leader's work. As I discussed in the previous chapter, the ultimate goal of the servant leader is to make themselves unnecessary. With this, the servant leader dies not for, but to, the work being done. By dying on the cross, Jesus became not a martyr dying for our personal salvation, but a servant leader dying to a radical social movement that God through him had begun. The crucifixion no longer marks the beginning of a static faith of waiting for a personal or global rapture. Rather, the crucifixion now marks the emergence of a radical social revolution that continues, however haltingly, to this very day (12).

The action of Jesus' reconciling Christians to God through his life and death has been described through the ages by various theologies of atonement. The last two ideas described here are known broadly as substitutionary and exemplary theories of atonement. Although much of the theology of the church had been established by about the fifth century, these theories of the atonement did not appear as doctrine until the twelfth century. Today, although it is considered controversial to question these and other ideas of God's reconciling action, the fact remains that multiple theories and controversy have surrounded the saving nature of Jesus' life from the time of his death till now.

To reimagine the work of the church, we must reimagine the meaning of Jesus' death on the cross. In our examination of the meaning and value of work, two types have emerged: the work of the entrepreneur and the work of the rent seeker. Here we recall that the entrepreneur's work brings an increasing social or physical order to our lives, while the rent seeker's work, rather than increasing order, keeps it the same or makes any mess worse. And while the entrepreneur as servant leader brings order by returning the work of the community to the people of the community, the rent seeker maintains his or her popularity by promising to bring an order that requires no work from anyone at all.

My belief is that the rent-seeking class rises from our unwillingness to do our own work, and in particular the work we are most likely to resist is that of existential suffering. For me the popularity of substitutionary atonement arises from our inherent inclination to favor the work of the rent seeker. In terms of the metaphors of this book, Jesus came as God's entrepreneur to show people what God's work is about. But in our propensity to laziness, we have transformed Jesus from someone who shows us what our work ought to be into a rent-seeking savior from whom we expect personal salvation and material prosperity without end.

The Christian's work shows its practical face in the banner theology that appears in many churches. In a church of my past, the post-Easter banner described Jesus' life as "He Came, He Died, He Lives," reflecting the atonement of Jesus' death and resurrection. In this statement, Jesus' singular act in time reconciles us to God in the living and resurrected character of Jesus Christ. In commenting on our banner a visitor described a banner in her home church as saying, "Jesus, taking you places you would not go by yourself." In the first banner, the work largely belongs to Jesus, and our work is to believe it; in the second the work is clearly ours as we follow the servant leadership of Jesus. Here the work of the new alchemy, the work of letting Jesus solve our problems for us, comes face-to-face with the new liturgy, the work of the people as given to the people by Jesus.

Mythology, Theology, and Christianity

No sooner was Jesus dead than his early movement began to evolve into a variety of Christian practices. Leading this evolution was the transformation of simple community practices based on the teachings of Jesus into new and complex practices based on the teachings of the emerging church. Today, steeped in layers of dogma and theology, the teachings and practices of the church have become so incongruent with the ministry of Jesus that for many they have become irrelevant, if not positively baneful.

Consider, for example, the stories of the virgin birth and bodily resurrection. The first voices of the Christian movement sprang from the teachings and ministry of Jesus, from the parables the Jesus Seminar found that would "call for a reversal of roles or frustrate ordinary, everyday expectations." But after Jesus' death, the Christian movement began to take on its own voice with stories of his virgin birth and bodily resurrection. In time these miracle stories took on such proportions that by the time the creeds of the church were formulated at the beginning of the fourth century, they had replaced the life of Jesus altogether. But neither the miracle of his virgin birth nor that of his bodily resurrection was unique to Jesus. On the contrary, it is most likely that these portions of Jesus' story were largely borrowed from the stories of other traditions.[13]

Throughout antiquity it was traditional that during the winter solstice, when things were darkest, heroic figures were announced by stars, born of virgins, and attended by magi. These heroes, after completing a requisite number of good deeds, would then traditionally ascend to heaven, prompting celebrations that coincided with the spring equinox and the return of light. For example, the myths of Attis and of the Persian savior Mithra include stories that are so remarkably like that of Jesus that it is likely that their stories became the evangelists' stories.[14]

It is useful to distinguish between what I mean by *miracle* and *myth*. Miracles are taken as literal events that occur outside the realm of physical reality and are believed to be true as articles of faith. A myth in contrast does not require suspension of belief in physical reality, but is rather taken as a nonliteral event that points to a greater truth. While miracles freeze events in time and hold us hostage to unchanging belief, myths are timeless and point to unchanging truths. Miracles happen once; myths happen never but always.

Today, few scholars put much credibility in the story of the virgin birth. Beyond this, there is a growing number of scholars and believers who acknowledge an ongoing life of Jesus in the resurrected character of Christ, but who believe that the bodily resurrection of Jesus is most likely a post-Easter story of the early Christian movement.[15]

From Christian teaching, it is easy to assume that the miracles associated with Jesus' birth and resurrection were unique to him and were facilitated by God as God's markers of Jesus' reconciling power. However, as we have seen, compared to the myths of the times, the narratives of Jesus' birth and resurrection made his life not unique, but just one of many. When we remove the virgin birth and bodily resurrection from the realm of the miraculous, the stories surrounding Jesus' life reveal new and greater truths that point the way to a more fully human Jesus. As myths rather than miracles, the virgin birth and bodily resurrection force us to ask the question of who was Jesus then that he warranted such acclaim and attention that today we remember *him* and not those from whom such myths were borrowed?

The scholar's reexamination of the origins and meanings of biblical tradition has led to the extensive demythologizing of Christian scripture. Although many find such work so threatening they excoriate it, others find such demythologizing so affirming they seek it out. For many, understanding biblical myths as pointers to timeless truths grounds their faith far better than being held hostage by what they believe to be fictitious miracles. Rather than demythologizing the Bible, the scholar's work remythologizes it. Freed from fictitious miracles frozen in time, a remythologized Bible allows the text to speak to all times and all people.

What is largely unknown today is that the unbelievable miracles that keep many from the church are found to be just as questionable by many biblical scholars. For those who are interested in renewing the church, the current knowledge gap between the scholar and the person in the pew constitutes a modern-day theological disconnect that makes going to church not nearly as engaging as staying in bed with the Sunday *Times*.[16]

Politics, Theology, and the Work of the Church

After Jesus' death, Christianity evolved over a period of five hundred years from a movement based on the teachings of Jesus and the ministry of Paul into an institutionalized church based on an increasingly complex theology. Although it is easy for non-Christians to avoid the faith by avoiding the church, the theology of the church is not so easily dismissed, because, like it or not, Christianity's ideas have in fact become integral to the way we think in America. Because they have, whether we are conscious of it or not, much of our work in America is directed by the Christian theologies of original sin and substitutionary atonement. Called "dead metaphors" by organizational leaders, they are far from dead but only made invisible by their sheer ubiquity.

Foremost to those who continued to follow the teachings of Jesus after his crucifixion was the need to bring meaning to his death. From this need sprang the ideas of substitutionary and exemplary atonement that we have already talked about. Yet earlier in the Christian movement, the work of Jesus on the cross was seen not necessarily as a substitutionary act, but as a victorious triumph over the powers that hold people hostage to the forces of evil. It was only later, during the Middle Ages, that the understanding of Jesus' death and resurrection shifted from a divine victory over sin to a human substitution for it. It was then taught that only the work of man *and* God could repay the sin of man, and so that God must send the God-man Jesus to do the work of both and to be God's redeemer in the world. Introduced into Christian theology by St. Anselm in the twelfth century, this understanding of the substitutionary work of Jesus on the cross remains central to Christian theology today.[17]

Acknowledged or not, all theology is created to meet the practical needs of the church and its people. To understand the popularity of substitutionary atonement, we now need to look at what I consider to be one of the greatest turning points in history: the legalization of Christianity.

From the time of Jesus' death to the beginning of the fourth century, Christianity was a subversive movement growing in many directions. As practitioners of a faith worshiping one God while refusing to worship either the state or the Roman emperor, the early Christians were regularly persecuted, and for those who refused to make pagan sacrifices, it was a martyr's faith. All this ended on October 28, 312, when Constantine routed the army of his enemy Maxentius at Rome's Milvian Bridge. Believing that his success in battle was directly attributable to the power of Christ that had been extended to him in a vision, Constantine and his coemperor, Licinius, moved to make Christianity legal throughout the empire. By the following June, with the issue of the Edict of Milan, Christianity became not only a tolerated practice, but a political force.[18] With the Edict of Milan, Christian bishops, who only the year before had been persecuted by the state, began to move into positions of prominence, patronage, and power.

Although the worst of the persecutions were over, they did not end immediately. Lacking Constantine's conversion experience, Licinius soon returned to Christian persecution. Constantine, seeing in this an opportunity to consolidate his power, then called Christians into a war more holy than civil against Licinius. Prevailing over Licinius, Constantine became sole ruler of the Roman Empire in 324.

With the church now a part of the empire, turmoil within the church became turmoil within the empire. For Constantine the problems of the church became the problems of the state. And the problem of the church in 325 was the divinity of Christ.

Valuing the power of a unified network of churches, Constantine called the first ecumenical council at Nicaea in the spring of 325 as a forum for the church to work out its differences. The divinity of Christ provided a twofold problem for the church. Somehow the divinity of Christ had to be defined so that the church remained both monotheistic and non-Judaic. If Christ were divine, there would be two divine beings, not one, and if he were not divine, Christianity would lose its distinction from Judaism. The solution was the Trinitarian God of the Father, Son, and Holy Spirit as described by the language of the Nicene Creed. Although the creed took on additional modifications and was not set until the middle of the fifth century, the creed formed at Nicaea was much like today's.

Soon after the Council of Nicaea, Constantine wrote to the church at Alexandria, "For the decision of three hundred bishops must be considered no other than the judgment of God."[19] Although Constantine and the bishops had spoken, the so-called Arian controversy continued on for several decades before the Council's creed became the established orthodoxy of the emerging church. And given this, the theological food fight of my youth was, in principle, over.

Still, the mystery of the Trinitarian God has been the theologians' problem throughout the ages.[20] No matter how useful it may have been for the early church fathers, it is for me today an unnecessary and perhaps even harmful theological and political construct. As a political and theological invention to distance the Christian church from Judaism by emphasizing the divinity of Christ, it has two negative practical effects.

First, by distancing Christianity from Judaism the Trinity causes the Christian to forget that the Judaic God, the ineffable, unnameable Yahweh, is also the Christian God. Second, the naming of Jesus as the divine Christ of the Trinity causes the Christian to forget about the historical and transforming ministry of the human Jesus. Through its theologizing of God, Jesus, and the Holy Spirit into the single Trinitarian mystery, the early church invented a teaching that simultaneously diminished both the Jewishness of Christianity and the humanity of Jesus. The separation of the Jew from the Christian and the Christian from Jesus in the theology of the Trinity constitutes two of Christianity's greatest losses.

Throughout the remainder of the fourth century, the church's tenuous unity under the theology of the Trinity allowed the now-legal church to further consolidate political power. But the theology necessary to consolidate the power of the church over the laity remained undone until the beginning of the fifth century and the work of Augustine.

Although Augustine is most remembered in the church for his autobiographical *Confessions* and his defense of Christianity, *The City of God*, his work of greatest practical importance was his theory of original

sin. Becoming ever more defensive in later life, Augustine claimed that
sexual desire was proof of original sin and that such sin is passed down
through generations by the sex act itself. To the pessimistic Augustine, the
"damned lump of humanity" was "wallowing in evil" and "falling headlong
from one wickedness to another."[21]

Such language comes not only from the fifth century, but also from
the 2008 edition of the United Methodist Church, *Book of Discipline*,
which declares:

> Original sin . . . is the corruption of the nature of every man,
> that naturally is engendered of the offspring of Adam, whereby
> man is very far gone from original righteousness, and of his
> own nature inclined to evil, and that continually.[22]

Such pessimistic theology could only have lasted fifteen hundred years by
meeting the practical needs of those affected. With humankind fallen in
body and soul, Augustine's theory provided emperors and bishops reason
enough to assert their secular and spiritual power over the people of the
empire and the church. For the heads of the church and state, Augustine's
fallen humanity begged for the application of an external authority that
they were more than willing to supply. And for those who worried about
the ever-growing interdependence of the church and the state, such
cooperation came to be seen as propitious, if not essential, for human
salvation.[23]

Although Augustine's assertion that humankind was beyond the pale
was reason enough for the state and church to claim authority, this alone
does not explain the success of his theology. Beyond its practical usefulness to the state and the church, Augustine's notion of original sin had
to meet the needs of the people as well. Augustine asserted that not only
humankind, but all of nature was corrupted by the sin of Adam, and that
the cause of all of life's sufferings, both natural and moral, was the fall of
Adam and Eve in the garden.[24] Made helpless by original sin, the people
of the empire and church were all too willing to accept the authority of
the state and church to save them, body and soul. By making us passive
participants in a mean and arbitrary world, Augustine's wretched pessimism readily accommodated our own human willingness to avoid the
work of existential living. By transferring the existential work of life from
us to the external authority of the state and church, Augustine's theology
of the fall institutionalized our natural laziness as no one had ever done
before, or since.

By the end of the fifth century the work that Jesus had given us had been successfully returned to the church through its emerging theology of original sin. But the church's transformation of Jesus' ministry did not end there. Because the early theories of atonement claimed Christ victorious over evil, such atonement could not be reconciled with Augustine's perpetual pessimism. Evil was permanent, and only the redemption brought by the God-man of Jesus could save us from our abysmal state of original and perpetual sin. With this the saving work of the church was returned to the Christ of the cross through the theology of substitutionary atonement. In short, the work of the people, the new liturgy, given to us by Jesus had finally been replaced by the new alchemy of the church, led by a rising and powerful class of rent-seeking priests.

In terms of the work metaphors of this book, the triumph of orthodoxy in the emerging Christian church had become largely the triumph of the new alchemy. Sinful humankind was now saved from itself by the governance of the state and the theology of the church. The work of the new liturgy that had been given to the people by Jesus had now been successfully returned to the Christ of the cross by Augustine's original sin and the church's theology of substitutionary atonement. The work of the people had become the work of the state and the church, and Augustine had become, without a doubt, the master of all alchemists. By the end of the fifth century the life and teachings of Jesus had been mythologized, legalized, and theologized. At last the radical transforming movement of Jesus had been contained, and the empire was without turmoil.[25]

Mythology, Theology, and the Serpent's Work

Our discussion now turns to a more optimistic, if not easier to live with, understanding of humankind, nature, and salvation. To begin we need to reimagine the oldest of our stories, that of creation.

The story of Adam and Eve in the Garden of Eden is Christianity's most essential myth. It is the second of two creation stories that appear in the first three chapters of Genesis. The first story simply states that God created humankind in God's image, "male and female he created them." And to these God gave dominion over the earth and "every tree with seed in its fruit." Given such blanket permission, this first story seems to imply that contrary to much of today's theology, none of the garden's fruit was forbidden.

Steeped in folklore, the second story is older, and although it is far richer in content, its primary interpretation has been one of the serpent's temptation and of Adam and Eve's disobedience and sin. I believe that today this simple and singular reading of the serpent's work in the Garden of Eden affects our own work more than we suspect.

In this second story, God creates man from the "dust of the ground," and for a companion God removes one of the man's ribs and from it creates woman. And although the man and woman were created naked, they were "not ashamed." The story tells us that before creating Eve, God told Adam not to eat of the tree of the knowledge of good and evil, "for in the day that you eat of it you shall die."

The serpent then enters the story and speaks to Eve. He challenges Eve to name the forbidden fruit by asking, "Did God say, 'You shall not eat from any tree in the garden'?" Eve tells the serpent that the fruit of all the trees, except that in the middle of the garden, may be eaten and then reminds the serpent of God's admonition: "You shall not eat of the fruit of the tree that is in the middle of the garden, nor shall you touch it, or you shall die." We are not told how Eve knows this, since Adam has all the information up to now. Either Adam told Eve about his instructions from God, or God told Eve without telling the storyteller. In either case, Adam also knows what God said but lets Eve do the talking.

The serpent then challenges both Eve and God, telling her, "You will not die; for God knows that when you eat of it your eyes will be open, and you will be like God, knowing good and evil." With Adam standing by, Eve hatches the deal. Knowing that the tree would "make one wise," she "took of its fruit and ate," and passes on some to the still silent Adam, who then eats some himself. And with this the "eyes of both were opened, and they knew that they were naked."

In this story, it is frequently thought that the serpent is a manifestation of evil and that Adam and Eve, in taking the first human test ever, flunk it without question. Seduced by the beauty of the fruit and the cleverness of the serpent, Adam and Eve disobey God and fall into original sin. In the New Testament, Paul uses this story to express his fear that the church at Corinth might be led astray by imposter preachers in the same way that "the serpent deceived Eve by its cunning."[26] Modern dictionaries define serpents as wily and treacherous, the devil or Satan, and even refer to the third chapter of Genesis as an example.[27]

Although evil images have been projected onto the serpent over the ages, in classical mythology the serpent is not particularly evil, but is clever or wise.[28] In the Genesis story of Adam and Eve, the word used to describe the serpent characterizes a creature that may be "crafty, subtle, shrewd, clever or ingenious."[29] Although such words do not imply unambiguous good, they do not necessarily imply evil either. Traditionally the serpent or snake by renewing itself through the periodic shedding of its skin represents an image of renewal or birth. As a mythical interpreter of physical reality, the serpent becomes a metaphor for the facilitation of rebirth and new life.

Using the serpent as a facilitator for the drama of the garden, Genesis scholar Terence Fretheim describes the serpent's work as a "divine sting operation."[30] Rather than being evil, the serpent here is grounded in God's creation and presents to Adam and Eve options for their lives. Fretheim explains that, far from deceiving Adam and Eve, the serpent is telling them the truth about the nature of God and life, and that the issue is not about the character of the serpent, but about what Adam and Eve will do with the serpent's truth. In the end, the serpent challenges Adam and Eve to trust God's truth and become open to knowing good and evil.

In contrast to a tale of disobedience and sin, the creation story now becomes a story of continuing creation as Adam and Eve become conscious of their nakedness. God created us as willful people, knowing that without such willfulness our species would certainly perish. But God also created humankind in God's image so that we would be conscious of God, self, and others. God set us up through the serpent, so that as willful people we could either reject or claim the consciousness that comes with being fully human.

God knew that by forbidding what was attractive, Adam and Eve as willful children in the garden would likely accept the serpent's offer. Like any parent, God knew that there is no easier way to motivate the action of a child than to forbid what is attractive. It is through the serpent that God invites us to trust God and claim our consciousness, to claim our very lives.

This interpretation leaves us not with humankind's original sin, but with humankind's original condition. Fretheim describes this not as a "falling down," but as a "falling out" from God.[31] By accepting the serpent's offer of consciousness, Adam and Eve have separated us from God not as people who are inherently sinful, but as people who are inherently human. Although we have been expelled from the garden to carry our consciousness into the world, our original sin is not that we ate the apple, but that we have failed to fully claim the consciousness, the knowledge of good and evil, given by it. Most compactly, the creation story is a story of creation yet to be completed. The work of completing creation requires that we claim our consciousness and act on the work that God gave us through Adam and Eve.

Believing creation stories is not as important as recognizing that they are frequently used as metaphors for how we choose our work. The metaphor of the evil serpent frequently plays out in the worst ways as we blame the hapless serpent for our troubles by claiming that the "devil made me do it." Yet on the far side of the serpent lies a new creation story, one that directs us to accept our consciousness and to get on with our lives. Our new creation story tells us that making the world a better place belongs not only to God, but us.

Jesus, Time, and Anxiety

Constantine's legalization of Christianity marked a turning point in history as the rising cooperation between the state and the church co-opted the power of the Christian movement. I have suggested that the reason for the success of this enterprise was the extent to which it accommodated our natural willingness to let others do our work.

The creation story reimagined above now turns the power of Augustine inside out as it tells us that our original sin is not our disobedience, but our unwillingness to do the work given to us in the garden. The success of the fall/atonement theology now becomes clear not as an answer to our sin of laziness, but as an accommodation to it. By accommodating rather than challenging the status quo, the theology of the early church simultaneously rewarded both the authority of the emerging church and the obedience of the laity. Without knowing it, the early church fathers produced a practical political theology without which the church would not have lasted a few centuries, much less two millennia. By accommodating rather than challenging its members, the church to this day has remained more of a compliant prop than a challenge to the state.

But more is addressed by the theology of the church than our unwillingness to do the work God gave us in the garden. By making us passive participants in the work done for us by the Christ of the cross, the theology of the church redefined the nature of time. Life was no longer uncertain and emergent, but was now marked by a resurrection event that divided time into a well-defined past and future. Time flowed in a linear fashion, and if we were just willing to wait for it, the kingdom would be ours. Such theology secured the authority of both the state and the church, and for the laity any loss of freedom to either was more than acceptable as a price for obtaining theological relief from the anxiety produced by the passage of time.

The church's theology of linear time and personal salvation stands in sharp contrast to the teachings of Jesus. For Jesus, time was simultaneously present and future. The kingdom was not announced by some future apocalyptic event, but was present among the people who did not understand or see it.[32] Jesus announced the kingdom this way: "The kingdom of God is not coming with things that can be observed; nor will they say, 'Look, here it is!' or 'There it is!' For, in fact, the kingdom of God is among you."[33] For Jesus the kingdom would be as present now as it was then.

A useful image here, rather than "kingdom of God," is "realm of God."[34] While "kingdom" carries a connotation of patriarchal hierarchy, "realm of God" describes an egalitarian world of servant leaders and self-organizing communities. In the realm of God, what God expects from us is not our adulation, but our cooperation. In the verses above, Jesus explains that the realm of God is the way the world is, and given this we can participate in a world that is a generous place today, tomorrow, and always.

For Jesus, the answer to the anxiety produced by the flow of time was the recognition that we live in a world that will be as present to us tomorrow as it is today. For Jesus, the existential security we all seek was to be found in a faith that the realm of God was continuous in time and that our present and future needs will be met by our participation in a hospitable world.

Jesus and Christian Practice

Regardless of what else the church has made of him, Jesus was foremost a Jewish peasant and sage announcing the realm of God among the people.[35] His most fundamental teachings were of love, not that of devotion, but of compassion, a word with Latin roots meaning "to suffer with." Jesus' compassion goes beyond conventional notions of love by directing us to suffer with those we would rather avoid all together: the sick, the poor, and those so different as to seem beyond understanding.

Jesus' teachings were radical. By going to the literal root of the law, he reduced its multiple instructions into a single teaching of compassion. Jesus directs Christians to the heart of the gospel with the great commandment: "The first is, 'Hear, O Israel: the Lord our God, the Lord is one; you shall love the Lord your God with all your heart, and with all your soul, and with all your mind, and with all your strength.' The second is this, 'You shall love your neighbor as yourself.' There is no commandment greater than these."[36] This one commandment of compassion to love God with all our being and our neighbor as ourselves embraces all other commandments. For Jesus, it was through compassion that we honor our parents and resist killing our neighbors. It was through compassion that we do not steal from them, lie to them, or covet their possessions. It was through compassion that we experience the whole of the law.

Through the great commandment, Jesus simultaneously freed people from the law and assigned to them the work of compassion. He freed people from the authority of the priests and gave to them the work of the new liturgy, the work of suffering with the other. But compassion as the whole of the law flew in the face of the social and political practices of Jesus' time. And given this, following Jesus became not only demanding, but dangerous.

The social and political practices of Jesus' day were directed by a system of purity, a framework of laws and cultural norms that separated the pure from the impure, the clean from the unclean.[37] Some portions of the law could be considered public health measures, such as avoiding disease-bearing animals for food or contaminated water for drink. Other portions declared as unclean species that crossed boundaries of earth, air, and water. Creatures of the water that stayed in the water, such as fish with fins and scales, were clean, but others that crawled as if on land, such as shellfish, were unclean. With such laws the Israelites brought order to their world by separating creation into classes determined by the physical boundaries between land, sea, and air.

This map brought order to the world in the same way that God brought order to the world in the creation story of Genesis. In Genesis 1:1, in the first three days of creation, "God separated the light from the darkness" to make day and night, "separated the waters that were under the dome from the waters that were above the dome" to make the sky, and "gathered together" the water to form seas and dry land. For the Israelites, life was ordered by naming boundaries.[38]

Although the purity system provided the Israelites with orderly and practical guidelines for living, the system became oppressive when its practice of naming physical boundaries became one of naming social and cultural boundaries as well. With the extension of the purity system to the social and cultural realm, whole people began to be named as either clean or unclean, pure or impure. Whether one was clean or not depended on one's birth, occupation, physical health, or economic standing. Illegitimate children were impure, as were tax collectors, the leprous, and the destitute.[39] The purity code went beyond the injunctions of Leviticus to new cultural and political dimensions. And with this the law of Moses went beyond personal religious practice to a public political practice of social, cultural, and economic exclusion.

It was into this world of social and cultural exclusion that Jesus brought his ministry of compassion. The core of Jesus' compassion went beyond the practice of the law as he entered into relationships that went beyond the accepted boundaries of his community. Jesus conducted his ministry as an open subversive to the purity boundaries of the day by extending compassion to all, regardless of personal condition or social class.

Jesus offered the people a new vision, one based not on exclusion, but on a new and radical equality. Rather than a system of social classification and boundaries, he offered a new map without either. His new map was that of eating at a table where boundaries disappear and new social order is created. While the purity system directed what should be eaten and with whom, Jesus taught his followers to invite all to the table and to eat what they were served. Jesus taught what John Dominic Crossan calls "open commensality," not only a practice for sharing a meal, but a model for all social and cultural relationships as well. Jesus opened the table to all people as both a sign and an example of his radical egalitarian ministry.[40]

Through his radical ministry, Jesus changed the social model of his day from one of purity to one of compassion. For him it was more important to be compassionate than pure, more important to value relationships than the law. For Jesus, the whole of the law was to value relationships over beliefs.

Christians and Christian Practice

Jesus' overturning of the purity system was short-lived as the rising church created a new boundary separating Christians into clergy and laity. This new boundary was created late in the first century of the Christian movement when Clement, the Bishop of Rome and Peter's third successor, wrote to the Christian community at Corinth in response to an uprising that had driven some of its leaders out of office. Clement wrote that "fools" had risen against the "wise" and the "young against the old." He argued that God delegates his "authority of reign" to his leaders on earth, specifically to the bishops, priests, and deacons, and that the people of the church at Corinth were to "bow the neck," and whoever disobeys God's authority on earth "receives the death penalty."[41] We do not know what issue disturbed the church at Corinth, but it may well have differed little from the issues that divide the church today. Whatever the reason, the church's obsession with order and obedience has remained unabated for nearly two millennia.

Jesus' call to trust God stands in sharp contrast to Clement's call to trust the clergy. The laity are now to trust the clergy and bring order to the world by the obedient conduct of their work. While the church brings order to the world by requiring the laity to obey the clergy, Jesus brings order to the world through his message to trust the realm of God in our midst. In the end, while Jesus calls us to trust God, the church calls us trust its authority.

The separation of Christians into clergy and laity in the first century marked the reemergence of the purity system into Christian thinking. Earlier, in our discussion of the Trinity, I suggested that the separation of the Jew from the Christian and the Christian from Jesus in the theology of the Trinity constituted two of Christianity's greatest losses. I now offer a third: the separation of the Christian from the spirit that informs the faith. Christian laypeople can readily experience such separation when the discernment of their faith leads to conclusions incompatible with the teachings of the church. Here the authority of the church can readily diminish the spiritual discernment of the person in the pew when it declares its teachings to be the only proper ones for all times and all people. Although I cannot deny the force of spirit experienced by the men of the first ecumenical councils and all those who have followed them, I can and must deny the church's assertion that their experience of the spirit must be mine also. The loss of spiritual discernment to the authority of the church constitutes Christianity's third and perhaps greatest loss.

The work of the Christian today is the same as it was for Jesus and his followers. We are to overturn the purity laws of our day and to set the table and welcome the stranger to share it with us. Since many of today's purity laws are maintained by the church itself, reformation of the church is as necessary now as it was then. The Christian revolution continues to this very day, and it lies at the heart of the coming schism.

The Coming Schism

While Jesus addressed the anxiety produced by the flow of time by telling us to trust in a benevolent God, the church has addressed such anxiety through the invention of ever more complex and bizarre theologies, theologies designed more to arrest the flow of time than to acknowledge it. For Jesus, salvation was not some future event that belonged to the obedient faithful, but was open to all—today, tomorrow, and always. For Jesus, the grace of God knew no bounds of time or place. Jesus' concept of time stands in such sharp contrast to that of the church that the teachings of the church are simply incompatible with those of Jesus.

Signs of this incompatibility are appearing with increasing regularity and intensity in today's Christian churches. For example, in my own United Methodist Church, some are calling for a return to the creedal basis of the church, while at the same time others are calling for a reimagined church that ranges far beyond the dogma of the creeds. While the first group is pressing for a confessional church based on historical creeds and beliefs, the second is pressing for a reimagined church based on contemporary relationships that mirror the ministry of the historical Jesus.

Throughout Christian churches today, both Catholic and mainline Protestant, issues such as the role of women in the church, the inclusion of gays and lesbians in the life of the church, and the social and political role of the church in the community are growing in intensity and number. Today, the best accommodation for America's Christian churches would be for advocates of all stripes to acknowledge the incompatibility of their theologies so that they could get on with who they are and how they wish to be in ministry.

This will not be easy, since much of today's understanding of denominationalism will disappear. For example, Catholics, United Methodists, and Lutherans who invite gays and lesbians into full participation in their churches share far more with one another than they do with members of their own denominations who believe otherwise. And within today's United Methodist Church, those who wish to freeze in time what they believe to be the true theology of the church stand in sharp contrast to those who believe that even though God is timeless, the praxis of faith is not. Today there is far more turmoil within than between denominations.

I suspect there will be little or no relief from this theological distress without a substantive schism within America's churches. Today the differences between Christianity's never-changing, belief-based practices and its ever-changing, relationship-based practices have become simply too great to either ignore or reconcile. By giving up the notion of unity at all cost and accepting the incompatibility of their differences, the emerging camps within America's churches could each begin the salutary work of getting on with their own ministries. Although establishing such distinctions within America's Christian churches would not be easy, if such accommodations were made, America's churches could begin putting their time, money, and energy into the local church where it belongs rather than spending endless time and countless resources on ever-more-removed national debates.

The Church and Christian Practice

Jesus gave the people a new map, one without boundaries, one of an open table in a closed society. Jesus' foremost message to his followers was that their work was to follow the new map, to set a new table, and to make it available to everyone. With these instructions Jesus established a radical and subversive movement to overturn the purity system of his day.

But as we have seen, starting with Clement and concluding with Constantine and Augustine, the movement of Jesus inexorably became the institution of the church. What is remarkable is that although most movements disappear when institutionalized, Christianity has not. Throughout history the miracle of Christianity has been its ongoing presence as an ever-evolving movement. Led more by heretics on the fringe than clergy at the core, the subversive movement of Jesus remains alive yet today.

Today the church's work is to recognize that its teachings and practices did not, full-blown, fall from the sky. The great unspoken fear of the church is that today's reexamination of the faith all too readily affirms what the laity have suspected all along, that the traditions of the church are as subject to negotiation now as when they were first founded. One needs only to review the recent activities of any of the mainline Protestant churches to recognize that the work of the church is grounded as much in political persuasion as spiritual discernment.

Such recognition creates fear within the church when it acknowledges that whatever has been won by negotiation in the past can just as readily be lost by renegotiation now. In her concluding remarks to *The Gnostic Gospels*, Elaine Pagels observes, "All the old questions—the original questions, sharply debated at the beginning of Christianity—are being reopened."[42] Today the work of the church is not to resist, but to invite such inquiry.

How then does the church do this new work? In *Texts Under Negotiation*, Walter Brueggemann offers a remedy in a word. It is the work of the church and the clergy, asserts Brueggemann, to "fund," that is, to provide the "pieces, materials, and resources out of which a new world can be imagined."[43] The new liturgy, the work of the people, is essential to this funding process. The work of the church now shifts from the clergy to the laity, a shift that is as dramatic for one as the other. Such a process is not easy, since many clergy are as reluctant to give up authority over the church as the laity are to accept responsibility for it. Yet, sooner or later, it will dawn on all that the church belongs to the laity. When the clergy learn they are to do the work of funding the laity, and laity learn they are to do the work of the church, a second coming of peace and reconciliation will be upon us.[44]

Good and Evil in God's World

In the world's bloodiest century just past, it is estimated that one hundred million or more people were intentionally and violently killed by others. In the face of such evil, it seems naive at best to claim that God's world is a fundamentally good place. Just spending a half hour with the evening news readily shows the horrendous suffering and daily misery experienced not only by our own neighbors, but by thousands of humans around the world. If God is so good, we ask, why does the world seem so filled with evil?

That so many people can so readily bring physical and emotional suffering to others and so blithely foster economic injustice through the unending accumulation of gratuitous wealth leads me to believe that much of the world suffers from remorseless Docetism (45). Driven by theological, political, and economic beliefs rather than human relationships, we live cartoon lives so removed from others that we have become immune to their suffering.

Such Docetic evil issues from our original sin when we refuse to carry into the world the consciousness given to us in the garden. Evil emanates from our refusal to be God's presence in the world. The work of bringing God to the world and relieving suffering is ours, and it will only happen when we begin to suspend our beliefs and enter into relationships that allow us to experience the suffering of others. Our original sin is our refusal to be the eyes, ears, and hands of God.

Today there is little practical difference between the complex political and theological constructs of the church and the equally complex structures of secular society. Both accommodate our original sin and serve to separate us from God and each other. At the end of our bloodiest century, it seems safe to say that our modern experiment to live without the consciousness of God has failed.

PART 3

WORK AND TRUST

CHAPTER SEVEN

The Chaos Paradigm

Trusting a New Covenant

How do we know that the creations of worlds
are not determined by falling grains of sand?
—Victor Hugo

The world is moved along, not only by the mighty shoves of its heroes,
but also by the aggregate of tiny pushes of each honest worker.
—Helen Keller

Community . . . cannot occur once and for all time:
always it must be the moment's answer
to the moment's question, and nothing more.
—Martin Buber

Consider the Ant

Go to the ant, you lazybones;
consider its ways, and be wise.
Without having any chief or officer or ruler,
it prepares its food in the summer,
and gathers its sustenance in harvest.[1]

Round and round, without purpose or accomplishment, a few hundred army ants will move in unceasing circles. Oblivious of each other and the basis of their being, they die without notice. Compared to humans and their brains of a hundred billion neurons, the army ant, with fewer than a hundred thousand neurons, is a creature both mindless and alive.

How then do ants make it in this world? Unable to figure it out by themselves, they survive by forming into massive social groups, collective organisms with minds of their own. Where a few hundred army ants will mindlessly perish, a few hundred thousand ants will organize themselves into a living organism that provides for itself and shelters its queen with better temperature control than most houses. By cooperating in ways that cannot be imagined from their individual behavior, army ants self-organize into mindful colonies that flourish.[2]

The collective mind of the colony emerges when the ants lay down and respond to trail pheromones. Although each ant remains unaware of the colony as a whole, through the reading and writing of chemical messages each behaves in a way that serves to the advantage of all. For example, in the transport of booty back to the nest, the ants move items of prey at a uniform rate to ensure an efficient traffic flow on the trail. If an item is moving too slowly, other ants join in until it is moved along the same as the rest. Without any awareness other than that a standard retrieval rate is desirable, an ant will join others to transport prey. By applying the simple algorithm of a standard retrieval rate to the group task of booty transport, each ant participates in a form of self-organization that serves the whole.

It is not known just how ants accomplish all the work required to maintain a colony, but it seems that two marks are necessary for the self-organization that leads to their success. The first is shared common information provided by the chemical messages of trail pheromones, and the second is local task shifting that serves the welfare of the whole colony. Although no single ant has an understanding of the whole colony, common information plus appropriate local action leads to the emergence of a living collective organism that simply could not be anticipated by looking at any single ant. The life of the colony cannot be examined through dissection, but only by considering it as a whole. The biblical injunction to consider the lilies tells us far more about life than does the scientific injunction that calls us to dissect them. Life cannot be understood by taking it apart.

The ant colony serves as a powerful metaphor for our own work. The task switching of the ants as they forage, transport booty, and maintain the colony shows us entropy work at its simplest.[3] When local order is maintained, global order emerges. The teach, equip, and trust work paradigm of Reell Precision Manufacturing as described in chapter 5 builds on the ant metaphor: the company teaches and equips its workers and then trusts them with the authority to make local decisions concerning tool maintenance, production planning, and temporary hiring. To "consider the ant" might not be a bad idea for any business.

Just like ant colonies, human communities also thrive on collective work. Tocqueville's observations in *Democracy in America* were those of an entomologist viewing the ant colony that was the United States. Reporting on the work of local associations in the promotion of America's social and economic goals, Tocqueville wrote:

> In the United States associations are established to promote the
> public safety, commerce, industry, morality, and religion. There
> is no end which the human will despairs of attaining through
> the combined power of individuals united into a society.[4]

Tocqueville's observation describes the work of America's nonprofit or third-sector organizations. In Tocqueville's America, the civil work of each member of the community enhances the civil order of the entire community. In human communities, like ant colonies, global order grows from local order.

Rules, Rules, Rules

Whether considering an ant colony or a civil community, one of the most powerful ideas of self-organization is that properly chosen individual work leads to the emergence of desirable community results. That is, beyond the need for each ant or citizen to stay busy lies the further understanding that the success of the enterprise turns on the actual tasks carried out. A simple example of self-organization is given by a computer simulation that captures the flocking behavior of birds.[5] In this computer simulation, birds, called "boids," form themselves into a natural-looking flock that flies around obstacles in a way closely resembling its natural counterpart. The birdlike behavior observed on the computer screen is achieved by charging each boid with the task of following three simple local rules. The first is to maintain a minimum distance from other boids and any objects placed in its way. The second is to maintain a speed and direction matching those of other boids flying nearby. And the last is for each boid to move toward the center of its local flock. Without any computer command to "form a flock," boids started randomly on the computer screen organize themselves into a natural-looking flock that flies in formation and avoids obstacles placed in its way. With no instructions other than to move under the direction of three local rules, the boids on the computer screen form a flock that gives the appearance of global organization.

Although it is easy to be captivated by these ideas and images and to claim that the flock has in some way come to life, a more prudent approach would claim that such demonstrations are best understood as metaphors rather than paradigms. The ant colony and the bird flocking simulation serve as metaphors for our lives when they direct our work by way of comparison. When a comparison becomes more concrete to our experience, it takes on the form of a paradigm, or example, for our lives. Whereas a metaphor tells us what something is *like*, a paradigm tells us what something *is*. Marcus Borg offers the very useful idea that a metaphor can be used as a bridge between paradigms. By giving us "a way of seeing," metaphors, suggests Borg, give us a way of moving from one paradigm to another, from one way of living to another. Importantly, Borg states that the point is not to "believe in" a metaphor, but to use it to see as we have not seen before.[6] Even without our complete understanding, ant colonies and computer simulations can well serve as metaphors as they inform our imaginations about new ways to live.

Self-Organization and Leaderless Work

The ant and boid metaphors demonstrate more than the power of self-organization under the direction of common rules; they show us the power of the leaderless organization. The notion that recognizable order can emerge from leaderless work illustrates my belief that, beyond leadership, the success of any enterprise lies in the work we each choose.

The order of the ant colony emerges from the work of each ant without any overall effort to get organized. For the colony, the organization of the whole is a free result of each ant's local work. The colony does not violate the second law of thermodynamics, since the total order of the colony and its environment is decreased by its presence. The foraging required to bring order and life to the colony simultaneously brings havoc to its neighborhood. For the colony to live, its environment must suffer.[7]

The hard work of laziness comes from our fond expectation that a desirable social order, like that of the ant colony, will spring up independent of our work and free of environmental consequences. But this is not the way the world works. Beyond the fact that life is work lies the further reality that the work of bringing local order to our lives necessarily brings disorder to the wider world. To bring order requires work, but to bring order that leads to the least overall disorder requires that we choose our work with discernment. It is only through the careful choice of our work that we can preserve both the earth and our life on it.

It might be argued that our work is really directed by others, or if not by others at least by circumstances that compromise our ability to choose just what our work should be. Both we and our leaders would like to believe this, since it removes from us the obligation of choosing our work while simultaneously granting our leaders the power and recognition they seek. Leadership fails because we have given our leaders responsibility for work that belongs only to us and no one else. Independent of the actions of leadership, we each need to become entropy workers bringing local order to our own households, neighborhoods, and workplaces. Without such work our families, communities, businesses, and environment all suffer.

The best leadership can do is to encourage behavior that self-organizes toward desirable goals. Required of such leadership is a tolerance for the ambiguity inherent in the self-organizing processes and for the anxiety that comes with waiting for something to happen. Since emergent results are not always clear from the start of anything new, there exists an almost overwhelming desire on the part of most leaders and followers to tinker with the system before it has had a chance to produce results. At this point, our impatience for success in the face of ambiguity becomes a principal source of failed leadership. We expect our leaders to make a difference *now*, and thus motivated, their work becomes more expedient than effective. Leadership fails because leaders fail to return our work to us. And they fail to return our work to us, because when they do, we all shout "no fair" and then promptly look elsewhere for those who promise us a lesser burden.[8]

What then is the work of the leader? The work of the leader is threefold. First, it is to be an exemplar of trust by maintaining an open organization where workers can trust what they hear, see, and, intuitively know about the organization. Like the trail pheromones of the ant, the value of congruent information to the success of the enterprise cannot be overstated. The second is to maintain a network of workers who share common experiences and values and to keep the purpose of the organization so visible to each worker that the larger goals of the organization emerge from their collective work. The leader's third and final act is to make the organization's work so self-organizing that his or her own leadership becomes unnecessary. With such servant leadership, good things can emerge in unexpected ways.

A simple and powerful example of servant leadership and the force of self-organizing work occurred during the World War II occupation of the village of Le Chambon, a small Huguenot community located in the mountains of southeastern France.[9] Here the work of the village in sheltering and saving the lives of five thousand refugees, mostly Jews, showed the robust power of self-organization. The work of the people of Le Chambon grew out of the leadership of André and Magda Trocmé. While Magda Trocmé readily welcomed visitors to the village, Pastor André Trocmé, through a combination of motivation and trust, maintained a network of safe houses in which refugees were just as readily sheltered. Even with the evil of the wartime occupation at their very doorsteps, the collective action of the Trocmés and the people of the village caused goodness to happen, and thousands who would have perished were saved. For goodness to arise in Le Chambon three resources were necessary: a shared common experience, an actively maintained network of safe houses, and a shared belief in the work that had to be done.

An important shared common experience was that the people of the village were themselves the descendants of people who had been persecuted for their faith. As Protestants in Catholic France, the members of André Trocmé's Huguenot congregation had a shared history of four centuries of persecution that had not ended until they were extended full religious freedom in 1905. This history left them well prepared to share with others who were suffering just for being who they were. But, beyond this, the success of the village's saving work turned on the utilization of thirteen Bible study classes that formed a network across its parish. It was through the thirteen leaders of these groups that André Trocmé kept his vision of nonviolent resistance in front of the people of the parish. And with this the parish leaders, called *responsables*, formed a network that became the center of a subversive system in which no records were kept or secrets shared.

But the heart of the work was done at the edge of the network in the homes of the villagers. It is here that people were sheltered. It is here that individuals, prepared by their history, led by their pastor, and directed by their parish network of *responsables*, opened their houses to the refugee. Far more pragmatic than heroic, the people of Le Chambon put aside their own indifference and fear to respond with compassion and shelter for all those who came.

A far simpler and less dramatic example of self-organization occurred during the construction of a superinsulated solar house I built a number of years ago. Although many techniques for building such houses are well known today, at the time the Northfield house was built, many of the ideas were new and unproved. Because of this, I decided to explain the general ideas of superinsulation to the carpenters rather than overdesign the house with numerous details. With the hope we would all learn as we went along, I told them, "Put in enough wood to keep it from falling down, but not so much that you put wood where you could put insulation instead." A week after this, on one of my regular site visits, I found the two carpenters engaged in a spirited discussion on the best way to frame the south corners of the house. I was encouraged to hear them having a conversation based on the design principles we had discussed the previous week, and to learn that between them they had arrived at a design better than any we could have come to by ourselves. By implementing an idea rather than following a blueprint, both carpenters became more engaged in the project, and I got a better house for it.

The Fractal Life

In chapter 1 I described how our desire for material things requires that our consumption be proportional to what we have already accumulated and that such constant percentage increases in our possessions leads to exponential, and therefore unsustainable, growth. Most needed today is the recognition that if we cannot sustain consumerism's growth, we cannot sustain any happiness based on it either. Today, with ever-greater incomes and ever more complex and time-consuming goods and activities to choose from, our lives have become far more active than rewarding.[10]

I believe our desire for more springs far less from genuine need than it does from a desire for variety—a desire that today is largely accommodated by the amount of money we bring to it. But if our desire for variety depends more on the nature of variety itself than on either its cost or its material content, then we have the markings of a new life.

Our desire for constant fractional growth in wealth, personal possessions, or social standing was quantified as early as 1738 by Daniel Bernoulli. Bernoulli suggested that transactions for people of various income levels are equivalent if the fractional changes in each transaction are the same.[11] For example, a raise of $100 a month for a worker earning $1,000 a month yields the same satisfaction for a low-income worker as does $1,000 a month raise for a person earning $10,000. For Bernoulli the satisfaction or social utility of each raise would be equivalent because each worker has received the same fractional increase of 10 percent. The phenomena of exponential growth that we observe in our culture occurs when we expect a constant rate of fractional growth, such as a 10 percent raise each year.

The idea that equal satisfaction comes from equal fractional raises illustrates what is called a scale-invariant phenomenon. Here, independent of the amount of his or her pay, each worker feels equally satisfied by the same 10 percent raise. Bernoulli used what he called a utility function to describe the fractional change required to produce such equal satisfaction. For Bernoulli, transactions with equal changes in utility provided equal personal satisfaction. A simple formula for Bernoulli's utility function can be written this way:[12]

$$\text{Change in utility function required for satisfaction} = \frac{\text{Change in what you have}}{\text{What you have}}$$

This equation tells us that maintaining a constant sense of satisfaction as we accumulate more stuff requires an equal fractional or percentage change in whatever we already have. For example, if I own one shirt and I get another, I have doubled the number of shirts I own. For this purchase, my change in utility is one, since I have increased the number of shirts I own by 100 percent. Bernoulli's claim is that if I desire to experience the same satisfaction with my next shirt purchase, I need to buy not just one shirt, but two, since two new shirts are now required to maintain my expected change in utility of 100 percent. Our ever-growing collection of clothes, or whatever, is an example of scale-invariant or scaleless phenomena. Regardless of how much we already have, we always want some constant fraction more.

Our human problem is not that we desire variety in our lives, but that we satisfy our desire for variety by ever increasing what we already have. To simply survive, we all need basic amounts of food, clothing, and shelter. Our problem today is that the food, clothing, and shelter we provide for ourselves frequently exceeds anything required for simple decent living. Without denying our need for it, our work is to bring variety to our lives in ways that our families, communities, and the world can all live with.

We need today to rescale our basic needs so that we get the variety we desire without ever-increasing our need for more stuff. With this, our goal is not so much to increase our personal affluence as it is to increase the well-being of our wider communities. Much of this work will involve recognizing how much richer we have all become as our general affluence has risen. For example, although I drive a bottom-of-the-line Volkswagen, in many ways it is a far better car than any of the luxury cars of my youth. Reliability, performance, safety, and sheer driving fun are all better in today's basic autos than they were in the best cars of the fifties. Although a family today might still buy a basic Chevrolet or Ford, their new car is likely to offer as many amenities as any luxury car of the past.

Learning to achieve satisfaction, not through constant growth, but by enhancing the pleasure we take from the huge variety of material things and experiences we already have will be the challenge of our lives. To begin we can use Bernoulli's utility function to arrange our experiences in a scaleless fashion so that our desire for variety is satisfied without the need to consume ever more resources. Given the impossibility of ceaseless growth, such a scaleless meeting of our desires offers us each a new way to live. Although the scaleless life may produce a tension of its own, for me it is far more desirable than one of constant debt or gratuitous accumulation.[13]

Scaleless happiness lies at the heart of voluntary simplicity, such as owning a house that one can afford not only to buy, but also to own. For example, although my wife and I could afford to buy a house larger than our current one-thousand-square-foot GI rambler, we could not afford to keep it clean, maintained, and furnished nearly as well. By owning a smaller house, we can furnish it with less but higher quality stuff and pay our entrepreneurial housekeeper a living wage to help keep it all clean. A house any larger would have us learning to like dust and cheap furniture. Our pleasure comes not from quantity, but quality, from a few pieces of fine furniture rather than a house full of plastic-veneered particleboard. None of this is particularly easy or cheap, and it was only in the past few years that we gave away the last of our budget furniture. Outside the house, Jan's small but fine flower garden brings as much pleasure to our modest yard as any country acreage, and the seasonal opening of our sun porch gives us as much pleasure as opening a cabin costing far more. Such reduced-scale living takes less time, money, and energy to keep up while giving us more time to enjoy it all.

The scaleless life, rather than giving us pleasure through the accumulation of more, lets us enjoy what we already have. Arranging our experiences so that the variety we seek comes by bringing variety to what we already have allows us to have satisfying lives that we all can live with. The scaleless life directs our actions so that our experiences, rather than constantly growing, are distributed in a scaleless fashion to vary as the inverse of what we desire. That is, to vary as 1/what we desire, so that the greater our desire, the less we should experience it. And with this we are led to lives that value the ordinary as much as the exceptional. I call such scaleless living the $1/f$, or fractal life. Arrangements in time or space that seem to have no one scale, but that appear the same at all scales of time or magnification, are said to be scaleless or fractal.

Beyond our own desires, nature itself prefers a scaleless geometry. As a tree grows to fill its space, each branch grows and divides and then grows and divides again, each division similar to the one that preceded it. Through such division, the tree develops a self-similar or fractal geometry from its beginning trunk to its last leaf. At each point of division, the tree does what it has done before, creating the canopy that is characteristic of its species. Such growth has a great practical utility because it does not easily resonate or go into an ever-increasing rhythmic motion with ever-increasing wind. With branches that are self-similar at all scales, a tree will bob and weave in ways that allow it to dissipate the energy of the wind rather than storing it to the point of self-destruction. It is the tree's fractal structure that makes it physically robust. Similarly, in our own bodies, the fractal branching of blood vessels creates a scaleless system that damps out the surges of the beating heart to keep our vessels from bursting. A likely explanation for the ubiquity of fractal order in nature is that it leads to the creation of robust organisms.[14] By assigning an equal value to all scales of growth, nature nurtures and maintains us within its own complex natural order.

Complex social institutions show similar behavior. For example, an examination of the stock market since 1900 shows that declines of more than 5, 10, 15, and 20 percent occurred with decreasing frequency, ranging from 318 declines of 5 percent or more to just 29 declines of 20 percent or more. An elementary analysis of these data shows that the number of declines as a function of size can be fitted with a simple function that is proportional to 1/size of the decline.[15] In practice this quantifies our intuition by telling us that there are a few large declines in the market and many small ones. What is unusual is how well it can be explained by an idea as simple as self-similarity at all scales. Here the yearly, monthly, daily, and even hourly records of the Dow Jones average all look remarkably similar. Unfortunately, although such a theory can tell us what to expect in the long run, it has no power at all to predict what is going to happen next.

In the same way that nature gives us robust bodies and self-similar markets, my belief is that the intentional practice of scaleless or fractal living can give us robust lives in a finite world. Learning to live intentionally in a finite world where our current lifestyles are not only improvident but impossible will call us into a new covenant with the only planet we have.

Toward a Fractal Life

Because the idea of fractal order or self-similarity at all scales is more descriptive than predictive, many people wonder if it is more an interesting curiosity than a scientific breakthrough.[16] After all, what good is a theory if it can't be used to calculate or predict? But even with these limitations, the science of complexity can still serve as a metaphor for understanding our own lives (17).

For example, a geoscience perspective in *Science* carried the arresting title "Earthquakes Cannot Be Predicted."[18] Data show that earthquakes, like the stock market, behave in a self-similar way, and the authors assert that the most we can know is that the earth will experience a small number of large earthquakes and a large number of small earthquakes. Without arguing the merits of this assertion, one can speculate what would happen if such a viewpoint became the dominant one. By accepting the idea that earthquakes cannot be predicted, building codes, zoning regulations, and insurance underwriting would all be affected. If complexity were to become the prevailing understanding of earthquakes—or, even more broadly, of nature itself—it would likely alter the way we live not only with earthquakes, but with all of life's vicissitudes.

More practically, I believe that we can use our understanding of the scaleless or fractal life to quantitatively distribute our resources so that we maximize our gratification for any given amount of time, money, or personal energy. For example, the fractal life would direct us to spend our money on eating out so that we would indulge in a few expensive meals occasionally while having less expensive ones more often. For this example, we can do a calculation using actual numbers. We start by deciding how many categories of meals we like to eat out, ranging from low-cost to pricey. For example, we can work out a budget for three types of meals; call them type A, B, and C. The A meals may be for special occasions or just pricy flings. B meals are simpler but frequently nearly as good, and C meals might be eating out at a simple ethnic place. It is reasonable for two to pay about $100, $50, and $16 for each of these meals, respectively. To find out how many of each is affordable, we need to set a budget. Let's say the budget is $100 per month or $1,200 per year, since this budget seems realistic and makes the calculation easy. Next, the annual budget is divided by the number of meal types, in this example three. To lead the fractal life, we then spend $400 per year on each sort of meal. This way we can have fine food four times per year, fair food eight times, and simple food twenty-five times. By budgeting equal amounts for each meal, the number of meals we get of each type goes in a fractal fashion as we divide the cost of each meal into its budget of $400. The less expensive the meal, the more often we get to eat it. The numbers tell us that much of the fractal life consists of simple experiences. In the fractal life, even if one's budget is unlimited, the relationship between the number and type of meals remains the same. In this case, the annual budget for 365 meals out becomes $11,800, with a fine meal each week or two, a fair meal or two weekly, and simple meals for all the rest. For the prices assumed here, independent of budget, nearly 70 percent of the meals out need to be simple. Regardless of budget, the fractal life clearly requires us to appreciate the ordinary if we are to find satisfaction in the special.

As a final example, I suspect one of the reasons I find sailing gratifying is that it requires constant attention to wind puffs that are distributed much like changes in the stock market or the size of earthquakes. By paying attention to the few large puffs that occur among the many small ones, I experience the fractal life as I keep my boat on an even keel and moving through the water. Yet, without watchful attention, one can readily capsize and experience a dunking similar to those that occur when we fail to pay attention to how we invest our money or where we build our houses. Beyond paying attention, a strong wind may also require me to reef down or reduce sail area. With this the chance of capsize is reduced while I continue to experience the pleasure brought by the variability of the wind. Such rescaling is a part of the fractal life. By rescaling our individual lives, we all can continue to experience the pleasure of the fractal life while simultaneously reducing the risk of either a personal or a global capsize.

Time, Theology, and Chaos

Although some claim that the study of complexity will be no more than a passing interest, it is my belief that over the next decades the science of complexity will inform our lives in ways we have yet to imagine. Leading this change will be the recognition that time is no longer a linear construct providing for a predictable future, but rather a quantity that ebbs and flows much as life itself. Even for the simplest systems, the science of complexity tells us that the future is unpredictable. For example, while the problem of two bodies gravitating around one another in otherwise empty space can be exactly solved, the addition of just one more body makes the problem impossible. While the path of a single planet going around a solitary star is readily shown to be a perfect ellipse, add a second planet and its gravitational attraction to the first, and no simple equation can describe the resulting motion.

None of this is particularly new. In 1889 French mathematician Henri Poincaré showed that finding an exact equation to describe the motion of a three-body system, such as two planets going around a solitary star, was simply beyond analysis. We now know that such systems, including all of the planets in our own solar system, are chaotic, unpredictable, in their motion. Although not a welcome finding, given Poincaré's observation of more than one hundred years ago, it should not be entirely surprising.

Today, through the use of extensive computer calculations, Gerald Sussman and Jack Wisdom of the Massachusetts Institute of Technology have demonstrated that the calculated orbit of each planet shows a great sensitivity to just where the planet is when the calculation is started.[19] If the calculation is started with just a one millimeter change in the initial position of a planet, the difference between calculated orbits increases geometrically, doubling about every three million years or so. Just as with compound interest, this constant doubling results in an exponential growth in the distance between the calculated orbits.

Not knowing where our planet will be within a millimeter or so in the next three million years seems like small potatoes until we remember that our solar system is about five billion years old and that our orbital uncertainty has gone through more than 1,500 doubling times. Thanks to the power of exponential growth, after about 50 doublings the uncertainty in the earth's orbit grows from one millimeter to a distance equal to about one trip around the sun. If we are so clueless as to where the earth should be on its yearly round, why does our planet remain going around the sun at all? This is unknown, but after five billion years, it appears to be our good fortune that our planetary chaos is more constrained than catastrophic. We may wander from our home, but we have not yet become lost.

As is true of many scientific discoveries, our inability to calculate the future was serendipitously discovered in 1961 by meteorologist Edward Lorenz. Working with a primitive computer in his office at MIT, Lorenz found that calculations that should have produced identical results did not. What Lorenz discovered was that changes in the numbers used to start his calculations, changes in his initial conditions as small as 1 part in 10,000, produced results so divergent that they called into question the entire enterprise of long-range weather forecasting.[20]

When first found, observations such as the unpredictability of next week's weather or of the earth's position in a few million years are just as likely to be dismissed as computational artifacts as they are to be accepted as findings of value. Because of this, as frequently happens in science, the study of chaos does not bring much of a "eureka" factor to the work of discovery. Fundamental discoveries may appear to be anything from profound to trivial to just plain wrong. Given such ambiguity, the discovery that initial conditions can dramatically affect long-term outcomes was necessarily slow to dawn. Such slowness is required to absorb the significance that three hundred years after Newton's *Principia*, we now know that the world is not nearly as deterministic as we would like it to be. Today the reassuring calculus of Newton has been replaced by the less-differentiated mathematics of the computer, with the unsettling result that as time goes by, we really cannot calculate the motions of the heavens after all. Frozen by the timeless theology of the church and then released by the elegant calculus of Newton, our understanding of time has now been shown by the sheer force of the computer to be not wrong, but dramatically incomplete.

Today the computer is transforming our most fundamental notions of time, and like Galileo's telescope, it is revealing to us a staggering new worldview. Galileo confirmed for himself and the world the solar system proposed by Copernicus. No longer did the sun, its planets, and the stars revolve around an all-important Earth and its people. Galileo demonstrated that as players on an ordinary planet traveling around an ordinary star, we were participants in, rather than central to, creation. The Copernican system, and in particular Galileo's defense of it, so challenged the church that he was tried, found guilty of sedition, and forced to live in seclusion the remainder of his life. It took over 350 years for the Catholic

Church to formally resolve the Galileo affair by renouncing in 1992 its 1616 prohibition that the Copernican system was a danger to the faith.

Three hundred and fifty years after Galileo's telescope transformed our understanding of space, the computer has begun to transform our most basic notions of time. While the Copernican revolution removed from us the comfort of living as all-important beings at the center of the universe, today's recognition that our position in space is beyond analysis has now taken from us any final comfort that the future is predictable.

Yet, in spite of all this, after five billion years of evolution, we are still here. That we as conscious beings on a friendly planet have somehow self-organized from a primordial soup is astonishing. For me it points to what I can only call the grace of God. It seems that somewhere within the notions of self-organization and the sensitivity of the future to where we are at the moment lies a crossing between faith and science. Complexity points to a God between one who has created and abandoned us and one who continues to rule the world. Complexity tells us that between the remote creator God of Newton's deterministic universe and the ever-present personal God who saves us from all our foibles and sins, lies a God of free will who graces us with a stunning array of options for making our own future (21).

Grace joins us with the universe to live out our lives as complex organisms in a complex social and natural order that we can neither explain nor deny. This was not lost on Jesus when he said, "Consider the lilies." Perhaps Jesus was speaking as an early chaos scientist when he tells us that life is emergent and that we should not be anxious about time. The genius of Jesus is that he addressed the question of the ages: what do we do about time? His answer, "Consider the lilies," is both unsettling and complete. It is an instruction to live lives of faith, to live lives of grace.

Work, Policy, and Chaos

The notion that leaderless work can lead to desirable results strongly supports the creation of policies that embrace rather than resist uncertain outcomes. The goal of policy should be not a sure or specific outcome, but rather a generally desirable result that is allowed to emerge from the work of the community. For example, in my twin towns the Urban Coalition of St. Paul discovered that only 30 percent of Southeast Asian women in Minneapolis and St. Paul were receiving adequate prenatal care. Still, even though these women had fewer clinic visits during their pregnancies, their babies were just as healthy as those of women whose prenatal care was much more extensive.[22] With an infant mortality rate 25 percent lower than the Minnesota state average, the Twin Cities' Southeast Asian mothers showed they had as much knowledge about having babies as that offered by the professionals assigned to serve them.

It is not that these Asian mothers are without resources; it is just that their resources are more cultural than clinical. Within their Southeast Asian community, pregnant women are cared for by an extended family of mothers and aunts who provide childbearing advice. Equally important for these new mothers is the recognition that pregnancy and birth are natural events rather than illnesses requiring medical intervention. Underserved by the medical community and for the most part defined by the government as living in poverty, the women of St. Paul's Southeast Asian community demonstrate that the poor and underserved have resources that money and prenatal programs cannot provide at any price.

In many cases, the success of such programs might be measured in terms of the number of prenatal clinic visits by each mother. After all, these data are easy to collect, report, and understand. Unfortunately, as just shown, these measures are meaningless when compared with the greater goal of a healthy baby. For example, although a documentable clinic visit might not stop a pregnant woman from eating junk food or having a drink and a cigarette, the unrecorded admonitions of an extended family of mothers and aunts will. Although their community may be defined by the government as living in poverty, they are not poor because they have resources within themselves to achieve socially successful lives.[23]

Although chaos-based policy may sound like the status quo, it is dramatically different. It does not mean a policy out of control, but rather a policy that lets go of control with the expectation that the goal of the policy will emerge from the affected community. In cases like the one above, we are learning that the best policy may be no policy at all. If there are any guiding principles, they are that policy ought to lead to desirable goals through work that is based more on trust than fear, more on relationships than regulations, more on capabilities than deficiencies—in short, more on abundance than scarcity.[24]

At heart, chaos-based policy puts the new liturgy into practice as it returns the work of the people to the people. With chaos-based policy the professional is no longer in charge but has the task of returning the work to the people and of providing resources for that work, for "funding" the work, as Walter Brueggemann said in chapter 6, and then getting out of the way.

Chaos-based policies are neither obvious nor easy to implement, since, for example, implementation might consist largely of resisting the urge that something must be done no matter what. Still, if there is a policy better than no policy at all, it is one that acknowledges the power of self-organization by returning the work of the people to the people. In other words, good policy encourages associations to serve the common good by bringing remedies, not programs, to the community. By encouraging community-based remedies that ameliorate rather than solve problems, we can all be motivated to transform rather than abandon our communities.

Life on the Edge of Chaos

Why is it that in the midst of all the unknowns, our lives continue to be filled more with hope than despair? More with optimism than fear? For me, hope and optimism spring from either the reality or the illusion of meaningful choice. Choice gives us a sense of control over our lives, even if we don't always know where life might lead. Here a little self-delusion can go a long way toward personal happiness. For example, even though I know that tens of thousands of new book titles appear each year and that of these only a few are widely read, I continue to write with the hope that what I'm doing will not only be read, but even make a difference. I work somewhere between the comfort of entitlement, where good fortune is certain, and the anxiety of fear, where it is not. And so, maintained by a hope, I continue in my ways.

Between the slack life of entitlement and the equally unproductive life of fear lies a life of work at the edge of chaos.[25] It is at the edge of chaos that we begin to trust the system, begin to trust grace, to bring desirable results to our lives. This is not easy, for it is difficult to see any immediate results of our actions. For example, *The Economist* reported that an American's chance of staying poor is less than one-half of 1 percent if just three behaviors are practiced: (1) finish high school, (2) get and stay married, (3) always work for wages (26). The notion that poverty can be avoided by adopting these behaviors is easily dismissed by youth or even many adults. After all, dropping out, getting laid, and knocking off a 7-Eleven each offer more direct rewards than studying, personal commitment, and showing up and getting to work. What makes life hard is that if one of these behaviors is missing, the risk of being poor grows greatly. Although these three behaviors may be sufficient for avoiding poverty, remove one, such as getting and staying married, and something else becomes necessary, such as avoiding having children out of wedlock.

We now know that success in life—the ability to feed, clothe, and house oneself; the ability to cope without becoming addicted to something; the ability to generate sufficient surplus in one's life to contribute to the life and arts of others—all require increasingly complex behavior. As we add more skills to our lives, they grow in complexity as well as in the capacity to produce happiness and wealth, or in the case of middle managers, a promotion to CEO (27).

Life on the edge of chaos is the work of the people. At the edge of chaos, the relationship between the laity and the professional becomes one of worker and mentor, as each carries out their work not from a position of original sin, but from a position of original consciousness, from what Matthew Fox calls "original blessing."[28] No longer are we people who are fundamentally sinful, sick, living in poverty, and worthy of constant suspect. Living lives of original consciousness, we become people living lives that spring more from blessing than sin, more from wellness than illness, more from our wits than our wealth, more from trust than suspicion. Gone are those who see deficiencies where there are capabilities and who would rather fix problems than ameliorate conditions—in short, gone are all those who advocate simple solutions over complex remedies, all those who promise us peace, abundance, and well-being without risk, work, or obligation. New are those who find us worthy of trust and who believe we are given to lives of grace, well-being, and inherent goodwill. No longer held hostage by the priesthood of professionals, we each begin to live lives of responsibility at the edge of chaos. And with this we each begin to trust that it is grace that directs our work and that it is grace that returns to us lives worth living.

Life on the edge of chaos requires that we give up both entitlement and fear and live lives of conscious discernment. Giving up entitlement will be one of the most difficult things we Americans will ever do. No longer can we wreck our bodies, our communities, our environment, our very well-being, and expect someone else to pick up the pieces. No longer can we lead sedentary lives and consume loads of tobacco, alcohol, sugar, salt, and fat and expect to have our health. No longer can we live in arbitrarily large houses and drive ever-larger vehicles and expect natural gas and gasoline to remain inexpensive. No longer can we flush the toilet, toss out the trash, dump fertilizer on our lawns, and expect not to assume responsibility for where it all goes. No longer can we not prepare for the future and still expect to have one. No longer can we give power that belongs only to us to the politicians, scientists, physicians, lawyers, or the theologically ordained of our lives and expect them to save our butts or pull our souls out of the fire.

Although giving up entitlement will be difficult, giving up fear will be even more so. If giving up entitlement brings us into a new relationship with our bodies and things material, giving up fear will bring us into a new relationship with our souls. To give up fear requires a new trust in the living system in which we find ourselves. To give up fear means trusting the world that has been created around us and our position in that creation. In the end, chaos tells us that we live lives of grace whose goodness comes from our own personal covenant with the creation that surrounds us.

CHAPTER EIGHT

A Crisis to Pray For

The End of Conventional Oil

*The question before the human race is, whether the
God of Nature shall govern the world by His own laws,
or whether priests and kings shall rule it by fictitious miracles.*
—Thomas Jefferson, 1815

*The present age of contentment will come to an end
only when and if the adverse developments that it fosters
challenge the sense of comfortable well-being.*
—John Kenneth Galbraith

*With scientific discovery and invention proceeding, we are told, at the rate
of geometric progression, a generally passive and culture-bound people
cannot cope with the multiplying issues and problems. Unless individuals,
groups, and nations can imagine, construct, and creatively revise new ways
of relating to these complex changes, the lights will go out.*
—Carl R. Rogers

The Lesson of the Roadmaster

Nineteen fifty was a good year. We were halfway through the twentieth
century. I was ten, the Buick Roadmaster was fourteen, and in America
twenty-five cents would get you a gallon of gasoline. General Motors'

Buick division had a record year with the addition of more than half a million of its toothy, chrome-grilled monsters to the forty million autos already on the nation's highways, and the Texas Railroad Commission kept them all going with a firm grip on the price of U.S. oil.[1] America's love affair with the automobile was taking off.

Buick's record production of 667,826 autos included my neighbor's Roadmaster. What a beauty. From its imposing chrome grill, portholed sides, and bulging rear fenders to its massive Straight-8 engine and Dyna-flow drive, it marked the beginning of the more-is-better school of U.S. auto design. The downside of all this glory was getting it all to work at the same time, and the hardest things to keep working seemed to be anything electrical. For most cars it was the clock or the taillights; for the neighbor's Roadmaster it was the fuel gauge. But even without a fuel gauge, the Buick's odometer worked, and while the amount of gas left was anybody's guess, the odometer at least told them how far they had come. Since they knew how far they could go on a tank of gas, the odometer became a default fuel gauge, something to be watched in expectation that the Buick would get filled before it faltered.

Like the neighbor's Roadmaster, our planet must also get along without a fuel gauge for its remaining oil. But unlike the Buick's driver, we do not know how much oil we started with, only how much we have consumed. Today, with limited information about our total oil supply, we are left with no more than our ability to make clever guesses about how much remains. The lesson of the Roadmaster is that without clever guesses and equally effective responses, our energy future will be dim indeed—not only immobile, but cold and dark as well.

Although a stalled car may not be a particularly welcome problem, it pales in comparison to that of a stalled planet. Both the Buick and the planet show us that our moment's work is frequently directed by our moment's problem. Such direction is called feedback, and in the case of the neighbor's Roadmaster, it may induce a variety of options, such as fixing the fuel gauge, filling the tank more often than a prudent watch would dictate, or living with the occasional empty tank and the adventure of meeting new people.

Similar actions, directed by the situation of the moment, directed by feedback, fill our lives. Finding ourselves cold, we put on a sweater; our cupboard bare, we go to the store; our basement flooded, we call the plumber. Although such feedback suits our daily needs, when it comes to comprehending the long-term requirements for our own survival and that of the planet, the signals we receive may be not only mixed, but contrary.

For example, at the beginning of the twenty-first century, we enjoyed real (inflation adjusted) gasoline prices that were about the same as they had been in 1950. Furthermore, thanks to growth in real income during the same period, gasoline had become more affordable than ever.[2] As an ever-decreasing portion of our household budgets, low-price gasoline encouraged Americans to buy heavy-duty, low-gas-mileage vehicles for the sheer fun of it. Today, as gasoline prices remain relatively cheap compared to income, it is easy to conclude that the good times, and our heavy vehicles, will roll on forever.[3] After all, if the minutes of work required to buy a gallon of gasoline have gone down for the past fifty years, why should we expect the next fifty years to be much different? This belief is so attractive that it is difficult to believe that it is also grossly wrong.

What is wrong with this picture is that the amount of what is called conventional oil is finite. And just because we have been pumping more and more of it out of the earth for the past one hundred years does not mean that we can continue to pump out ever-greater amounts for the next hundred. Although it is likely that conventional oil will be produced for the next fifty to one hundred years, it will be produced not in ever-increasing, but rather in ever-decreasing quantities. As with the production of any finite resource, what goes up must come down.

We now know that the production of conventional oil follows a bell-shaped curve that rises and falls about a finite peak. As consumers who have only experienced the increasing availability of oil, it is not surprising that we will be surprised when we reach the peak of oil's bell-shaped production curve. The bell shaped curve, beyond not giving us any sort of feedback that oil is finite, positively misleads us by giving us the most oil at the least cost at the very moment it is about to start its inevitable decline. The coming peak in the production of conventional oil will mark the end of cheap and abundant oil and will be the Roadmaster lesson felt around the world.

Hubbert's Last Peak

The idea that oil production follows a bell-shaped curve was first suggested by M. King Hubbert in 1956 (4). Hubbert's principal idea was that the full production cycle of oil in the United States would follow a bell-shaped curve from its first discovery to its last barrel's recovery. According to Hubbert, as years went by, the rate at which oil is recovered, say, in billions of barrels per year, would rise from zero, pass through some maximum annual production rate, and then fall back to zero, tracing a symmetrical pattern of rise and decline.

It is important to acknowledge at this point just how misleading it is to describe the pumping of oil from the earth as the "production" of oil. Such extraction does not produce oil any more than pumping fuel from a filling station produces gasoline. While it seems clear that the neighborhood gas station extracts gasoline from a tank buried in the ground, we seem less ready to accept the fact that oil, rather than being "produced," is simply extracted from geological reserves left to us by the providence of nature. The notion of oil production becomes particularly dangerous when we apply the economist's invisible hand to the problem of providing energy to an ever-expanding world economy. No matter what we might believe about the forces of market economics, the forces of economics have never, and will never, produce oil or any other form of fuel or energy. The most economics can do is to direct our capital investment toward the best means for the extraction of energy from what nature itself provides. Hubbert's curve is not so much a measure of our ingenuity as it is of nature's bounty.[5]

The most important property of Hubbert's oil production curve is that the area under the curve is equal to the total amount of oil expected to be extracted. Thus, in 1956 Hubbert reviewed the estimates to date of the amount of oil that would be produced in the lower forty-eight states and prepared bell curves with areas corresponding to ultimate productions of 150 billion and 200 billion barrels of oil.[6] To the shock of many, Hubbert's curves showed that oil production in the lower forty-eight states would peak somewhere within the next ten to fifteen years. By 1970 at the latest, Hubbert predicted, the lower forty-eight would begin to produce less and less oil. Although Hubbert's simple analysis was met with incredulity, in March 1971 the Texas Railroad Commission allowed for the first time in decades an all-out production of U.S. oil.[7] This action marked the peak of U.S. oil production and the end of America's control over the price of oil. Hubbert had been vindicated, and while America's romance with the automobile continued unabated, its ability to extract the oil required for its own gasoline use had ended. A decade of oil scarcity was to follow, with the price of oil increasing more than fivefold by the early 1980s.

The value of institutional control of the production and hence the price of oil was not lost to the world's oil-exporting countries. A decade earlier, in September 1960, the Organization of Petroleum Exporting Countries (OPEC) was formed in response to a unilateral reduction by

Standard Oil of New Jersey in the so-called posted price of oil.[8] While market prices were usually discounted to be less than the posted price, it was the posted price that was used to compute the tax and royalty revenue of the producing country. Threatened by loss of revenue, the oil-exporting countries created OPEC, an organization that would provide for them the same force of price control that the Texas Railroad Commission was providing so well in the United States.[9] Although OPEC was formed ten years before the oil-price crisis of the 1970s, its force in the market remained in check thanks to America's great capacity to pump as much oil as needed to keep its price at a constant $10 a barrel (in 1997 dollars).

Ten-dollar-a-barrel oil ran out when America ran out of capacity to pump oil in 1971. OPEC was now in the driver's seat, and with this the rest of the world was suddenly motivated to develop the new oil provinces of Alaska, Mexico, and the North Sea.[10] Between new sources of production and decreases in demand produced by $50-a-barrel oil, the price of oil began a steady decline to less than $20 a barrel by the mid-1980s. Like the United States in 1971, OPEC had lost its margin of control due to the increased pumping capacity of the rest of world. Thus, from about 1970 to 1985, the privilege of controlling the price of oil shifted from the United States to OPEC and finally to producers whose provinces were outside of both. While America has now experienced Hubbert's peak in its own ability to extract oil, OPEC and the world have yet to experience theirs.

A Crisis to Pray For

Learning to live with the vicissitudes of the world's emerging oil market will be one of the principal challenges of the twenty-first century. Yet, given our reluctance, our existential laziness, to pick up this challenge, it's likely that only a crisis will get our attention. Crisis does not necessarily mean a negative event, but an event that is so pervasive that it gets everyone's attention at the same time. An example of such an event would be a severe gasoline shortage, and like the two-part Chinese word for *crisis*, it would present both a "danger" and an "opportunity."

The extent of the danger and opportunity provided by any crisis depends on the basic nature of the problem from which it comes. Earlier we talked about two kinds of problems, convergent and divergent. Convergent problems were the dead batteries of our lives, those problems for which there are clear and ready consensus solutions. Problems of this sort appeal to us because they allow us to passively participate in their solution while selected experts do the work. Divergent problems are those that are not resolvable by consensus, such as health care, abortion, public education, or use of the natural environment. For these problems well-meaning people can be found on several sides of any issue, and there are no single solutions, but only remedies that allow individuals of all persuasions to participate in a community response to the problem.

Remaining still are problems of a third type, those that, even though they appear convergent, require the work of the community as well as that of the expert.[11] The coming crisis in the supply of conventional oil is such a problem. The problem here is clear and convergent: conventional oil is finite, and our ability to produce it is entering a period of permanent decline. But the solution becomes divergent when we realize that the problem is about not only the production of oil, but also its use.

The two most direct responses to the shortage of anything are for those who produce to produce more, and for those who use to use less. A shortage becomes a crisis to pray for, not only because it is clear, but also because it invites—if not demands—us to actively participate in its remedy. Although we may have little control over the response of the larger system, we do have control over our response to its effect on our lives. By controlling our response to crisis, we can bring meaningful participation to our lives. Acts of meaningful participation become acts of grace as we bend our wills to cooperate with a natural order that is at heart indifferent to our existence.

Crisis, then, is feedback writ large, and the crisis to pray for comes from feedback that is more instructive than fatal. When my stepchildren were adolescents growing into young adults, my constant prayer was that they would not do something irreversibly stupid, harming themselves or others beyond the repair of love. Today we are planetary adolescents growing into an adult relationship with the life system that supports us, and like adolescents we find ourselves feeling invincible, an invincibility that, depending on our choices, may be fatal or not.

Why Us, Why Now?

Losing our global capacity to pump oil could be only one of many crises that gets our attention at the beginning of the poised century. Others could be global problems of adequate freshwater, hunger, public health, climate change, financial collapse, or wars prompted by such global distress. It is reasonable to ask, why these problems, and why now? After all, Cassandras of all sorts have been predicting the end the world for centuries.[12] What is happening today that has not happened in the past?

The short answer is nothing. And that's the problem. Today, as in the past, we continue to grow at a rate that is proportional to where we are at the moment. And given this, because we go from moment to moment in our lives, we become easily immune to the fact that what is going on all around us is exponential growth without end.

When anything is growing exponentially, it doubles and doubles and doubles again in a regular pattern that is easy to calculate. If something is doubling at a regular rate, all we need to know is the percent by which it grows in any given time to figure out the doubling period. Here's the equation:

$$\text{Time to double whatever} = \frac{70}{\text{Percent rate of growth per period}}$$

So if you have a bank account that is paying 7 percent interest per year, it will double your money in about ten years. Better yet, at 10 percent interest per year, your money will double in seven years.[13]

For the first eighty years of world oil production, from 1890 to 1970, the growth in global oil output was close to exponential. With production growing at the rate of about 7 percent a year, the annual global output of oil doubled every ten years for eight decades, a remarkable growth in resource extraction and use.[14] What makes it even more astonishing is our next and last mathematical lesson of this book: in any doubling period, the amount of anything produced or consumed is equal to all that has been produced or consumed in the past.[15] Thus, over the ten-year period from 1960 through 1969, the amount of oil produced in the world was equal to all the oil ever produced from its first discovery through 1959. The world's ability to produce as much oil in a decade as ever produced in the past stopped abruptly in the 1970s.

Although the above notion of production may seem abstract, it may be readily demonstrated with paper and pencil. Start by drawing a straight line across your paper. Now mark the top left of the line "present amount" and the bottom left "sum of previous amounts." Next, above the line, write a series of doubling numbers: 1, 2, 4, 8, 16, and 32. Finally, below the line, write a second series of numbers. Under the 2 write the sum of all the previous amounts above the line (in this case 1), under the 4 write the next sum, 3, and continue this process, ending with the number 31 below the 32 on top. Comparing the upper and lower numbers shows us the remarkable fact that when anything is doubling, the upper number is always one more than the sum of all the numbers preceding it. In any doubling period, the amount of any resource extracted equals the total of all that has ever been extracted. This is the way constant growth works, and it ought to be understood by every schoolchild and adult in America.[16]

Our last observation allows us to answer the question "Why us, why now?" Through 1970 the world had enough oil-pumping capacity to double the production of oil every decade for eighty years. But even with this prodigious growth in output, by the early 1970s just one-eighth of the world's oil had been extracted.[17] With seven-eighths of the world's ultimately recoverable oil remaining after eighty years of production, one could easily be led to believe that any oil crisis would take place far in the future. Yet, as we have just seen, the mathematics of exponential growth makes such optimism unwarranted. With production growing at 7 percent a year, and thus doubling every ten years, each decade marks a doubling in total amount of oil ever produced. That is, with one-eighth of the world's oil produced through 1970, during the next decade, by 1980, an additional one-eighth would have to be produced to maintain an annual growth rate of 7 percent. With this, two-eighths, or one-quarter of the world's oil, would have been produced and consumed by 1980.

Continuing our calculation, a constant 7 percent growth in production would then predict that one-half would be gone by 1990 and that by 2000 all the world's oil would be gone. While the first half of the world's total oil supply would take a full century, from 1890 to 1990, to produce, the last half would take but a single decade. Such is the power of exponential growth.

So the answer to "Why us, why now?" is simply this: when anything is growing exponentially, even a doubling of the total resource puts off the day of reckoning by no more than one doubling period. In the case of world oil production growing at a rate of 7 percent a year, the reckoning is put off just ten years. In reality, world oil production has been relatively contained since 1970, and as of today we still have roughly half of the world's recoverable oil still left in the ground. The purpose of my idealized argument is more to temper unbridled optimism than to predict the actual peak of oil. Today, to our good fortune, Hubbert's curve for world oil production has more the shape of a plateau than a peak. And, due to world demand for oil remaining below our capacity to pump it, oil prices have remained moderate, with price spikes driven more by political and economic unrest than resource scarcity.

A conservative estimate of the total amount of world oil that will ever be produced stands at about 2,000 billion barrels, and of that amount about one-half remains as we start the twenty-first century.[18] Because oil production is roughly symmetric in time, with half of the world's resources of oil already consumed, no one should be surprised if the amount of oil produced begins to decline in the near future. How near a future depends on the total amount of oil that is expected to be produced, but the emerging consensus suggests sometime between 2010 and 2030 (19). Since two-thirds of the world's remaining oil lies under the OPEC countries of the Middle East, the ability of the world to produce oil will depend critically on how much pumping capacity the Middle East countries are willing to bring to bear.[20] More certain than OPEC's future decisions, however, is that the oil production capacity of the world outside the Middle East will peak shortly after the turn of the century. When this happens, the present buyer's market will come to a halt as the countries of the Middle East assume a permanent and singular control of the world supply of oil. The control of the oil market that moved from the Texas Railroad Commission, to OPEC, to producers outside of both, will finally and permanently return to the OPEC countries of the Middle East at the beginning of the millennium.[21]

The Builder, the Broker, and the Banker

Over the years I have found three recurring responses to a future that requires, if not demands, our participation in the world oil problem. I call these the responses of the builder, the broker, and the banker, all given me during the early 1990s oil crisis. The builder's response was that we have had many predictions of looming oil scarcity in the past, and since they have all proved wrong, so will this. He cited Daniel Yergin's *The Prize* and observed that the exploration of oil had always been full of good surprises and that the future would likely be the same.[22]

The builder's observation of oil's history makes the point that looking for oil is a complex and competitive business and therefore relatively efficient. It is the sheer complexity of the oil business that allows us to use ideas as simple as the Hubbert curve to draw conclusions about the future of oil.[23] Two factors are important: the way oil is distributed around the earth and the way those who look for oil cover the world to find it. The most arresting characteristic of the earth's oil is that the vast majority of it, 94 percent, is found in just the top 12 percent of the world's oil fields.[24] Conversely, it is sobering to note that the remaining 88 percent of the world's oil fields contain just 6 percent of the world's oil. Like the magnitude of its earthquakes, the earth's oil is distributed among a few large fields and many small ones.

Beyond these known fields, the record oil prices of the late seventies through the mid-eighties prompted a worldwide surge to find yet more. That no new major oil fields were discovered as a result of this intense effort serves as another sobering reminder of just how thoroughly the earth has been explored for oil.[25] Given such exploration, it is highly unlikely that much oil has been left undiscovered. To assume otherwise is to discredit the skill and knowledge of those whose business it is to find oil. Like a Sunday school egg hunt after a flurry of youngsters has explored every square inch of turf, it is unlikely any eggs go unfound.

More fundamental than the sheer intensity of oil exploration is the growing understanding of how oil is formed and where it is likely to be found. Knowledge of tropical seaways maintained over geologic time by the coming and going of tectonic plates has given us a broad understanding of where petroleum can be expected to be found around the world. Based on this understanding and the results of modern exploration, Masters, Root, and Attanasi report in *Science* they are "substantially confident" no new oil resources are "likely to be found" that would tip the balance of oil production away from the Middle East.[26] Like Hubbert's oil production curve, the curve for oil discoveries is also bell-shaped, and today, after decades of exploration following the 1973 oil crisis, its peak remains firmly fixed in the early sixties. With most of the world's oil now found, the builder's optimism becomes tempered by the reality that the world contains a finite amount of conventional oil. With Hubbert's curve for discoveries now firmly fixed in the past, oil's finite future seems more certain than ever.[27]

Not to be discouraged, the broker bargains, "Can't we make oil out of rocks?"[28] The broker's observation is reasonable in that it is possible to literally mine oil. Such oil is found in the tar sands of Canada, where the province of Alberta alone has about three hundred billion barrels of recoverable tarlike oil, or bitumen. So thick it needs to be dug out of the ground like so much oil-bearing ore, bitumen is recovered through a process that involves crushing the ore and then extracting the bitumen with hot water and steam. Left behind are tailing ponds requiring careful management and a product that requires further processing to produce chemical and fuel feed stocks. Although retrieving oil from the tar sands of Canada is a dirty, complex process requiring extensive environmental safeguards, producers claim that its price is competitive with that of conventional oil.[29]

Competing with the broker's technology for making oil out of rocks is technology for enhancing the recovery of oil from existing fields.[30] Such technology converts oil from resources that are believed to exist into reserves that can be recovered.[31] Two technologies are of primary importance: three-dimensional seismology, which shows where oil might be found, and directional drilling, which allows it to be extracted. While the art and science of finding oil using acoustic reflections is more than fifty years old, only recently have such techniques been refined to the point where they can be used to rework known fields to find oil previously missed.[32] Once found, such oil can be recovered more easily than ever by using steerable drills that can travel downward and then horizontally through the field to recover oil that earlier had been left behind. Applied to old fields, improved seismology and directional drilling can enhance recovery factors by up to 20 percent.

Beyond enhancing recovery from existing fields, advanced exploration and drilling techniques have found further application in the development of offshore oil. Previously beyond the reach of exploration or development, offshore fields of 100 million to 1 billion barrels of oil are now common. Placing platforms the height of a fifty-story building above water one-half to one mile deep at a cost of $1 billion or more is neither simple nor cheap. But even with technologies like these, the cost floor for complex projects appears to be between $60 and $70 per barrel, a price below oil's current trading range.[33]

With so much good news, the banker now joins the chorus, asking, "What's there to worry about?" What distinguishes the banker from the builder or broker is the sheer passivity of his position. "If I need to change the way I do things, so be it, but I will only do things differently when I have to."[34] The banker represents all those who choose to remain unengaged: those who seem willing to accept whatever may be, who seem willing to muddle through whatever bad planning has to offer. In the end, like the builder, broker, or banker, we are each optimistic in our own way about the future and our ability to cope with whatever scarcities may come our way.

America's greatest scarcity today is not one of physical resources but of political will and imagination to do something positive about our next, and final, oil crisis. Beyond the need to find new sources of energy and more efficient ways of using them lies the even greater need to find sufficient capital to develop the capacity required. Our greatest scarcity in the future will be not only of fuel resources but also of "patient capital" in amounts massive enough to fund the long-term development of new technologies whose short-term returns may be as uncertain as the price of the commodity displaced. Required for the poised century will be investors as interested in the future and communal as the personal and immediate.

Numbers in the News

My Sunday paper carries the headline, "Astonishing trove of oil is waiting in Caspian Sea."[35] At first blush, this appears to be good news, since it tells us we still have time to decide whether we might have a real global oil production problem or not. But good news becomes bad news when it causes us to believe that we have no problem at all. Going only by good news, we find it easy to believe our energy problems are just a thing of the past. Fortunately, it takes only a few numbers for us to compare such claims to reality.

Consider the above-mentioned article. It goes on to say that "proven" and "possible" oil deposits in the Caspian basin add up to an "astonishing 178 billion barrels of oil." First consider the words *proven* and *possible*. "Proven" oil is oil that can be recovered now, and "possible" oil is oil that might be recovered sometime in the future. The article may claim a find of 178 billion barrels, but estimates in the literature of the amount of oil in the Caspian basin range from 50 billion to 186 billion barrels.[36] While time will tell who is right in this case, it is useful to know that quoted estimates can easily vary by factors of two to three, or even more.

Let's now assume that 100 billion barrels of oil will be ultimately recovered from the Caspian Basin. Is this really an "astonishing" amount of oil? Three comparisons can be made. First, compared to a conservative estimate of the amount of ultimately recoverable oil in the world, 2,000 billion barrels, Caspian oil will add only 5 percent more, a small fraction compared to the 100 percent required to add just one doubling period. Second, compared to the current world extraction rate of about 30 billion barrels a year, Caspian oil will add a little more than three years' production. However, this is generous, since this oil will, in reality, be produced over a period of many years, during which time oil production is expected to grow about 2 percent annually.

More realistically, the 100 billion barrels that might be extracted from the Caspian Basin will appear as just one small curve under the much larger Hubbert curve for global oil production. Given that the area under the global Hubbert curve is equal to all the oil that will ever be extracted, the effect of adding Caspian oil will be to make Hubbert's peak a little wider, higher, and slightly moved forward in time. Albert Bartlett of the University of Colorado has mathematically modeled this behavior and found that the peak of the curve is moved outward by about 5.5 days for each billion barrels of oil added to the area under the curve.[37] Thus, a Caspian find of 100 billion barrels will move forward our day of reckoning by 550 days, or about a year and one-half. By comparison to the world's one-hundred-year history of oil development, a year and a half is fleeting.

Finally, consider the estimate of total recoverable oil given by the Cambridge Energy Research Associates (CERA). CERA claims that more than 3 trillion barrels of recoverable oil remain in the world. Let's now assume that between the more conservative estimate of 1 trillion barrels cited earlier and CERA's 3 trillion, that 2 trillion additional barrels of oil remain to be recovered. With an outward move of oil's peak by 5.5 days for each additional billion barrels, CERA's additional trillion will move out our day of peak oil by 5,500 days, or very close to fifteen years. Although such optimism buys us time, it does not change the fundamental fact that we need to plan for a future without oil.[38]

Although journalists may use words such as "astonishing" to finds such as those around the Caspian Sea, and others such as CERA may report resources more than double current reserves, we each need to do our own numerical, and thus sobering, reality checks.

Energy and Imagination

If we are to imagine any sort of decent life tomorrow, we must begin to imagine life without conventional oil today. How we do this work, or whether we do it at all, will play a large role in determining the civility of our collective life on the planet. What we know now is that our greatest natural subsidy of the twentieth century, conventional oil, a substance that built and currently maintains our present global development, is going to simply trickle out during the twenty-first century. The end of nature's most generous subsidy will be the Roadmaster lesson felt around the world, and how we respond to this most natural of all feedback effects will become a primary measure of our future lives.

The sheer ubiquity of energy in our culture mandates that we pay attention to where it comes from and how we use it. Most significantly, we need to remember that neither perpetual motion nor spontaneous heating and cooling has ever been observed. In short, it has always been observed that without energy, everything stops. We need to remember, too, that energy is a physical variable that depends on the size of the system involved. For example, if we want to boil water, it takes twice as much energy to bring two quarts of water to boil as one. Of greater consequence, however, is the reverse. If we reduce the amount of energy used to bring our water to a boil by a factor of two, we can boil only half as much. Whatever it is we desire, if we use half the energy, only half of the work gets done.[39]

Our vast capacity to extract fossil fuel resources from the earth has left us with the notion that we have some vast capacity to produce energy. We need to disabuse ourselves of this idea by remembering always that energy cannot be created, but only transformed from what we have been provided. By confusing our ability to exploit the natural order with the notion that we have the capacity to produce energy, we have come to believe that it is our ingenuity and not the bounty of nature that has got us thus far.

Energy is the ultimate consumable. Once used, it is gone forever, never to be of use again.[40] Even energy from renewable resources is consumed, only to be restored by the earth's daily supply of wind and sun. When we learn that there is no substitute for energy and that no amount of genius can create it, it will mark the beginning of a massive paradigm shift from our exploitation of the natural order to our cooperation with it.

Since old ways of doing things are rejected only in the face of crisis, paradigm shifts are never easy. Thomas Kuhn, in *The Structure of Scientific Revolutions*, describes one thing that scientists "never" do, and that is to reject an existing paradigm, no matter how troublesome, until an alternative paradigm becomes available.[41] For Kuhn, paradigm change requires a crisis that is propelled by a failure of present understanding together with the occurrence of new thinking that simply works better. Like those of us who hope for perpetual motion or a refrigerator that cools without being plugged in, scientists too will generate ad hoc explanations in order to bring order to their lives. These theories frequently become ever more complex and bizarre until someone comes along and offers a better explanation. Such was the work of Copernicus when the ad hoc epicycles of Ptolemaic astronomy proved too much to handle.

Imagining the sun rather than the earth at the center of the solar system did more than create a revolution in our geometric understanding of the solar system; it fundamentally changed our own position in creation. No longer at the center of things, we were forced by the Copernican revolution to see ourselves as lesser participants in some greater whole. Although such a change in understanding was revolutionary at the time, it demanded little of us other than to accept it, and whether or not we did, life went on unchanged. While the revolution of understanding our place in space required little of us but acceptance, the coming revolution in understanding our place in time will engage us in ways we have never experienced.

Time Will Tell

We are now experiencing the last years of an abundant age that has provided for our livelihoods from the start of time. Resources of fuel, food, and space to grow, abundantly supplied by nature, will come under greater and greater stress as we try to maintain perpetual growth in a finite world. Most important is the nature of exponential growth, which tells us that with each doubling in our rate of consumption, we consume as much as we have ever consumed in the past. As casual observers on a friendly planet, we may look out our windows and see nothing but an abundance of resources. Yet, as exponential growth shows us, when even half of a resource remains, it is but one doubling period away from exhaustion. The power of exponential growth is so large that it makes little difference if one has half or even three-quarters of any resource left. Whatever remains will be gone within one or two doubling periods.

Today, our habit of exponential growth will separate past from future in an unmistakable way that will present us with unprecedented choices for our future life on the planet. Not only will our supplies of conventional oil finally run out, but our ability to feed a growing world will diminish as well. Although substitutes may be found for oil's energy, there are no simple substitutes for our own energy—food. Today's need to feed ever more people is sorely testing the world's food production resources, particularly water and arable land. Without continued improvement in the efficiency of food production, we are simply going to run out of these critical resources.

The cultivated earth provides us with about three Calories of grain per square meter each day.[42] Because it takes between 1,800 and 3,000 Calories to maintain each of us, between 600 and 1,000 square meters (about the size of a city lot) of arable land is needed to grow the minimal food for just one person. Given an arable land area of about 10 trillion square meters, the world's maximum population is today limited to about 10 to 15 billion people.[43] With a present world population of about 6.5 billion people, we are, as with oil, about one doubling period away from the earth's capacity to provide. Using our previous formula for calculating doubling time from growth rate, our present population growth rate of 1.4 percent a year yields a population doubling time of fifty years.

Today, our persistently doubling consumption provides a natural clock that is ticking out our collective future on a small and finite planet. With each doubling period that ticks by, we are one less tick away from extinction. With only a single tick, one doubling period, remaining for our supplies of food and oil, nature's great clock will without doubt be sending us wake-up alarms within this, our poised century.

Avoiding Catastrophe:
The Need for New Worldviews

Our discussion has now brought us full circle to again encounter what we all try to avoid: suffering. Yet suffering is not all bad, because it tells us that something is wrong, and if we just listen, it will direct our lives in new ways. Seen as feedback whose purpose is more to inform than punish, suffering can become a positive force in our lives. The feedback of running low on fuel or food, while not entirely welcome, should be seen not as the end of the world, but as a sign that we need to do things differently.

Although we have no choice but to find energy resources beyond oil and to limit our growth before we overrun our finite world, we do have choices as to how we will live through these experiences. The choices we make in addressing these inevitable changes are far more important than the problems themselves. Above all, rather than constantly looking to the scientist, politician, or preacher to bail us out with pain-free solutions, we need to embrace the reality that our problems will require complex and likely messy remedies that will demand as much of us as of the experts to whom we would like to defer. In the end, we will find that the problems of our age are as much social as scientific and that the work of bringing civility and sustainability to our communities belongs to each of us. You and me. We're it. And if we don't begin this work by enhancing the consciousness and civility of our own daily lives, it won't get done.

Most important for us today is whether we will collectively make timely and sustainable decisions or let the larger natural order make its own decisions for us. Surprisingly, as the planet's most rapacious and conscious species, we seem to have little interest in which way it will work out. As a species that has yet to raise its level of consciousness to much beyond itself, we remain largely ignorant of the global consequences of our individual behavior. Producing and consuming in a world we perceive as boundless, we carry on with our lives as if there were no tomorrow. Like the petri dish in the laboratory, our planet in space, whether we are conscious of it or not, will simply use its own mechanisms to make those decisions we defer to it. Like bacteria in a laboratory petri dish that flourish and disappear, so may we.

One way to prepare for the emerging order of things is to conduct our lives so that in the long run they are more robust than fragile. For example, by living in smaller and better-insulated houses nearer our work and driving more fuel-efficient vehicles, we can all act to reduce the impact of increasing energy prices on our lives. By investing in efficiency now rather than later, we can all robustly prepare ourselves for the inevitable ebb of conventional oil and natural gas (44). It might be claimed that acting this way comes from special class privilege not available to most Americans, and that such suggestions should be dismissed as elitist claptrap. Still, even if many cannot afford to do these things, many of us *do* have the resources to make similar choices, but choose instead impressive size over good design, gratuitous consumption over simple living, and exclusive remoteness over shared nearness.

Although many of us would consider running out of oil to be a major problem, it pales in comparison to some of the far more complex responses that the earth could have to our presence. For example, the issue of global warming revolves around whether or not human activity is causing a general warming of the planet. Most data presented to argue the point for global warming show that the earth's average temperature has risen about 1 degree Fahrenheit over the last century.[45] Most people agree that global warming is possible, since the growth in atmospheric greenhouse gases, such as carbon dioxide, is well documented and accepted.

But the simple existence of a possible mechanism leaves others unconvinced that the true cause of this century's warming is actually related to human activity.

What we are learning now is that the planet's climate, and ultimately the weather in our neighborhood, is determined by many interacting factors that make the job of sorting out climate change exceedingly difficult, if not ultimately impossible. As a complex self-organizing system, our planet's climate is sensitive to initial conditions. Because of this, small changes today may have large effects within the lifetimes of many.

When most of us think about weather, our primary concerns are the temperature and whether it is raining or snowing, and perhaps, during the summer, how humid the day might be. As creatures of comfort, we prefer warm, dry, and sunny over cold, wet, and gray. But the local weather we experience is controlled by the much larger elements of global climate, of which global temperature is only one measure among many. What we now know is that within the past ten to fifteen thousand years, our climate has changed dramatically and rapidly, with North Atlantic air temperatures changing 10 to 15 degrees Fahrenheit within decades.[46]

There is now overwhelming evidence that our current warm climate is about ten thousand years old, and that at the end of the last cold period, the so-called Younger Dryas period, the various parameters used as proxies for temperature fluctuated over several centuries from colder to warmer with periods ranging from a few decades to a few years. While our current ten-thousand-year warm spell, the Holocene, leads us to experience our climate as something rather stable, the historical record, based on cores of polar ice and midlatitude ocean sediment, shows that simultaneous worldwide climate changes have been far from exceptional. Although global climate change may be driven by changes in the absorption or magnitude of solar radiation, the rapid and large-scale changes observed in the geologic record indicate that some larger effect must be operating as well.

One large effect proposed is the "great conveyor," a globe-encircling ocean current that flows from the Pacific Ocean to the North Atlantic at a rate equal to more than ten times the flow of all the world's rivers.[47] By transporting heat to the North Atlantic that is then carried by prevailing winds to Northern Europe, this great ocean current indirectly warms Europe by as much as 10 to 15 degrees Fahrenheit.[48]

It is now believed that the ocean current that carries this heat around the earth is part of a great solar-powered thermal engine that periodically cycles off and on. Warmed in the topics and midlatitudes, the conveyor travels north toward Greenland, where it loses heat and moisture to prevailing winds that moderate the climate of Northern Europe. Made colder, saltier, and thus denser by heat loss and evaporation, the conveyer's water sinks and begins a deep southward flow that travels as far as the southern oceans, where it circles Antarctica and eventually winds its way into the North Pacific. There it begins to warm and rise, gathering heat for the return journey along the tropical latitudes between Australia and Indonesia, and then, rounding the cape of Africa, it completes its path with a final flow to the north.

Like a great thermal engine, the earth's ocean conveyor transfers heat from a warm source to a cold sink. It is now proposed that as this current has run over the millennia the heat brought north melts existing ice, sending freshwater on top of saltwater. With freshening, the water current diminishes in density to the point where it fails to sink and the great conveyor stops. With this, ice age conditions prevail, stopping both freshwater flow and further dilution. The ice age ends when, without the dilution of freshwater, the saltiness of the ocean is restored, and the great conveyor begins once again to bring warmth to the north.[49]

Predicting the conveyor's flow is made complex by the observation that although the current may remain stable for thousands of years, given the right conditions its flow can change dramatically within ten years or less.[50] We usually like to think that the relationships between cause and effect follow some linear pattern, and that a change in cause always produces a proportional change in effect. For example, in stretching a simple spring, a two-pound force causes twice the stretch as a one-pound force. If the earth's ocean currents behaved in the same way, their motion could, in principle, be predicted. But for the great conveyor, freshwater inflow to the North Atlantic produces little or no change in the current flow until, by dilution, some critical water density is reached at which point a disproportionally large change happens: the conveyor slows or even stops (51).

The on-off character of the conveyor can be thought of as an emergent property of a complex self-organizing system that consists literally of earth, air, fire, and water. Because of its complex response, the global conveyor adds a large and unpredictable component to the whole issue of global climate change. The issue becomes deeply entangled with global warming, since such warming not only melts ice and snow, but may also deliver loads of tropical water vapor to the North Atlantic in the form of rain, snow, and continental runoff. With this, global warming may accelerate the dilution of the conveyor, causing its next slowdown to happen sooner rather than later. Thus, because of its nonlinear response, the earth's great conveyor acts as a large amplifier of any global warming effect. For example, could just one more degree of global warming mark the beginning of another ice age? This we do not know, but compared to a worldwide oil shortage, it is clearly not a crisis to pray for.[52]

If we accept that gradual global warming might actually produce something else—global cooling—then our options for living on the planet become more sharply focused. With our growing understanding of the fundamental unpredictability of complex self-organizing systems, it is becoming increasingly evident that we have built our civilization on the tail of a sleeping dragon, a dragon that we are now poking with the sharp stick of global development.[53] With the advent of new understandings, we need to come to a new relationship with the only place we call home—planet Earth. Avoiding catastrophe will require new worldviews that are only now beginning to emerge (54).

Toward a New Paradigm

Little is certain about our future life on the planet other than this: that within the twenty-first century we will begin to tax our natural capital to its limit. Although many people, particularly economists and engineers, will dismiss this as far too pessimistic to take seriously, I believe that the growing human demand for fuel, food, and water will simply overwhelm the capacity of the earth to provide. While this might surprise many, it is nothing more than the observation that the most we can expect of any unconscious species living in a closed system is that without natural predators it will grow exponentially until limited by the miseries of starvation and conflict over who gets the last crumb. Our saving grace, of course, is that the earth is not a closed system and we are given to consciousness, if we would but claim it. As a large, living, thermal engine in space, our planet receives energy from the sun as high-temperature radiation, or light, stores a tiny amount in living things, and then returns the difference to space as low-temperature radiation, or heat. And although today we seem to be blindingly unconscious of tomorrow, we do have the capacity to learn. Whether or not we learn to make the choices required of us to preserve the earth, and in turn our own lives on it, is the question of the poised century.

As adolescents coming of age on a finite planet, we remain blithely oblivious of our vulnerability. Changing our individual lives and our relationships with one another and with the natural order around us will require a crisis that may or may not be reversible. Like my stepdaughter and her date, who rolled and totaled his family's new coupe on prom night and then walked home to tell about it, I pray that our experiences will be more instructive than fatal. For us and our planet, they may or may not be.

It is remarkable that today, just as we have begun to tax the earth's capacity to provide, we have, thanks to chaos and the new science of complexity, an entirely new way of understanding how the world works. The whole notion that the world is self-organizing and far more sensitive to what we are doing at the moment than ever before imagined provides us with a radical new perspective for the conduct of our lives. The coincidence of finding a new metaphor for life as a complex self-organizing system, together with the need to find a new way to live on a finite planet, presents us with choices for transforming our worldview from one of domination to cooperation. Today with a new metaphor for how the earth and our lives upon it work, we can begin to form new paradigms, new patterns, for living.

CHAPTER NINE

The Poised Century

Abundance or Despair?

*The arch enemy of an open society is no longer the Communist threat
but the capitalist one. It is wrong to make survival of the fittest
a leading principle in a civilized society.*
—George Soros

*When we stop demanding more than nature can logically provide,
we liberate ourselves to look within.*
—Stephen Jay Gould

Transcendence is the only real alternative to extinction.
—Václav Havel

Your Money or Your Life

One of comedian Jack Benny's great trademarks was his endless self-deprecating humor. Besides his being perpetually thirty-nine years old and a lousy violin player, he also delighted in being an unremitting cheapskate. In one sketch he was mugged at gunpoint and presented with the ultimatum, "Your money or your life?" After being asked this several times, Benny, with his usual deadpan delay, responded, "I'm thinking, I'm thinking."

Like Benny's mugger, life presents us with options, some of which are likely to be better for our collective well-being than others. While Benny's humor turns on the delay of what would seem to be an obvious answer, today when presented with similar choices for our own future, we, too, seem equally reluctant to act. By living lives unconscious of the natural order and oblivious to the collective results of our individual actions, we, like Benny, invite ruin.

Today our most fundamental challenge is to so live our lives that our collective future is both assured and desirable. Creating such a future will require servant leadership, the appropriate use of technology, and an extensive rethinking by each of us as to who we are and how we live on our planet. As the most rapacious members of the earth's most rapacious species, we Americans will be particularly challenged by any emergent new order. Learning that we must find satisfaction without continually increasing the level of our consumption or the extent of our activity will lead us to lives that not only we, but also our neighbors and the planet, can live with.

From what we know today, I am convinced that the twenty-first century will mark a time between cultural ages of the earth. Still, although things are likely to get worse, perhaps much worse, I remain hopeful that we Americans will, sooner or later, come to our senses about where we stand in the natural order of things. To be hopeful is to be neither pessimistic nor optimistic. Hope springs from being pessimistic enough not to be surprised by the worst, optimistic enough to have an abundant vision of the future, and free enough to know that a desirable and sustainable future can be ours. Hope grounds us, sustains us, and directs us to do not only what is possible, but what is desirable as well.

How Much Is Enough?

Beyond bringing the question of chapter 3, "Can we all do it?" to each of our activities, we must also ask, "Even if we had wealth sufficient to always get more of the material, would such use of wealth actually be desirable?" By placing so much emphasis on the possibilities of the material realm, we have grown dismissive of all the wealth offered to us by the realms of the natural, social, and spiritual. Only by embracing the whole of creation's pleasures will our collective future be assured. Our work today is not to accumulate material wealth, but to transcend it.

Fortunately, beyond America's material wealth, lies a bounty of natural, social, and spiritual well-being.[1] The difficulty of leaving behind our habit of material accumulation lies not in the absence of other choices for leading our lives, but in our difficulty of leaving behind our bent to comparison. When it comes to material goods, bigger is better, particularly if they are bigger and better than what our neighbors or colleagues have today or what we ourselves had the day before. Giving up our need to compare, whether with our neighbors or ourselves, will be essential for our survival, and since giving up something is itself a measure of growing up, our fundamental need today is simply this: we need to finally grow up.

I once had a colleague who was told by his physician to "diet or die." Today, a similar life-saving admonition of "scale down or perish" needs to go out to all Americans. Foremost to our growing up is that we must scale down by answering the question, "How much is enough?" As *Homo sapiens* we need to live up to our name, *sapiens*, Latin for having wisdom or discernment. Discerning how much is enough is actually rather easy, since as a species we are much more alike than different. As humans we require food that provides each day, depending on sex and age, from 1,800 to 3,000 calories and from 45 to 60 grams of protein. This is what "enough" means for our diets.[2] A livable standard of housing provides 150 square feet each of private and public space for each occupant, or 300 square feet per person. With an additional 300 square feet for a kitchen and bath, a family of two would be comfortably housed in 900 square feet, a family of four in 1,500 square feet. These are about the sizes of houses built during the years immediately following World War II. This is what "enough" means for our housing. And from personal experience, I know that for no more than a few hundred dollars a year I can minimally clothe myself with purchases from a mail-order merchant. This is what "enough" means for adequate clothing.[3] Although these numbers are very modest by current American standards, they are, by world standards, far closer to luxury than deprivation.

Even so, thanks to the vast commoditization of many consumer goods, our standards for luxury continue to rise. Today's high-quality computer-aided design and manufacturing has turned the market for material goods into a bidding process for the lowest-cost producer of a uniformly high-quality product. While we Americans have yet to experience a futures market in December minivans or September refrigerators, many basic consumer goods are now of such high quality and so universally available that even people of modest means can drive autos with power everything or cool their sodas with ice from automatic home dispensers. Such ready availability of high-quality consumer goods has led to competition for ever more expensive designs and finishes in our products. For example, when the latest thing in kitchen or bath gear becomes available at Sears or Home Depot, the upper class rapidly abandons it for equipment that is yet more unique. The goal here is not to have more of something, but to have something that others cannot. Such exclusivity is not entirely bad, since the incremental material and energy input required to compete at this level can be nil.

Competition in the material realm becomes more harmful to the human enterprise when it alters the basic scale of material goods desired for living. What compromises the 6,000-square-foot house is not its expensive designer floors, but its large floor area that requires an inordinate amount of lumber to construct and an inordinate amount of energy to heat in the winter and cool in the summer. And, while a luxury sports sedan may have about as much material in it as an auto costing far less, it is compromised not by its material construction, but by its beefy low-fuel-economy engine that enables it to accelerate to sixty miles per hour in less than six seconds. These examples demonstrate what I consider to be an unacceptable use of scale to meet human desire.

For anyone to say that another's material province is beyond the pale is surely an invitation to derision. But beyond inviting dismissal, these comments are meant to invite an examination of what we buy and why we buy it. More important, they are meant to invite an examination of how our desire for the material affects the larger natural and social world in which we live. For example, a local advertisement for a new rural housing development paints a romantic picture of the aroma of fresh-baked bread wafting from homes as neighbors visit on front porches. This idyllic picture is shattered by the description that each country home sits on its own two-and-one-half-acre lot, a scale of land use totally incongruent with the social values offered by the ad's image. With lots over 200 feet wide and nearly 500 feet deep, one wonders just how far aromas can waft or porches invite. Similarly, the cover art for the annual Parade of Homes visitor's guide shows a simple and inviting cottage that belies the mini-mansions shown inside. Still other advertisements show large, low-gas-mileage vehicles carrying happy family members on outdoor adventures, bounding through clouds of dust or snow with little regard for either the natural environment or the time required to earn whatever it takes to keep the fun going. The tension between the material, the social, and the natural is palpable as developers and automakers present what is largely material as if it were social and natural as well.

In the end, the question "How much is enough?" is a highly personal challenge to discover what it means to live an abundant life. An abundant life begins with adequate food, clothing, housing, transportation, and health care, and it continues with self-reliance, rewarding work, meaningful relationships, creative expression, and a place in the community. When we all have these and know it, we will have arrived at abundant living.

Freedom, Choice, and the Common Good

Freedom of choice, whether it brings abundant living or not, is a clear value of American culture. It has become such a measure of who we are that choice denied has become tantamount to freedom denied. For example, in my town we have an extensive system of ramp meter lights to control freeway access during peak traffic periods. Such control has long been a bone of contention for those who see their freedom to use the public domain as an unassailable personal right. Studies of various control strategies indicate that as a practical matter, most drivers, when given the choice of having the ramp meter lights either on or off, would prefer to have them off. As citizens of a democracy, people in my town would rather be delayed by their fellow freeway users than by a freeway entry light, even when their transportation department's light offers them a faster and safer drive.

Freedom on the freeway is just one example of our desire for freedom in the commons, freedom to use those resources held by the community for the common good of all. The irony of freedom in the commons is that unlimited individual freedom compromises the freedom of all. For example, drivers who persistently alter traffic flow as they incessantly change lanes for individual advantage compromise everyone's safety and travel time. As we have learned from the second law of thermodynamics, there is no free lunch, just socialized costs.

The difficulty of cooperative living was examined several decades ago by Garrett Hardin in his classic essay, "The Tragedy of the Commons." Hardin uses the example of a free and open grazing commons to illustrate his point. He points out that in a totally open commons, individual herders are motivated to add more and more animals, since the profit from each additional animal accrues to the herder's own benefit, while the additional cost of each animal is shared by all. With such an enormous incentive for the individual herder, all are motivated to do exactly the same. Given perfect freedom to privatize gains while socializing costs, the commons's inevitable end is overgrazing and reduced productivity. Hardin's conclusion is simple and direct: "Freedom in a commons brings ruin to all" (4).

To avoid the tragedy of the commons in our own lives, we must each value what is good for our communities as much as we value what is good for ourselves. To continue our freeway example, bringing cooperative behavior to the commons of the freeway requires each of us to extend the personal boundaries of our own driving to include those drivers beyond our own fenders. With such driving, safety and traffic flow are enhanced and shorter travel times emerge. Although we may have to give up our personal freedom to drive as we please, any compromise in our freedom is amply rewarded by a faster and safer drive. Freedom in the commons is not the freedom to exploit the commons, but the freedom to use it for the benefit of all.[5] This is the opportunity of the commons, and all that's needed to seize it is to join with others who wish to do the same.[6]

The Coming Revolution

Rethinking the way we Americans live on the planet and our effects on the common good will most likely be initiated by a crisis in material resources, although global climate change, the spread of virulent disease, financial collapse, or similar events could just as easily prompt us to new understandings. Today our crisis lies not as much in the environment, the availability and use of energy, or meeting human needs as it does in the imagination of our leaders and in the will of the people. Our best hope for the present is that we each experience what I have called a "crisis to pray for," a crisis of such a proportion that it affects almost everyone's daily life, and of such a nature that its resolution requires the cooperative action of all. A crisis to pray for is one produced by, and resolvable by, local behavior. For example, a shortfall of transportable fuel, that is, of gasoline and diesel fuel, would be such a crisis. Whether such an energy crisis would cause each of us to reduce our own energy use, or to merely complain about it and expect it to be solved by someone else, will be a measure of our American character and a test of our willingness to move beyond the ever-increasing self-indulgence of our collective adolescence. In short, a test of whether we are ready to grow up or not.

In the coming revolution, America will need to transform itself from a culture of consumption to one of moderation. Within such an emerging culture, natural, spiritual, and social well-being will be sought along with material well-being, and maintaining a moderate material life will be seen not as an act of denial, but of positive abundance.

Living abundantly with less is hardly the American way of doing things, and the above suggestion that we will evolve toward a culture of moderation seems naive at best. After all, in America bigger is always better, more is always more, and less is always less, period. Surviving and, yes, prospering in the twenty-first century will mean that America will need to practice what others have advocated for years—that scale is important and design matters.[7] From the size of our houses to the size of our autos, to the size of our food portions, a fundamental rethinking of the design and scale of America's material life can no longer be avoided.

As participants in the natural world, our survival requires that our lives reflect the natural order itself. Design for the abundant life is thus a design for a fractal life that includes material, social, and spiritual niches for all people. With such design, food, clothing, housing, transportation, and health care become available to all. This is not a description of some social utopia of equality, but of an inclusive and sustainable culture based on equity, on the availability of the fundamentals of life to all. My purpose is not to denigrate wealth, but to encourage abundance, an inclusive social order that brings a sense of well-being to all people, rich or not. If material abundance is to follow the natural order of things, income will follow a fractal distribution too, with a few millionaires and many thousandaires.[8]

The Social Cost of Entropy

To create a more inclusive social order, America must answer one of the most pressing questions of the day: "How will we socialize the cost of entropy in our culture?" Although this is not a common way to address the problems of housing, transportation, work, poverty, crime, and incarceration, these problems and more can be addressed by examining how we socialize the costs of maintaining the most fundamental functions of our society, that is, how we pay, directly or not, for the order provided by the low-income worker.

To examine the social cost of entropy, we first must remember that entropy is a measure of order and that, like the child's bedroom, the greater the order, the lower the entropy. This leads us to life's most resistant lesson, that reducing entropy—creating order—requires work. Preparing a cheeseburger, making up a room, cleaning an office, selling merchandise, entering data, and packaging poultry all require work. Depending on the circumstances, these tasks may be pleasant or even engaging, but most often they are not. Low-paying, repetitive, and not highly valued, these tasks are held in cultural disdain, even though they are America's most ubiquitous, fundamental, and important work.[9]

Whether we pay directly or not, we all pay in some way for the cost of the entropy work required to maintain our most basic social order, and the way in which we socialize the cost of this work is a measure of the equity and civility of our economy. Today, while the benefits provided by the low-income worker accrue to the middle and upper class, it is the worker who pays for them through his or her poverty-level living. By doing America's most fundamental work for a nonliving wage, low-income workers build social and material wealth that is not shared with them in proportion to the order their work brings. Through the economic devaluing of these most fundamental contributions, we set ourselves up for problems far costlier.

Regardless of how the work of the low-income person is valued, in some way we all pay for the economic and social well-being it brings. Whether we pay the low-income worker a living wage now or pay the greater costs of poverty, welfare, and incarceration later, we cannot avoid the expense of keeping our communities running. Although it may seem that my life is made better by the subsidy of the nonliving wage, any savings I might realize in the price of my cheeseburger, hotel room, or sport shirt is more than lost through my country's ongoing, inefficient, and therefore costlier, subsidies of poverty, welfare, and incarceration. While the costs of our most fundamental and essential work may be deferred or redirected, they cannot be avoided. What is required of us in America is that we provide the opportunity for everyone to do their best, and this starts with a living wage.

Moving beyond our current low-income, poverty-wage, system will require transferring the cost of low-income work from the taxpayers— that is, all of us—to the user of the goods or services produced. This would be accomplished most ideally through wages enhanced by improved productivity. This is the way the middle class has made its money. With enhancements from robots in auto factories to personal computers in offices, the productivity of the American worker has led to an ever-rising standard of living. But it is hard to increase the productivity of the worker who prepares our cheeseburger, cleans our office, or sews our shirt. Such labor-intensive work is resistant to productivity improvements other than driving workers harder or paying them less.

We come down to two ways to pay for the entropy work that gets done in America: the customer pays, or we all pay. Under the present system, we all pay through our indirect subsidies that support lives of poverty, welfare, and incarceration—the primary niches we have created for the low-income worker in America. A better way for everyone to pay is through the direct subsidy of the negative income tax.[10] For bosses who are too cheap to pay a living wage or can't compete if they do, we can all pitch in and transfer some of our positive income tax to the low-income worker through the subsidy of the negative income tax. Better yet is for each of us to support the institutionalization of a living wage by simply paying more for what we already buy. By increasing the purchase price of labor-intensive goods and services, the customer both benefits from and fully pays for the labor provided. Would it ruin any of us to pay a few dollars more each year for our fast food, vacation hotel, or sport clothes? Finally, there is a third way: we could just tell low-income people that their reward is in heaven, and that even though they're poor now, by and by everything will work out for the best. If such blessed assurance could feed, clothe, and house the working poor, then this would be the way to go. But it can't and it isn't.

The goal of the new economy is not to make all equally rich, but to allow all a place at life's table—a place that provides for us the security, belonging, and self-actualization that we each need. And if the niches of life's table are to follow the natural order, they, like nature, will be arranged in a fractal order. That is, not all will be equally wealthy. To accommodate all people within our economy, we need to give up the idea of ever growing wealth for all for the more accessible notion of simple abundance for everyone. Such an arrangement allows for not only the wealthy, but also the middle and lower classes, to prosper. Each person, independent of wealth, would have adequate food, clothing, and housing, and ready access to transportation and health care. Creating economic niches for all people will require a fundamental rethinking of how we pay those who provide our most basic goods and services. This will move America's response to poverty beyond the usual solutions of welfare for those who work within the system and incarceration for those who do not. America needs a nonpoverty niche for all people in the economic scheme of things, an unapologetic position that moves beyond the notion that the poor would have a better life if only they would apply themselves. Low-income abundance need not be an oxymoron.

Toward a Sustainable Economy

To ensure our survival, the work of the poised century will require us to vastly accelerate our present but halting shift from mindless consumption to sustainable living. Although it would be best if our unceasing desire for material wealth could be reformed through the natural limits on our time to consume and the voluntary action of everyone choosing a scaled-down and simpler lifestyle, this is so unlikely to happen by itself that we cannot rely upon it to encourage the substantive lifestyle changes required today. While earlier I suggested that such changes would likely require a crisis to motivate us toward new ways of living, there remains yet a third path for our collective future. Between trusting the collective goodwill of individuals and waiting for a motivating crisis lies the use of reordered incentives to encourage new behavior.

One of the most effective ways to incentivize new behavior is to tax what is deemed undesirable while providing tax relief for what is to be encouraged. For example, our present tax system effectively directs us toward being the most overhoused and underinvested developed country in the world. By promoting large houses and long commutes through mortgage interest deductibility, low-cost gasoline, and ever-expanding freeways, and by discouraging investment savings through taxes on capital gains, dividends, and interest, we have got just what we have incentivized—a country capitalized to consume. Much could be accomplished through a reordering of our tax system to tax consumption and encourage moderation in our lives. For example, an increased gasoline tax, along with the elimination of mortgage interest deductibility on all but modest housing, would be a good start. These plus compensating reductions in income tax and the establishment of income-qualified tax-free investment accounts could initiate a redirection in the way money is spent and invested in America. Rather than buying as much house as one could afford, one would be encouraged to buy as much house as one needed and to invest the difference (11).

In the same way that the wages of low-income workers who increase order may be called entropy wages, taxes on activities that bring disorder can be called entropy taxes. By using the economic forces of tax policy to encourage moderate living, America could begin making strides toward a sustainable economy.

Toward a Conscious Economy

America's Declaration of Independence and Adam Smith's *The Wealth of Nations* both materialized in 1776. Since then we have experienced an economic run of more than 225 years guided by our own unparalleled freedom and Adam Smith's unfettered invisible hand. During this period the amount of wealth generated by the American free enterprise system has been enormous, and the belief that the only viable economy is a constantly growing economy has remained unabated.[12] Today, America's principal economic task is not to maintain a continually growing material economy, but to create an abundant economy we can all live with.

Moving from an economy of perpetual growth to one of abundance and moderation will require conscious living that embraces not only what is good for us, but also what is good for our neighbors, whether next door or around the world. Rather than engaging in things that are ever larger, faster, or more prestigious, we must now learn to take pleasure in things of a smaller scale. For example, in my state of ten thousand lakes, sailboat marinas are a common sight. Yet on even the finest summer weekends and holidays, most of the boats remain dockside—unsailed, unused, and seemingly unappreciated. On such days, our twelve-foot dinghy attracts the attention of those who would "rather be sailing" but don't seem to have the time. That so many own boats so much grander than ours and yet not sail them on such splendid days confirms for me that in today's America we have far more money than time.[13] Moving from consumption to abundance will require the development of a new economic consciousness of how we use our time, money, and personal energy.

We need a new economics, what might be called conscious or Buddha economics. With the simple inquiry, "How many Buddhists does it take to change a lightbulb?" we can begin to examine just how the new economics might work. In this case, the answer is two, one to change the lightbulb and one not to change the lightbulb.[14] By embracing such opposites we are led to what Buddha taught as the "middle way," a way between wealth and poverty in which resources are used to maintain an "optimum functioning but no more."[15] Buddha economics tells us that we should pay as much attention to achieving a goal as to not achieving it.

With a name meaning literally the "Awakened One," Buddha taught that the origin of life's suffering is desire, and that desire can be transcended through a series of eight right actions known as the Eightfold Path, a practice of reflective choice and intentional living.[16] As a "wakeful" enterprise, Buddha economics is an economics of consciousness that is grounded in paying attention to the way we live. In practice, Buddha economics becomes "wakeful economics" when it tells us that we ought to spend as much money on insulating our house as heating it, direct as much care toward spending, giving, and saving our money as earning it, devote as much time to nurturing our children as working to support them (17).

For example, wakeful economics can direct one's retirement savings. In today's information-saturated economy, the stock market has become so efficient that performing better than the average of the market over any extended period of time, say five to ten years, has become exceedingly difficult for most people, including even those who make a business of it. Applying Buddha economics to the problem of market investment leads to the idea that as much effort should be given to making money as not making money. Remarkably, this seeming indifference to profit still leaves the investor an option for doing better than the average, not by increasing growth, but by reducing expenses. The problem of how to invest is now turned around simply by asking the question, "How does one invest in the market at least cost?" This question naturally leads the investor to low-cost, passively managed index funds. By accepting average, or literally the "middle way," as good enough, one can use low costs to achieve superior performance over the long haul. Given efficient markets, time is a great equalizer. Over any long period of time, say that required for retirement planning, people who pay attention to expenses, taxes, and inflation will do just as well, if not better, than those who constantly chase market moves. Interestingly enough, "wakeful economics" ironically leads to what is known as couch-potato investing. It tells us that while those who believe they can do better work up a lather over whether Procter & Gamble is a good buy or not, we of the couch-potato school can relax and enjoy the fruits of their labor—the efficient markets that make passive investing so attractive.[18]

Buddha economics can also improve your health with the question "How many physicians does it take to set a problem right?" Of course, the answer is again two: one to do something about it and one to do nothing about it. For example, while recovering from hip surgery, I managed to pinch a nerve in my arm, leaving the fingers of my left hand weak and numb. When I explained this to the surgeon on one of my follow-up visits, she became animated over the prospect of further surgery that would move the offending nerve from the outside to the inside of my left elbow. Practicing Buddha economics, I chose not to proceed with her recommendation, but instead went to a massage therapist. At Vi's Massage, with a treatment infinitely more pleasant than surgery, the problem was solved. Not only was the treatment far more pleasant, but it also posed a far lower risk of complication and cost far less to boot. Yet I was not financially rewarded for my prudent money-saving action. While insurance would have paid for all of my surgery, I paid for the massage therapy out of my own pocket. Thus, the system is set up to favor the complex and the costly. Ideally the surgeon should have recommended massage as an alternative worth trying, but such recommendations are bad for business, and surgeons have to eat, too.

Applied to material things, Buddha economics asks questions such as "How many cars does it take to get across town?" Again two: one to drive and one not to drive, which leads to either ride sharing or bicycle riding. Even though bicycle riding may seem slow, when the total time required to own and operate an auto is included, the distances traveled per hour of effort for the bicycle and auto are comparable. Compared to a car, riding a bicycle pays a living wage. What would Buddha do? Buddha would ride a bicycle.

Applying this idea to housing, we may ask, "How many rooms does a person need?" Two: one to share and one not to share. And with this we are led to moderate housing.

Although the above ideas may appear chimeric, they illustrate that our lives may be lived as much on the side of reduced demand as on that of increased consumption. Building an economy based principally on consumption builds an economy with no natural limits. In such an economy more is always better, and unsustainable growth without limit is the natural result. Buddha economics invites us to build an economy based not on ever increasing our consumption, but on a middle way that challenges our need for always more of the material. It asks us to reconsider our desire for more, whether it is living in ever larger houses, driving ever larger autos, or of comparing in ever more ways, such as having more heart bypasses than the guy next door. By bringing the demand side into the picture, we can begin to evaluate our lives based not only on our personal consumption, but also on what they cost the larger world. For example, employers who consider a minimum workweek to be sixty hours or more and expect their parking lots to be half full on evenings and weekends are extracting a cost of work unlikely to be of aggregate benefit to the communities in which their workers live. By comparison, even though it might reduce each worker's weekly productivity, a forty-hour week leaves workers more time for enhancing the overall well-being of their families and communities in ways that simply cannot be provided by the corporation, the marketplace, or the state (19).

Finally, Buddha economics allows us to reconsider the two-income family. Would family economics be served just as well if one parent earned income while the other reduced demands on income by caring for a child or preparing a meal?[20] Has the movement to empower both men and women advanced enough that we can begin to value work beyond building and maintaining personal careers?

We need to recognize today that there is wealth to be had in moderation. Between America's unprecedented prosperity and the grinding poverty of much of the rest of the world lies a third, middle way of having wealth—simple abundance. Simple abundance starts with a living wage for all workers and requires each of us to rethink how much is enough. Beyond today's never-ending economic hubris lies a new economy that is both equitable and abundant.

Participation, Relationships, and the New Economy

Today we need what Ivan Illich called convivial tools: tools that maximize freedom by freeing us from grinding labor while simultaneously keeping us out of the grasp of the rent seekers who wish to own all the tools and then charge us for their use. Convivial tools are social in the sense that they engage the worker with the enterprise and with those served by it. The relationship created by this engagement can be as much spiritual as material, and it includes the consumer as an active participant in the process. With this the consumer is not just a passive recipient of education, medical services, legal advice, food, a place to live, or a car to drive, but instead becomes a person who positively assumes responsibility for his or her own learning, wellness, contracts, nutrition, housing, and transportation.[21]

Tools mean not only hand tools such as wrenches and screwdrivers, but also household appliances, cooking utensils, musical instruments, democratic processes, social institutions, and more. Tools may be anything we use in our daily work, the entropy work that brings order to the world, and may include goods, services, or personal interactions that make our daily entropy work efficient, even pleasant, without taking from us either our personal power or our social responsibility. Because they may contribute as much to our collective as to our individual lives, convivial tools may be as much civic as personal. For example, universal public education is one of America's most powerful convivial tools. Yet without a classroom of students who come from families and communities where learning is valued, little learning may be accomplished. Attendance at any school open house readily shows what separates families who value education from those who do not—families who value education show up and pay attention, just like their sons and daughters do every school day. Beyond convivial families, enhancing the education of America's children requires more—it requires enhancing the conviviality of their communities. It's hard for both children and parents to pay attention or even show up when they are living in poverty, being harassed, or even shot at. If we do not improve the conditions of our most vulnerable communities, there is little hope for improving the conditions of their schools.

One of the most effective convivial tools we have in America is the sidewalk.[22] Yet with the predominance of the automobile, sidewalks have taken a backseat in our transportation system. For example, try, just try, walking to a shopping mall in the United States. Designed without regard for pedestrian traffic, malls require us to be seasoned athletes just to make it into the place. The sheer inhospitality of America's malls keeps me well anchored to my local merchants, even if the prices are higher and the selection smaller. But beyond this, the greatest compromise of the public walkway has been its privatization within the confines of the mall itself. By separating material glitz from the social throes of society, the mall isolates us from life itself and becomes little more than a sterile incubator of the consumer culture. Although some may hail the shopping mall as America's new main street, it has none of its conviviality. What would our urban landscape look like today if it were primarily designed to accommodate the pedestrian rather than the automobile?

Other convivial tools are policies and procedures that promote community welfare. For example, zoning ordinances that promote mixed use create communities on a smaller scale than those that create separate sites for working, shopping, and living, as if manufacturing, retailing, and housing were at such impossible odds they demanded separation. In my neighborhood I can easily walk—and on sidewalks, too—from my home to an upscale urban grocery store, an auto-assembly plant just over the fence from the grocery store, or an art deco movie theater, all the while passing by a wonderful neighborhood library and recreation center. This is the way cities should be built. And finally, my favorite example, the

United States tax code, of course, could be made convivial by making it simple enough so that the average person could figure their own taxes without needing a passel of professionals to tell them what it's all about.

From neighborhood to nation, the possibility of making our lives in America more convivial is boundless. Capitalizing on such endless opportunity is the work of a new generation of convivial workers: the nonprofit entrepreneur. Called to unwrap the excesses of our consumption, the duplicity of our churches, and the unconsciousness of our lives, their work is that of the new liturgy, the work of returning the work to the people. Extending Walter Brueggemann's idea from chapter 6, the work of our leaders and institutions is not to dogmatically construct an alternative world, but to provide the "pieces, materials, and resources" out of which a new world can be imagined and constructed by those who live in it.[23] The leader's work and moral obligation is to return the work of reconstructing the world to the people, and it is the people's moral obligation to imagine and construct a future in which all may live abundant lives. Such work requires servant leadership and conscious living of the highest order. It is not for the fainthearted.

A Last Lesson from Physics

Today we must begin to act on the reality that life lived outside the realm of natural law is not only improvident, but impossible. While the bad news is that the second law of thermodynamics tells us that there is no free lunch, the good news is that it also tells us how best to eat the lunch we have. While the first law tells us what is necessary, the conservation of energy, the second law tells us what is possible, how to best or most efficiently use the energy we've got.

Energy efficiency is usually determined by dividing the amount of useful heat or work obtained by the amount of energy required to provide it. This is called first-law efficiency. For example, an efficient furnace or boiler might be advertised to be 90 percent efficient, meaning that of all the heat available, 90 percent enters the house and 10 percent goes out the flue. Measures of input and output are frequently used to determine economic activity, and the more labor, material, or energy that flows through the economy, the greater its activity. While this measure may seem a good one for the person receiving professional services, material goods, or energy, it ignores the larger system we live in. By equating economic activity with improved personal circumstance while ignoring the economy's affect on others, we may be easily led to believe that overall things are really getting better. Even though our lives might appear to be individually improving, they are, when combined with the lives of other people and the resources of the world, actually deteriorating. As participants in a living system, we need to learn that each enhancement to our personal well-being requires the larger system to suffer.

The second law of thermodynamics describes this observation when it tells us that any order that comes to our lives must come through a simultaneous decrease in the order of the world.[24] The big lesson here is that planning a sustainable future for the next generation requires a balanced life that can come only from valuing the whole as much as we value ourselves.

We can begin to value the whole by reducing the amount of disorder we each bring to the world. While the second law of thermodynamics tells us that as living beings we must run the system down, it also tells us how to get the most out of the disorder we create in the process. Most people don't consider such effects in their lives, but the simple act of burning fuel for heat, such as heating a house with a natural gas furnace, provides a good example of what actually happens when we burn fuel for any purpose. In this case, even though the sticker on our furnace might claim that it is 90 percent efficient at turning natural gas into space heat, it is, from the point of view of the second law, far from being as efficient as it could be.

The problem arises because our house needs to be kept at room temperature, around 68 degrees Fahrenheit, by a gas flame that has a temperature several thousand degrees greater. Lost in the flames of combustion is the fuel's availability to do something more useful, such as powering an engine that could be used to produce either mechanical or electrical power. While electrical power could be used to directly heat a house, a better alternative is to use the engine's mechanical power to drive a heat pump, a device that works like an air conditioner in reverse. By using the engine to power a heat pump, low-temperature heat may be extracted from outside the house, raised in temperature, and then used inside for household heating. Burning fuels to produce mechanical power or electricity makes better use of the potential availability of the fuel than simply burning the fuel to produce low-temperature heat.[25]

Although burning fuel for any reason will always produce disorder, burning fuel for its high-temperature heat to produce ordered energy, such as mechanical or electrical energy, provides as much energy with as little disorder as nature allows. An economy based on the ideas of the second law would, through private investment, public policy, or a combination of the two, encourage those processes and services that create the most order (or cause the least disorder) for the amount of material, fuel, or labor used. Because current measures of economic activity such as gross domestic product fail to account for disorder created, new measures of economic activity are needed.

The Poised Century:
Learning to Live Today As If Tomorrow Mattered

When I was a youngster in grade school, one of our favorite playground activities was to load up the seesaw with as many kids as possible to see which side could keep its end on the ground, with the hope that a winner would be declared before the seesaw failed. The metaphor of the seesaw brings us to the question of the day: how much can we load the earth's multiple seesaws before some of them begin to break or tip in unexpected ways, dropping large portions of humanity heedlessly on the ground? Today our multiple seesaws of population, water, food, disease, energy, and climate are becoming increasingly stressed as competing forces strive for ever more advantageous balances. Bringing abundance and sustainability to the twenty-first century—the poised century—will require each of us to consciously consider how the weight of our lives affects the balances of the world.

Finding an abundant and sustainable way to live on the only planet we've got will require an effort unprecedented in both the greatness of its scale and the brevity of its time. Balancing the burgeoning stresses of the poised century will require the work of all and demand of us a personal transformation that values the future and communal as much as it does the immediate and personal. Living today as if tomorrow mattered is the work of the poised century.

As citizens of an ever more interdependent world and as participants in our own local communities, we each have the power to choose simple abundance over gratuitous wealth, mindful cooperation over unending competition, and conscious relationships over uncritical belief. The poised century will turn on how we make these choices. Within the lifetime of today's children, it will be clear how well we have done.

PART 4

WORK AND TASK

CHAPTER TEN

Sing a New Song

Ten Remedies for the Poised Century

The day will come when, after harnessing the ether, the winds, the tides, gravitation, we shall harness for God the energies of love. And, on that day, for the second time in the history of the world, man will have discovered fire.
—Pierre Teilhard de Chardin

We don't receive wisdom; we must discover it for ourselves after a journey that no one can take for us or spare us, for it is a point of view about things.
—Marcel Proust

We're neither pure nor wise nor good;
We'll do the best we know.
We'll build our house, and chop our wood,
And make our garden grow.
—*Candide* (Leonard Bernstein)

The Need for Remedies Now

There are no simple solutions to today's most pressing problems. Far beyond the solutions of the expert, today's problems require remedies that demand the work of all. Low educational achievement, homelessness, poverty, crime, addiction, bad diets, obesity, poor health, personal and national debt, rising costs of education and health care, global climate change, peaking oil production, and a dearth of national leadership all call for remedies that can only be carried out by the combined work of each citizen. This is the work of the new liturgy, the work of the people.

None of the ten remedies suggested here can by itself ameliorate the problems facing the United States and the world at the beginning of the twenty-first century. Yet put all together and carried out by motivated people of goodwill, they might well have the power to move mountains. Choose a remedy from those listed here or create your own. Either way, get busy with bringing sane and sustainable living to your life, to your community, and, most important, to your country.

1. Sing a New Song: Craft a singable national anthem.
2. Junk the Tax Code: Simplify America's revenue system.
3. Craft a New Measure of National Well-Being: Dump the GDP.
4. Live Better with Less: Scale down or die.
5. Expand America's Living-Wage Economy: Create an economy for all of us.
6. Tax Waste, Not Work: Make waste expensive, work attractive.
7. Get Off Coal, Oil, and Uranium Now: Reframe the nuclear option.
8. Keep Congress Working: Get the money out of elections now.
9. Develop a Civil Economy: Value the universal.
10. Live Today As If Tomorrow Mattered: Consider the children.

Sing a New Song

It's high time we all learned how to sing our national anthem. The problem, of course, is only half ours. The other half is a tune that stretches the range of most singers, including all the ballpark divas who dishonor it with tricks designed more to disguise than demonstrate its noteworthy difficulty.

The National Association for Music Education has taken upon itself the daunting task of remedying this situation through its National Anthem Project, a program to promote the singing of "The Star-Spangled Banner" (www.thenationalanthemproject.org). As commendable as this is, are we all really ready to sing out for a full octave and a half? With most church hymns ranging over no more than an octave plus a few notes, this effort seems difficult at best. With half the crowd croaking over each note above an octave, it is no wonder that the "rockets' red glare" and the "land of the free" have become as much a test of personal fortitude as the defense of Fort McHenry itself. While the defense of our flag from assault by some unhappy Brits may be worthy of honor, must we repeat the challenge with each sing? Perhaps such a song builds character, but without full participation, our efforts weaken. Set to a British drinking tune written more to showcase the talent of its composer than to be sung by the common citizen, "The Star-Spangled Banner" as an article of national participation has outlived its usefulness as our national anthem.

What better way to publicly announce America's reclamation of its national work and heritage than for all to join in singing a new and singable national anthem? Group singing can be inspirational, even moving. And what better way to start a ball game or any public event? Somewhere in America there is an organization or individual with the talent and resources to make this happen. What better project than to organize America's choral leaders, music teachers, church choir directors, composers, and lyricists into a national effort to produce and teach us a new national song? And what better celebration than for all to sing along as the president throws out the first ball at the first game at which America's new song is first sung?

A new national anthem, beyond scaling down the opportunity for the less talented to embarrass themselves, would have all of America singing not only better, but all together. Who knows? We might start cooperating on even more things, such as sane driving or going to school meetings. Singing civilizes the soul, and today, without doubt, we need a new national civility more than ever. Surely a singable national anthem would be a worthy start.

Junk the Tax Code

Craft a new and simpler tax code. For a good look at just how bizarre and complex the U.S. tax code is, take a gander at IRS Form 6251, the Alternative Minimum Tax—Individuals. Here lies enough work to keep dozens of K Street lawyers in the chips for decades. With special interest piled on special interest, it becomes impossible to tell where good governance ends and personal favor begins. It is time, simply time, as IRS commissioners have been saying for decades, to replace America's tax code.

Today's tax code is far more useful as a political pawn for Congress to curry favor than it is as a means for collecting revenue to run the country. It is a grossly inefficient and embarrassing sham of personal interest and little more. Enough! With improved transparency and the possibility for hundreds of billions of dollars in annual savings from simplified compliance, a new and well-crafted tax code would vastly increase the effectiveness of America's revenue collection system. To this end, a high-exemption flat tax would be a good start (see chapter 3, endnote 18). Few, if any, arguments can be brought against the broad social, economic, and political benefits of this remedy.

Craft a New Measure of National Well-Being

Between the end of World War II and the turn of the century, America's gross domestic product (GDP) per capita (adjusted for inflation) tripled. Yet during the same period, even as real personal incomes increased, the number of Americans who reported being "very happy" remained at a steady 30 percent. Today, America's GDP is a far better measure of wealth produced than satisfaction achieved. By confusing activity with progress, by valuing the incarceration of a youth as much as the education of a child, and by excluding the degradation of the environment altogether, today's ever-increasing GDP could just as well be taking us toward social and environmental ruin as economic abundance.

Beyond today's GDP, we need new economic and social measures that reflect not only America's national income, but also the efficacy of its use. For example, consider the much-debated idea of universal health care. How much would the well-being of America's workers and their families be enhanced if we eliminated all the kitchen table conversations about who is going to have the job with health-care benefits? And how much would universal health care enhance labor mobility, self-employed entrepreneurship, personal happiness, and productivity? For example, one estimate based on multiple studies indicates that potential loss of health-care benefits reduces U.S. job mobility by as much as 50 percent.

Without new measures of economic success that go beyond the social and environmental indifference of the GDP, the value of universals such as health care will remain unknown. Today we need a new measure, one of gross domestic well-being, GDWB, a measure of how our economy affects actual lives. Beyond national income, life qualities represented by the GDWB could include not only access to affordable health care, housing, transportation, and early childhood education, but also measures of outcome such as income equity, educational performance, longevity, and infant mortality. By using a measure of GDWB that values the resources and outcomes affecting the lives of real people, the United States could begin to extend opportunities of well-being to all its citizens.

Somewhere in the United States there is an academic department or economic outfit that could craft such a measure and market it to opinion-makers such as the *Wall Street Journal* or the *New York Times*. In time a growing GDWB could be used to demonstrate America's progress toward equitable opportunities and desirable living for all.[1]

Live Better with Less

America's greatest happiness occurred during the post–World War II prosperity of the 1950s and was due as much to our record rate of growth in abundance as it was to the abundance itself. Since World War II we have lived with the belief, quantified as early as 1738 by Daniel Bernoulli, that what makes us happy is not the just accumulation of ever more stuff, but the accumulation of more stuff ever more rapidly. With material happiness requiring constant material growth, meeting our needs for happiness through the accumulation of ever more stuff is not only improvident, but impossible. But more important, after decades of experience, we now know that, absent poverty, having more stuff makes us no happier. While our ongoing belief in Bernoulli may drive us to ever greater consumption, such consumption brings only fleeting happiness at best. Living better with less requires us to find satisfaction not in material accumulation, but in the arrangement of our lives around pleasures of a lesser scale.

To live better with less, we need most to live within the earth's capacity to provide energy. Living in well-designed, well-insulated, not-so-big houses, driving high-fuel-mileage autos fewer miles per year, and living less material-intensive lives in general will all become desirable, if not imperative, in the twenty-first century. We now know that spending as much money on saving energy as using it—that is, spending as much money on efficiency as energy—leads not only to an optimum use of resources, but to better living as well (see chapters 4 and 9). Reducing energy demand through massive investments in efficiency is half the solution to the coming energy crisis.

Beyond living within the earth's capacity to provide energy lies the challenge of living within its capacity to provide food. For example, today's large-scale production of meat consumes more grain and water than can be justified by the amount of protein produced.[2] Even more, thanks to its prophylactic use of antibiotics, such production compromises our public health as well. As Americans who get most of our protein from meat, we each have the option to enhance not only nature's capacity to provide

food, but also our own health and well-being by getting more of our protein from beans, grains, vegetables, and nuts (chapter 9, endnote 2).

Living better with less also means valuing the order brought by those
who do not work outside the home. By valuing work in the home as much
as that in the marketplace, the work of the family and community as well
as that of commerce may be accomplished. Providing help for teachers, assisting a neighbor with an errand, volunteering in the community,
managing household finances, planning and preparing meals, and most
important, rearing children, all have value beyond the credit presently
assigned to them. Simple abundance and community order begin with
valuing the ordinary, no matter who does the work or in what setting.

Finally, the new science of chaos has shown us that to remain happy
with finite goods in a finite world, we need to arrange our experiences so
that they, like nature, follow a scaleless or fractal order. We need to learn
to consume as nature provides and to consciously arrange our lives so that
they contain far more small experiences than large (see chapter 7). With
such remedies, living better with less will become an act not of denial, but
of positive abundance.

Expand America's Living-Wage Economy

Bringing equity, or simple abundance, to an economy driven by vast
inequalities in the capacity to create wealth will force us to rethink how
we value our most fundamental work: the day-to-day labors of America's
service workers. Today we are learning that the capacity to create wealth
increases not from the addition of skills, but from their multiplication.
That is, for better or worse, life geometrically favors the high-resource,
high-skill professional. Yet, even though the professional may create
wealth founded on complex order, it is the old and familiar simple order
maintained by the service worker that makes such wealth creation possible—an office cleaned, a fast-food meal prepared, a shirt sold. Work
that, left undone, would compromise the work of all. Such work has value
not because of its complexity, but because of its ubiquity and the order it
brings to daily living. By paying people in proportion to the order their
work brings to our daily life, we can begin to justly compensate those
whose work supports the creation of all our wealth. Needed today is a
living-wage economy for all of America's workers, professional or not.

Henry Ford invented the living-wage economy when, in 1913, he
revolutionized auto production by doubling his workers' daily wage. Not

only did his company's productivity soar, but Ford's workers began to earn enough money to buy what they were making—the automobiles that became the backbone of America's growing middle-class economy. Ford's genius was in knowing that every worker was somebody's customer, and with this all of America prospered (see chapter 3). It is time now for a second wage revolution in America—one that creates a living-wage economy for all of America's workers.

Done well, the daily round of the service worker cleaning offices, preparing fast food, or selling merchandise can readily bring as much order to our lives as the complex activity of the far better paid but less productive professional. For example, consider all of the unproductive activity surrounding America's complex tax code. By valuing the service worker who brings simple order as much as the professional who promotes more complex, if not always more productive, activity, a new balance between low- and high-income earners can be established. It is time for everyone to be justly compensated for the basic order their work brings to our collective life.

Tax Waste, Not Work

Since most of us would rather pay lower than higher taxes, taxes will always incentivize tax-avoiding behavior, no matter how they are applied. Given this, one remedy for improving both the lot of the planet and our life on it is to tax those activities we want to discourage while giving more desirable activities a pass or even a credit. If order-enhancing work or activity, a desirable thing, should be rewarded with wages or credits, then order-diminishing activity, a less desirable thing, ought to be penalized with taxes (for example, energy-efficiency credits and carbon taxes). Wages, taxes, and credits tied to the order or the entropy of our lives (see chapter 2) would direct our individual behavior from unsustainable consumption to an economy growing in abundance and simple living. From reduced trash to increased household and auto efficiencies, taxes and credits that reflect the true social and environmental effects of our lives would enhance both our social and our natural order.

The idea to tax waste and not work, to tax bads and not goods, as economists say, is easier to talk about than to implement. Still, bringing wages, taxation, and credits into alignment with the natural order should be seen as the challenge of the age by scientists, economists, and policymakers alike. Aligning the primary measure of our natural and social order, entropy, with the conduct of our lives on the earth is a sure and necessary remedy for finding our way through the poised century.

Get Off Coal, Oil, and Uranium Now:
Reframe the Nuclear Option

The twenty-first century's rudest awakening will be the realization that fossil fuels are a finite resource that will be recovered in ever lesser amounts with ever greater effort. Along with this will come the growing understanding that, although economic investment may be applied to recover energy resources, it has never *produced*, nor will it ever, a single Btu of energy. Impossible to create, energy can only be obtained from nature's own generous providence. What we must understand is that the only energy-producing materials we will ever have are those nuclear materials given to us in the first few moments of the creation of the universe. Now condensed into the heavy radioactive elements of the earth's crust and the protons of the sun's fusion reactor, these nuclear materials power all life on the planet. The fossil fuels that make our lives possible today are just yesterday's fusion-powered sunshine, finite and depletable.

For example, consider the production of oil. We now know that the recovery of oil follows a bell-shaped curve, and that of all the oil represented by the area under this curve, about one-half has been recovered to date. With half left, why worry? It is here that our fond hopes get dashed on the rocks of exponential growth. It is here we need to realize that with each doubling of consumption we consume as much oil as all that produced in the past. With half of the world's oil left, we are but one doubling period—decades, not centuries—from the exhaustion of nature's most generous subsidy. What the sun's fusion reactor has provided for us over eons, we will consume in a lifetime. Our day of reckoning is at hand (see chapter 8).

Beyond oil, coal has long been thought to be America's most abundant fuel. So abundant, in fact, that it could fuel our electric power generation for another century or more. Yet, in another rude awakening, the U.S. Geological Survey has recently disabused us of this hope with a study of America's largest remaining coal reserves.[3] Found here was the arresting estimate that of these largest reserves, just 6 percent could be profitably recovered. Still more, a 2010 study predicts that world coal production will peak in 2011.[4] Although estimates of ultimate production are fraught with uncertainty, such radically reduced estimates of ultimate production show us that the future of coal, like oil, will be measured not in centuries, but in decades.

However, just in time and to our good fortune, America's natural gas production, which a few years ago appeared to be in permanent decline, has recently been reprieved through the application of horizontal drilling and hydraulic fracturing (fracing or fracking) to recover natural gas from deep shale gas formations.[5] As a bridging fuel between the age of fossil fuels and the energy age to come, natural gas has the potential to fuel America's transition from coal-fired electrical generation to a new era of nuclear, wind, and solar power. Wise use of these newly found, but still finite, natural gas reserves is crucial to America's energy future.

Still, as we proceed we need to be conscious that in the end we are left with only the primal sources of life given to us in the creation of the universe. The choices we make today of how and in what proportion we use these primal sources—the radioactive elements of the earth, nuclear energy, and the fusing protons of the sun, solar energy—will without doubt determine our future life on the planet. Deciding how we will capitalize our ability to recover, store, distribute, and, just as important, use these most generous gifts of nature is the challenge of the poised century.[6]

Our present uranium-based nuclear energy technology has suffered from decades of study with little to show in terms of acceptable solutions to the problems of safety, spent fuel storage, nuclear proliferation, and cost. Lacking the development of socially acceptable and cost-effective passive safety designs and a closing of the nuclear fuel cycle, today's nuclear promise remains uncertain at best.

Yet with new thinking there is an often cited, but just as frequently neglected, way forward—thorium as a nuclear fuel.[7] Recognized early as a potential source of nuclear power, but then forgotten in the imperatives of World War II and the Cold War that followed, thorium as a proven reactor fuel has remained out of favor.

During World War II, uranium won the day with its demonstrated weapons potential and, in particular, its capacity to produce plutonium. At the end of the war, with an abundance of uranium know-how and the ongoing need for plutonium to build the nuclear arsenal of the Cold War, uranium and its progeny, plutonium, became the fuels of choice for both the U.S. Navy and the civilian power generation that followed.[8]

But yet, if we were starting over, confronting not a cold war, but a war on terrorism, a growing trade imbalance, and a pending end of cheap coal and oil, we might have taken a different path. As an answer to uranium's problems of safety, spent fuel storage, nuclear proliferation, and cost, an energy future based on the element thorium is not only attractive, but compelling. Although not directly usable as a fissionable reactor fuel, thorium as a so-called fertile element has the capacity to be transmuted into a form of uranium that is fissionable. By absorbing a neutron and then emitting two electrons, fertile thorium transmutes itself into the fissionable nuclear fuel, U-233.[9] The fact that thorium does this is an absolute gift of nature that calls for far more than a simple nod of good intentions.[10]

The use of thorium and its progeny, U-233, particularly as a molten salt reactor fuel, offers so many advantages beyond today's uranium reactors and resolves so many of the problems that plague our present weapons-derived nuclear energy program, that failure to consider thorium as a source for America's base electrical power would be to miss a monumental opportunity for enhancing both our economic well-being and our national security. For example, consider safety. In the 1960s the Oak Ridge National Laboratory (ORNL) demonstrated that, as a molten salt fuel, U-233 is self-regulating. ORNL discovered that as the liquid fuel's temperature increased, its nuclear reaction rate declined, an intrinsic self-regulating safety feature of great value.[11] Furthermore, in case of a system failure, the molten salt can neither melt down nor blow up. As an unpressurized liquid, any breach of its containment vessel would result in a controlled leak to a holding area where it would cool to a nonreacting solid. Unlike the superheated vessels of conventional pressurized hotwater reactors, it cannot produce a violent steam explosion driven by the depressurization of superheated water.

Just as important, thanks to the molten state of its fuel, fission products that normally contaminate solid-fuel uranium reactors may be continuously removed. Given this, a thorium-based reactor "burns" to heat 100 percent of its fuel rather than the 15 percent or less burned by even the most efficient uranium reactors. Such complete burning results in waste that is less than 3 percent of that produced by a uranium reactor. But even better, these much reduced waste products decay far more rapidly. By decaying to one ten-thousandth of the radiation level of uranium reactor waste, and doing so within three hundred years rather than the hundreds of thousands of years required of uranium, thorium reactor waste may be returned to the earth it came from within a few hundred years rather than the near million required for uranium.

Beyond this, the fact that a thorium reactor's fuel, U-233, is continuously created and consumed in a closed cycle greatly reduces its possible proliferation. Most important, while a full year's operation of a large (1000 megawatt) uranium reactor produces 600 pounds of plutonium, a thorium reactor of the same power produces less than a pound, again greatly reducing thorium's proliferation potential.[12]

Finally, costs are much reduced because it is intrinsically easier to build an ambient-pressure reactor vessel than a high-pressure one. Even more, because there is no chance of a phase-change–driven explosion of superheated water into steam, massive concrete containment domes are not required to contain breaches in the reactor vessel. Beyond these construction cost savings lie reduced fuel costs, since much less fuel must be prepared and handled. A 1000-megawatt uranium reactor requires the processing of 250 tons of natural uranium to fabricate 35 tons of reactor fuel that then become 35 tons of waste. In contrast, a 1000-megawatt thorium reactor would annually burn 1 ton of thorium and produce but 1 ton of waste.[13] Given a production efficiency per ton of fuel 250 times greater than that of uranium and a 4 times greater natural mineral abundance, thorium as a nuclear energy source outpaces uranium by a thousand to one. Still more, beyond these savings, fuel costs are dramatically reduced because thorium fuel requires no processing beyond refining thorium ore. Such thrift allows a year's supply of thorium for a 1000-megawatt plant to be delivered by a Ford F250 pickup in a single load.[14] Given all these cost advantages, it is predicted that thorium power will cost less than coal.

With so much capacity for a thorium future, what becomes of wind and solar power? Although the sun's nuclear energy is by its very nature intermittent and diffuse, its life-giving intensity, absolute abundance, and zero cost makes it an extraordinarily attractive energy source. In fact, the sun's energy is so abundant that in a single hour our earth receives enough solar radiation to power the entire planet for a year. With such solar abundance, combined with present technology, America's total power demand of a trillion continuous watts could be met by covering just 3 percent of our land with solar panels and wind turbines.

Although solar energy is frequently dismissed for its intermittent nature, we have today advanced ways of using solar energy that make its extensive use not only possible but, like thorium, compelling. For example, recent advances use solar energy to extract valuable chemical feedstocks such as hydrogen and carbon monoxide from everyday water and carbon dioxide.[15] Given these new sources of hydrogen and carbon monoxide, decades-old processes can be used to synthesize a wide range of liquid fuels including diesel fuel and gasoline. With nearly all of America's transportation sector dependent on oil, and with well over half of our oil imported, solar-derived transportation fuels would not only reduce our trade deficit, but robustly enhance our energy security as well. Finally, although wind turbines can run through the night, they too experience periods of calm. It is here that the judicious use of readily dispatchable natural-gas generation can be used to complement wind for the production of base load electricity as America moves from coal, oil, and uranium to thorium, solar, and wind.

A more certain and cost-effective "source" of energy is efficiency. We now know how to build houses that use less energy to heat and cool by a factor of two to three or more. Such enhanced efficiency, plus the adoption of well-designed smaller houses, can be used to reduce America's household energy use by a total factor of at least four to six. Smaller autos, designed for efficiency and safety rather than power and performance, combined with driving fewer miles per year, can just as easily reduce our major petroleum demand, personal transportation, by similar amounts. For example, advanced rechargeable hybrid autos and light trucks that are for the most part electrically powered can reduce the amount of fuel required for regular daily transportation by a factor of five or more.

All of this is made economical by the fact that the optimum way to invest in any energy-using device is to spend, over its lifetime, as much on saving energy as providing it.[16] The savings available through the massive application of efficiency offers America one of its greatest opportunities not only for getting us off oil now but for promoting what should be, along with the development of alternative energy resources, our fastest-growing business sector—sustainable, secure energy. To this end, America's greatest requirement will be for "patient capital," capital investment in great enough amounts for long enough times to build a new energy infrastructure—an infrastructure whose return on investment may depend as much on the uncertain prices of the commodities displaced as on the alternative technologies brought to bear.

Today our greatest dearth is not of energy, but of imagination and will to plan for an age beyond the age of fossil fuels. For our individual well-being, our national economy, and, most important, our national security, there is no remedy more urgently needed than the initiation of a long-range national energy plan, starting now. Central to this plan will be efforts leading to the production of electrical power and transportation fuels grounded in the development of thorium, solar, and wind technologies. Accomplishing this will require an extensive government and business effort carried out with all the fervor that American science and engineering brought to the Manhattan Project. Today, more than ever, we need a second industrial revolution that will build America's twenty-first-century energy infrastructure (17).

Keep Congress Working

Many of the remedies given here can be readily initiated by an informed and willing public. Others will involve policy changes provided by an equally well informed and willing Congress. This means, in short, that Congress has to rise above its current political rancor and get down to the actual business of governing. For many in Washington, such work will be a new experience. For those who can't or won't provide the leadership required for the poised century, we their constituents have the moral obligation to elect those who will.

Democracy is a messy process rising out of the natural conflict between America's entrepreneurial and rent-seeking classes. Entrepreneurs bring order to the world by enhancing our lives and communities through the creation of material and social wealth that improves the economic and social condition of all. In contrast, the rent-seeking class moves around the resources of others while leaving their condition unchanged or making any problem worse. Entrepreneurs and rent seekers may appear in any walk of life. What distinguishes them most is that whereas entrepreneurs work to enhance the human condition, rent seekers work, knowingly or not, to largely cash in on it (18). Because it is the work of Congress to enhance the human condition, it is their obligation to work as entrepreneurs to provide opportunities whether through money, programs, or equitable governance so that the people of the country may do the work of the people. In short, it is the work of Congress to fund the new liturgy, the work of the people. And even more important it is the obligation of the people to do this work.

Since much of the work of Congress is to allocate the nation's wealth, its work is redistributive regardless of political intent. Washington is a pot of money, and Congress hands it out, if not as cash, then as opportunity.[19] Because distributing money, or the opportunity to acquire it, is central to their work, members of Congress need to be distanced from those who desire to cash in on its largess. For the preservation of democracy, money needs to be distanced from politics—and this means elections must be distanced from money. The single best way to keep Congress working for the common good of the people is to finally get serious about the public funding of election campaigns.

Today the average annual cost of campaigns for the presidency and Congress is pretty much peanuts, or chewing gum, compared to the amount of money that currently flows through or because of their hands. For example, with a federal budget now over $3 trillion, the average annual cost for all Senate, House, and presidential campaigns would be a mere one-half of one-tenth of 1 percent of America's annual spending. Although this "mere" amount is $1.5 billion, it is, as the authors of *Freakonomics* point out, about what Americans spend each year on chewing gum.[20] In terms of money spent or opportunity given, $1.5 billion is just 10 percent of the $15 billion Congress doled out in 2010 as special-interest earmarks (pork) or 1 percent of the estimated $150 billion or more spent annually on complying with Congress's equally accommodating and ever-more-complex tax regulations.

Public funding of campaigns would have the salutary effect of keeping Congress working as advocates for the people who elected them, rather than as envoys delivering favors and chasing dollars in anticipation of another election. With a typical Senate race costing $10 million to $20 million, a senator must raise $5,000 to $10,000 a day, every day, for six years just to get reelected. With so much effort required to stay in the race, there is little incentive to provide the sort of leadership that might cause one to lose it. Raising money diminishes courage to tell the truth, and today as much as ever we need truth-tellers of the highest order. For those who want to bring servant leadership to the Congress, the present road is rough indeed. More than ever, publicly funded campaigns are a worthy start for bringing new leadership to Washington.

Finally, since we are trying to get the foxes out of the henhouse for which they make the rules, it will fall to an energized public to make publicly funded campaigns the law of the land. Step up, folks; it is finally time for the Congress of the United States to become a Congress for all the people. Conscious evolution, the cry of this book, calls for a conscious Congress elected by a conscious public.

Develop a Civil Economy:
Valuing the Universal

A civil economy begins with bringing equity to inequality—with bringing fairness to an economy that inherently favors the entrepreneur and the creation of wealth. Guided by Adam Smith's invisible hand, America's entrepreneurs have generated much of the material well-being we all enjoy. Yet, while the invisible hand has adroitly created enormous wealth in America, it has failed miserably at its equitable distribution.

Today we have, broadly, a three-class economy in America: the working poor, the getting-by to middle, and the professional to very wealthy, comprising, respectively, the bottom 40 percent, the middle 40 percent, and the top 20 percent of the population. With the lower class limited by lack of upward job mobility, and both the lower and middle classes limited by growing costs for housing, health care, and education, the upper class continues to accumulate an outsized portion of America's growing wealth (see chapter 3). With the top 20 percent now receiving 50 percent of the national income, it is no wonder that the wealth of the upper class continues to grow. But even with the top 20 percent receiving half of the national income, the top 5 percent receives close to one half of this, or nearly one-quarter of the national income. With those in the top 5 percent receiving, on average, more than twice the income of those in the next 15 percent, the haves and the have-mores of America clearly demonstrate the skewness of our national income. More disconcerting than America's rising economic tide lifting its yachts more than its boats is the threat such inequality poses for maintaining a civil, engaged, and democratic society.

What to do? Both top-down solutions of the government and bottom-up remedies of the people are required. Top-down redistribution is required to extend to all Americans access to such universal needs as housing, health care, education, and transportation. Many people, particularly conservatives and the very wealthy, recoil at such a suggestion. Yet in *Growing Public*, an extensive study of developed countries, Peter H. Lindert argues that the net national costs of such social transfers are "essentially zero." Rich countries do not tax and spend less, reports Lindert, and there appears to be no clear negative relationship between social spending and GDP per capita.[21] Other universals, such as affordable housing, adult education for skill improvement, and health care, all seem to add not only to the national well-being, but to the economy as well. In short, investing in people pays.

But if top-down universals can help everyone, bottom-up remedies are required to further support the working poor who need living-wage jobs and upward mobility if we are to have a truly equitable society. But, because poverty may grow as much from improvident behavior as lack of progressive circumstance, more is needed. Bringing transformation to the ill-fated habits of all classes is the work of the third or nonprofit sector. If the work of the for-profit sector is to enhance the material wealth of the country through a new and improved product or service, it is the work of the nonprofit sector to enhance the country's social wealth through a transformed person or a redeemed social condition (see chapter 5). In the end, we all need an affirmation of the spirit that will allow for the poor to grow out of their poverty, both systemic and personal, and for the rich to transcend their ever-growing need for gratuitous wealth.

The reality is that progressive policies are just as necessary for a robust national wealth as conservative economics. Lindert's *Growing Public* supports the broad argument that affordable housing, universal health care, worker education, and public transportation all add to the productive capacity of the country by bringing a more equitable and secure life to all of the country's workers, low-income or high. In an ever more competitive world, it is just as necessary to provide "universals" for enhancing the productivity of workers as it is to provide "particulars" for improving the circumstances of commerce (for example, trade agreements and subsidies). When it comes to governance, it's the efficacy of taxing and spending that matters. Housing, health care, and transportation trump welfare, incarceration, and incomprehensible taxes in improving the lives of people and the abundance of nations.

Again, much of the work of bringing civility to our economy and our lives will be led by the nonprofit organizations and servant leaders of the twenty-first century, as described in chapters 4, 5, and 7. While previous generations have suffered largely from the effects of poverty, twenty-first-century America will confront entirely new forms of social and physical distress, growing not out of poverty, but out of bounty ill-spent. Today, with record incomes, we lack savings for retirement. With abundant food, we lack good nutrition. And with ever more of everything, we are no happier than when we had far less. The problems of the poised century will stem as much from affluence as poverty.

Live Today As If Tomorrow Mattered

A common scene today: a hundred-twenty-pound woman steps aboard her three-ton sport utility vehicle as the carry-out clerk places twenty pounds of groceries in the back. If we do not soon learn just how fleeting a scene this is and begin to act on it with new imagination, our lives will surely suffer. While the SUV driver makes an easy mark, she is just one example of America's larger cultural response to more than a century of ever growing world oil production. But world oil production is peaking, and years from now, when its peak is clear, it will be equally clear that the weight of our vehicles, like the production of oil, has followed a bell-shaped curve of its own. Riding prosperity, clueless of consequence, we are today consuming oil as if nature were generous beyond measure. Yet however sweet, our ride will be brief. What nature has provisioned for us over eons, we will today consume in decades. Learning to consume within what nature provides will be the learning experience of our lives. On whether and how well we do this turns the poised century.

The peaking of world oil production is just one of several crises that could get our attention within the first decades of the twenty-first century. Others, such as unpayable American debt, global pandemic, irreparable climate change, food and water shortages, or war brought on by any of these could occur just as well. What distinguishes these crises is that while an energy crisis may be reversed by the concerted action of many, the others could just as well end in catastrophe. Given this, the coming oil crisis becomes a crisis to pray for—a reversible crisis of such proportion and effect that it will compel each of us to change our ways from consumption to sustainability.

I believe that our personal fate hangs in the balance today, and that by the turn of the next century we will know, without a doubt, how well we have done. Have we grown into a sustainable life of diverse communities, or have the wealthy garnered within gated enclaves the remaining resources of a once-abundant earth, while far removed from the gates of the wealthy poor masses huddle in hunger around civilization's last fires? Although this may sound like apocalyptic hyperbole, today the top 10 percent of the U.S. population has a net worth of over four times that of the remaining 90 percent.[22]

Finding our way through the twenty-first century—living today as if tomorrow mattered—will require behaviors that value the future and communal as much as the immediate and personal. Much of this work will be informed by the ideas of self-organization, which tell us that the repeated application of simple and proper behaviors—habits—leads to desirable living. Habits such as finishing school, committing to relationships thoughtfully, exercising regularly, eating lower on the food chain, reducing the scale of our houses and autos, accumulating savings rather than debt, working to improve the world whether it's making up a hotel room or finding a cure for cancer; habits that, in short, create lives that honor life. The abundant life flows far more from mindful living than boundless consumption.

Living within our personal means and the capacity of the earth to provide requires us to appreciate the ordinary if we are to find satisfaction in the special. Such living gets quantified when we arrange our life experiences in a natural or fractal way. Such natural living directs us to arrange our lives so that among our many ordinary experiences we indulge in a special few. By scaling our lives after nature's own example, we maintain not only the health of the earth, but our happiness on it (see chapter 7).

All of this work will be informed by a new and conscious evolution. Central to the new consciousness is a rethinking of time that will cause us to value the future as much as the present. Today, by overvaluing the present and undervaluing the future, we maintain houses and garages filled with material indulgences, all the while mortgaging our future to acquire yet more stuff. With the expectation of ever-increasing wealth, and ignorant of nature's demands, we diminish our equity by taking on yet greater, and what may well be unpayable, debt. Such living cannot end well. Conscious evolution tells us we can no longer discount the future and expect to have one.

Rethinking the future will include rethinking how we wait. As we watch our lives on the earth, do we actively respond to the natural and social feedback we receive from the earth and its people, or do we naively proceed as always? How long do we observe global warming, world population growth, rising demands for daily food and water—diminishing oil and increasing environmental distress—before we act? Will we go on believing that the discoveries of science, the economics of the market, or the programs of government will solve our problems, or will we begin to live as if all life on the planet were as important as our own? Although we cannot know what our lives will be like at the end of the century, if we value the future, it is essential that we begin to act today as if the answer mattered.

Living today as if tomorrow mattered will require of us habits of the spirit grounded in the intentional practice of gratitude and sabbath. Only by bringing to our lives the habits of gratitude, an appreciation for the daily, and sabbath, an intentional time for rest and reflection, will we be led to lives of happiness and meaning. Without practicing sabbath, we have no time for gratitude, and without gratitude our lives remain captive to getting-and-spending that strips our souls, weakens our communities, and destroys our planet.

Today we know that, absent poverty, more of the material makes us no happier. Our challenge today is not to garner more of the material, but rather to use our capacity for producing wealth to enhance the social and natural wealth of our communities and our country. There is little hope of us Americans getting off our hedonic treadmills without a return to lives of community—lives that grow from an appreciation of the ordinary and the regular practice of gratitude. Start today—give thanks and be glad.

GRATEFUL THANKS

Many have contributed to the experiences and the ideas that have formed this book, and to them I offer my grateful thanks. To Don Anderson and Mike Scott, my thanks for opportunities in passive solar research and the application of simplest-things-first design. To Ross Stickley for mentoring in how to write a winning proposal and to manage the research that followed. To Jackie Lind, Gary Nelson, Martha Hewett, and Michael Noble, whose skill and hard work helped me to learn much about how the world of energy efficiency really works. To Jim Reierson, who got me a position teaching in Fiji, an opportunity that continues to inform my life. To those who pointed me toward ideas that have informed this book— Lee Bajuniemi, Sharon Brown Christopher, Robert Nevitt, and Phyllis Wilcox—and their recommendations for the works of E. F. Schumacher, Walter Brueggemann, Viktor Frankl, and Terence Fretheim. To Toby LaBonte and Harry Boyte for bringing to my consciousness the powers of framing and agency. To those who mentored me in my writing, Dan Odegard and Stephen Wilbers, without whom this book would have never seen print. To Elizabeth Jarrett Andrew for mentoring in the business of writing and books. To my patient readers of various parts of the text, Mary Robinson (no relation), Roger West, Betty Schilling,

Nancy Victorin-Vangerud, Richard Ireland, Chad Koppes, Tom Townsend, Jean Pfeifer, and Chuck Pfeifer. To Jim Cederberg and Julia Thornton Snider, who read with an eye to the physics and economics of the text. The responsibility for any variation between reality and the text is, of course, mine. And for weekly conversation over the years, I give thanks to Steve Ozanne, Bob Sellers, Al Edgar, Waldron Lowe, and Jim Schlaeppi. To Beth Wright and Zan Ceeley of Trio Bookworks, many thanks for your expert design and project management skills. And finally, my greatest gratitude to my ever patient wife, who has lived with and contributed much to a project that seemed to have no end. Until now. My grateful thanks to all.

NOTES

1. The Addiction to More

1. It was never clear what Mr. Sommers' complete invention might have looked like. Years later his nephew reported that he frequently talked about coupling a steam engine to an air compressor in some fashion that would run perpetually. My colleague Jim Cederberg, who met with Mr. Sommers over a period of two years, conjured as a youth a similar perpetual motion machine consisting of an electric motor coupled to a generator that would, in turn, power the motor. Given a starting spin, such a device would just keep picking up speed until it spun itself into oblivion.

   When I was ten or so, I tried to make my own perpetual motion machine, a pair of bedsprings coupled in a two-cylinder arrangement that would swap energy from spring to spring for ever and ever. I soon discovered that my curtain-rod crankshaft operating in wood-block bearings resulted in a machine that would keep going for no more than half a turn at a time. My contraption would have worked far better as a door closer than a perpetual motion machine.

2. *The Graphic Work of M. C. Escher*, new, revised, and expanded ed. (Hawthorn Books, New York, 1960), plate 76. Many images of Escher's *Waterfall* may be found on the web by searching with the keywords "Escher" and "waterfall."

3. Elisabeth Kübler-Ross, *On Death and Dying* (Macmillan, New York, 1970).

Although today some are dismissive of Kübler-Ross and her work, many others nevertheless continue to find her steps to be informative in the face of loss.

4. One system in nature that appears not to dissipate its energy is a superconductor in which an electrical current can flow in a closed loop without resistance—friction—for an indefinite time. Although it seems to be as close to perpetual motion as nature allows, superconductivity, because of its quantum nature, is not generally regarded as perpetual motion.

5. Because energy measurements are difficult, particularly when measuring heat, it is easy for the enthusiastic inventor to make errors that favor the desired result—free energy.

6. Changing our frame of thinking from the immediate and personal to the future and communal is made difficult by the fact that it is intrinsically easier to frame the immediate and personal. For example, consider the conservative frame "tax relief." Such a frame is readily conceived as both immediate and personal, since a quick change in tax law can readily provide me with personal relief from my implied "tax burden." While it is possible to reframe this with more progressive terms, such as "tax fairness," such a frame is far less compelling than the words "tax relief." Central to the progressive agenda in America is the challenge of reframing the future and communal into frames that appeal to the immediate and personal interests we all have. See George Lakoff, *Don't Think of an Elephant! Know Your Values and Frame the Debate: The Essential Guide for Progressives* (Chelsea Green Publishing, White River Junction, VT, 2004). It is hard to overestimate the understanding that Lakoff's work has brought to the recent conservative successes in the United States. Through the use of simple yet powerful framing language, the conservative movement in America has captured not only the attention but also the votes of many.

7. Carl Jung said it this way: "Neurosis is always a substitute for legitimate suffering." Quoted in M. Scott Peck, *The Road Less Traveled: A New Psychology of Love, Traditional Values, and Spiritual Growth* (Touchstone, New York, 1978), p. 17.

8. Or, as scientist, mathematician, and religious philosopher Blaise Pascal wrote in the seventeenth century, "All the troubles of man come from his not knowing how to sit still." Quoted in George Seldes, comp., *The Great Quotations* (Citadel Press, Secaucus, NJ, 1983), p. 549.

9. Viktor E. Frankl, *Man's Search for Meaning: An Introduction to Logotherapy* (Touchstone, New York, 1984), p. 82.

10. Earnie Larsen, *Stage II Relationships: Love beyond Addiction* (Harper and Row, San Francisco, 1987), p. 12. See also Earnie Larsen, *Stage II Recovery: Life beyond Addiction* (Winston, Minneapolis, 1985).

11. Anne Wilson Schaef, *Beyond Therapy, Beyond Science: A New Model for Healing the Whole Person* (HarperSanFrancisco, New York, 1992), p. 128.

12. Peter D. Kramer, *Listening to Prozac* (Penguin, New York, 1993), p. xvi.

13. Juliet B. Schor, *The Overworked American: The Unexpected Decline of Leisure* (Basic Books, New York, 1992), p. 115. Schor reports that the percentage of the population who reported being "very happy" peaked in 1957. For a thoroughly engaging description of America's postwar happiness, see Bill Bryson, *The Life and Times of the Thunderbolt Kid* (Broadway Books, New York, 2006), pp. 5–6.

14. "Money Isn't Everything," *Science*, March 24, 1995, p. 1765. This article presents data showing that although average U.S. real income more than doubled between 1957 and 1992, the percentage of "very happy" people remained nearly constant at 30 percent. For most Americans, more money does not buy more happiness. According to this report, "the real ingredients for a contented soul have to do with inner resources and personal relationships."

15. *Wall Street Journal*, February 16, 1989, p. C22.

16. Successful indeed. Over fifteen years later, Nabisco's Teddy Grahams are still occasionally displayed on an aisle endcap at my local grocery store. They're actually pretty good—it's easy to see why they would appeal to parents and kids alike.

17. For a ready example of the proliferation of unnecessary choices in America, one need look no farther than beverage and breakfast cereal aisles of the local grocery store.

2. The Ultimate Limit to More

1. Depending on climate and costs, the least-cost amount of insulation works out to be about two to three times that of current building practice. David A. Robinson, "Life-Cycle Cost Economic Optimization of Insulation, Infiltration, and Solar Aperture in Energy-Efficient Houses," in *Thermal Insulation, Materials, and Systems for Energy Conservation in the '80s, ASTM STP 789*, F. A. Govan, D. M. Greason, and J. D. McAllister, eds., American Society for Testing and Materials, 1983, pp. 176–88. Most needed to save energy today is not new or complex technology, but personal will.

2. One of the first presentations of these findings caused a small riot. The chair of the meeting had to gavel the group to order so I could finish. The second speaker for the evening talked about heating a log cabin with an incredibly complex system of tracking solar receivers along with gobs of pipes, pumps, valves, and controls. The crowd loved it. Solar had become another energy source to waste.

   Beyond "How do you heat a house for the least cost?" a second and equally important question is, "How do you heat a house using the least energy?" In this case, the total energy provided is not only that required to heat the house, but also that required to fabricate its insulation. Interestingly, this question leads to the same sort of answer as when the least cost way to heat a house is considered. That is, for any given time period, as much energy should pass through the house's insulation as was used to fabricate it. Just like dollars used for heating, as much energy should be used to heat the house as to not heat the house. Both calculations assume some time period for the investment of either money or energy. The calculations here use factors of about twenty-five and fifty years for the cost and energy calculations respectively. For a fifty-year period, easily within the lifetime of most insulations, the optimum thickness for even a fairly energy-intensive insulation such as fiberglass is about three to four feet. Although the installation of several feet of insulation may be prohibited by the cost of the wall cavity needed to hold it, the amount of insulation required in this case does show that the lesser thickness of insulation required for the least-cost case is quite reasonable.

3. David Bohm, *On Dialogue*, Lee Nichol, ed. (Routledge, New York, 1996), pp. 16–17.

4. For compelling worldwide photos of just such an effort, see Peter Menzel, *Material World: A Global Family Portrait* (Sierra Club Books, San Francisco, 1994).

5. I should talk. I have got lots of stuff of my own, particularly tools. I keep it at bay by regularly asking myself whether or not a particular thing continues to be either beautiful or useful. If it brings pleasure to look at or use, the thing remains; if not, it is given away. Careful selection helps, too. We keep clothes finite by not buying new until we know what needs to be replaced. Buy one item; recycle or give away another. For good ideas concerning your own personal clutter, see Don Aslett, *Clutter's Last Stand: It's Time to De-Junk Your Life!* (Marsh Creek Press, Pocatello, ID, 2005). Offering more than simple recommendations for spring cleaning, Aslett engagingly addresses why we collect so much stuff in the first place and what we can do about it.

6. Not everyone in America has this choice, since many need multiple jobs and constant work just to get by.

7. For example, a simple lentil and sausage stew when compared to a frozen pizza costs less per calorie of serving yet provides more protein and fiber along with less fat.

8. Repair-or-replace timelines for common household products can be found in "Repair or Replace It?" *Consumer Reports*, August 2011, p. 29. Reported here is a "consider repair" period for a push power mower that extends into just its third or fourth season of use. Beyond this period, replacement is recommended. This can be contrasted with my own power mower, now twenty years old, which con-

tinues to start on the first pull and perform as new, all thanks to routine maintenance and a simple, periodic carburetor repair. Based on an estimated engine life
of 1,000 hours and a seasonal use of 25 hours per year, my mower should serve
me well for at least forty years, ten times the *Consumer Reports* estimate. Their
estimated lifetimes for other household products seem equally brief. Planned
obsolescence is alive and well in America.

9. United States Census Bureau, historical income tables for households, available
at http://www.census.gov/hhes/www/income/income.html. Click on Historical
Data, then Households, to find tables H-2 and H-3 for all races.

10. Juliet B. Schor, *The Overworked American: The Unexpected Decline of Leisure*
(Basic Books, New York, 1992), p. 125.

11. "I cannot conceive a successful economy without growth." Economist and former
presidential adviser Walter Heller, quoted in Garrett Hardin, *Living within Limits: Ecology, Economics, and Population Taboos* (Oxford University Press, New
York, 1993). For this quote and others on economic growth, see page 190.

12. For example, if we expect a real annual growth rate of 3 percent, in one hundred
years our real wealth will grow by a factor of nearly twenty. Can any of us use, or,
more importantly, can our planet tolerate, more than ten times of anything we
have now? With "flat growth" economic thinking, retirement planning for fifty
years of work and twenty-five years of retirement would require an annual savings rate of one-third. Like any living organism, a flat-growth economy would
not be a dead economy but rather an economy that has finally grown up—an
economy alive yet free of the cancer of constant growth.

13. Even if the average low and high income levels grow at the same rate, the rich
still get richer faster because they can more readily save. Once this occurs, low-
and high-income families become separated not only by income, but also by net
worth. With this, high-income families have not only earned income but also
investment income, and their money, now leveraged by the market, can grow yet
more. Those who have, get. The more money you've got, the easier it is to make
even more, and so inequality grows.

14. Robert D. Putnam, *Bowling Alone: The Collapse and Revival of American Community* (Simon & Schuster, New York, 2000), sect. 4. A notable exception is that
church attendance is "essentially uncorrelated" with Putnam's Social Capital
Index, n. 9, p. 487. See figure 92, page 360, for a scatterplot of income equality
versus Putman's social capital index.

15. For example, see Ichiro Kawachi, Bruce P. Kennedy, Kimberly Lochner, and
Deborah Prothrow-Stith, "Social Capital, Income Inequality, and Mortality,"
American Journal of Public Health, Vol. 87, September 1997, pp. 1491–98.
Kawachi et al. conclude that income inequality leads to increased mortal-

ity due to a reduction in social capital. See also Martin Daly, Margo Wilson, and Shawn Vasdev, "Income Inequality and Homicide Rates in Canada and the United States," *Canadian Journal of Criminology*, April 2001, pp. 219–36. Daly et al. combine U.S. and Canadian data to show that America's five times higher homicide rate can be largely explained by its greater income inequality. It is also interesting to note that the United States experienced a decade-long postwar decrease in income inequality that reached its low point in 1957, the same year in which Americans reported their greatest happiness. See page 199, note 13. See also U.S. Census Bureau, "The Changing Shape of the Nation's Income Distribution, 1947–98," available at http://www.census.gov/hhes /www/income/income.html. Click on Income Inequality to find this and other resources.

16. You can find your own personal discount rate by answering the following question. How much more than $1,000 would you need to receive one year from now to make getting that sum as attractive as getting $1,000 today? Say that your answer is $1,500. If $1,500 is required to make the transactions equally acceptable, then your personal discount rate, or expected interest rate, is 50 percent. As impatient people, it is easy to compromise our future in expectation of such outsized rates of return. As a nation, we seem to be on a path of gross public and private underinvestment as we remain captivated by Wall Street and its ever more seductive and reckless get-rich-quick financial products and the bubbles required to finance them.

17. *Wall Street Journal*, March 21, 1994, p. B1.

18. Studies on multitasking show that such attention to information is ineffective at best. Stanford professor of communication Clifford Nass reports that multitaskers are "actually extremely bad at multitasking." Moreover, says Nass, those who claim to be the best at multitasking are among the worst. Nass cites the importance of being able to filter information but notes that multitaskers are "suckers for irrelevancy." Such a mind-set leaves us ill prepared for our present century. Quoted in "Why Multitaskers Stink at Multitasking," *Wall Street Journal*, August 26, 2009, and "Media Multitaskers Pay Mental Price," *Stanford Report*, August 24, 2009.

19. It happens. Presentation photo of piano breaking through house floor into crawl space from *Bugs, Mold, and Rot,* a workshop on residential moisture problems sponsored by the Building Thermal Envelope Coordinating Council and Oak Ridge National Laboratory, May 20–21, 1991.

20. James O. Berger and Donald A. Berry, "Statistical Analysis and the Illusion of Objectivity," *American Scientist*, Vol. 76, March–April 1988, pp. 159–65.

21. Or, as H. G. Wells wrote, "Statistical thinking will one day be as necessary for

efficient citizenship as the ability to read and write." Cited in *Wall Street Journal*, April 24, 2003, p. A1. Although the complexity of the global warming problem may make its calculation uncertain, what is not uncertain is that we need to learn how to formulate policy based on incomplete information. Decisions about when to stop analyzing and begin acting will necessarily be subjective, and in this sense they will be Bayesian. For example, see "Scientific Uncertainty: When Doubt Is a Sure Thing," *Nature*, August 1, 2002, pp. 476–78.

22. Robert Ornstein, *The Evolution of Consciousness: Of Darwin, Freud, and Cranial Fire: The Origins of the Way We Think* (Prentice Hall, New York, 1991), chap. 25.

23. Since, no matter what, some would most certainly survive, the total extinction of our species is highly unlikely. However, without a great awakening in the world today, particularly in the West, it is not impossible that we will experience a 50 to 90 percent reduction in the world's human population, along with a vast decline in our own Western standard of living. If one were to place a date on the beginning of our extinction, I would choose February 12, 2010. On this date *Science* magazine published a special issue on food security. With no mention of population limits and dismissal of lower input diets for the well-fed, the issue proceeded to address the problem of world food security through a singular inquiry of how to feed nine billion people by the year 2050.

24. The Sentencing Project, available at http://www.sentencingproject.org. Click on Incarceration, then click the Publications tab. For U.S. prison statistics, see Bureau of Justice Statistics website, http://www.ojp.usdoj.gov/bjs/prisons.htm.

25. Bruce P. Kennedy, Ichiro Kawachi, Deborah Prothrow-Stith, Kimberly Lochner, and Vanita Gupta, "Social Capital, Income Inequality, and Firearm Violent Crime," *Social Science and Medicine*, Vol. 47, July 1, 1998, pp. 7–17. Kennedy et al. summarize their findings this way: "The profound effects of income inequality and social capital, when controlling for other factors such as poverty and firearm availability, on firearm violent crime indicate that policies that address these broader, macro-social forces warrant serious consideration."

26. Peter L. Benson, *The Troubled Journey: A Portrait of 6th–12th Grade Youth* (Search Institute, Minneapolis, 1993). Benson examined both youth assets and at-risk behavior and concluded, "The more assets a given teenager reports being present in his or her life, the fewer at-risk behaviors that teenager displays." Available at www.search-institute.org.

27. Sue Shellenbarger, "Dad Takes Home a Tough Day at Work," *Wall Street Journal*, June 29, 1994, p. B1.

3. The New Work

1. At very cold temperatures, quantum effects become evident. Atoms cannot sit perfectly still, since we would then know exactly where they are, a violation of the Heisenberg uncertainty principle that tells us we cannot simultaneously know both the position and the momentum of a particle.

2. When I see the "Freedom Now" signs of those who desire less government in their lives, I think it would be good to know what, if any, are the communal obligations that come with the freedom they advocate. Beyond this call for freedom, one of America's most popular political accommodations these days seems to be the recommendation to keep shopping.

3. Robert Ornstein, *The Evolution of Consciousness: Of Darwin, Freud, and Cranial Fire: The Origins of the Way We Think* (Prentice Hall, New York, 1991), p. 267.

4. Abraham H. Maslow, *Toward a Psychology of Being*, 2nd ed. (Van Nostrand Reinhold, New York, 1968).

5. In these agrarian communities, the similar daily routine and lower mobility got acknowledged not with the question "And what do you do?" but with the greeting "And where are you from?" Today much of our sense of belonging has moved from the local to the corporate.

6. For example, see David Halberstam, *The Reckoning* (Morrow, New York, 1986), pp. 71–73. Using Taylor's ideas for industrial production, Henry Ford reduced the time to assemble a Model T from thirteen hours to ninety-three minutes. Just as important for America's growing industrialization were the equally dramatic increases in agricultural productivity that freed up farm workers for industrial labor in the cities. Farm population as a percent of total U.S. population decreased from 41 percent in 1900 to less than 2 percent in 2000. See Carolyn Dimitri, Anne Effland, and Neilson Conklin, "The 20th Century Transformation of U.S. Agriculture and Farm Policy," *USDA Economic Information Bulletin*, No. 3, June 2005, available at http://www.ers.usda.gov/publications/EIB3/EIB3.pdf.

7. Although describing these vocations as insidious specializations may be an overstatement, they are unfortunately becoming more so with each year. The problem arises when we give to those who practice these vocations work that belongs only to us, and in doing so we greatly compromise their capacity for doing their own good work. The next chapter explores this phenomenon in detail: we will see that those who have sought to be agents of change for ameliorating the human condition have become, thanks to our outrageous expectations, practitioners cashing in on it. And so today we have smiley-face "What could go wrong?" financial advisers, teachers expected to perform more like parents than like educators, and elected officials who offer us freedom without obligation.

8. John Kenneth Galbraith, *The Affluent Society*, 4th ed. (Mentor, New York, 1985), chap. 2.

9. Adam Smith, *Wealth of Nations* (Prometheus Books, Amherst, NY, 1991), chapter 2, book 4, p. 351.

10. For a glimpse into the life of the low-income worker, see Tony Horwitz, "9 to Nowhere," *Wall Street Journal*, December 1, 1994, p. A1. Horwitz examines the lives of workers in a number of low-income jobs, including those who clean poultry, sort trash, and process envelopes. It's not pretty. In 2008 the lowest fifth of U.S. households (about twenty-three million) received a mean annual income of a little over $11,650. In total, the lowest fifth of U.S. households received 3.4 percent of the nation's aggregate household income. For income data see page 201, note 9.

11. Or as Barbara Ehrenreich has written, "The 'working poor,' as they are approvingly termed, are in fact the major philanthropists of our society." Barbara Ehrenreich, *Nickel and Dimed: On (Not) Getting By in America* (Henry Holt, New York, 2001), p. 221. Ehrenreich makes a compelling journey into the life of the working poor and discovers for herself and her readers the unworkability of low-wage life.

12. This is a broad assertion, and I give a broad response based on the historical distribution of household income in the United States. Since 1967 the lowest fifth of households has received between 3.4 and 4.5 percent of the aggregate household income. Doubling the income of the lowest fifth households would require shifting about 4 percent of the aggregate income to these households. This could be accomplished if the average household incomes of the third through the highest fifth households were each reduced by 4.5 percent. The income of the lowest fifth could be doubled, increased by 100 percent, if the highest fifth reduced its income by 8 percent. Because of savings in welfare and incarceration, actual costs to increase the household income of the lowest fifth would likely be much less. For income data see page 201, note 9.

13. The lowest-income fifth of U.S. households has taken home about 3.4 to 4.5 percent of the total household income since 1967. While low-income households increased their real income by 29 percent between 1967 and 2008, the top fifth increased their income by 70 percent. With a mean annual income in 2008 of $11,650, the bottom fifth have become not more rich so much as less poor. In 2008 the income ratio between the top fifth and the lowest fifth households stood at about 15 to 1, growing from its 1967 value of 11 to 1. Over the same period, the top 5 percent of households saw a growth in real income of 86 percent to a ratio of twenty-five times that of the 2008 income of the lowest fifth, a substantial increase from its 1967 ratio of 18 to 1. For income data see page 201, note 9.

14. For example, see "The Low-Wage Labor Market: Challenges and Opportunities for Economic Self-Sufficiency," prepared by the Urban Institute for the U.S.

Department of Health and Human Services, Washington, DC, December 1999. This multiauthor review paper describes, among other things, the U.S. labor market as divided into a primary and secondary portion, with the primary portion providing those jobs that offer stability and upward mobility along with fringe benefits, while the secondary market provides jobs that offer low income, little stability or upward mobility, and few, if any, benefits. Needed today is either a single labor market or a sustainable secondary market offering living wages and basic benefits. A frequent counterargument is that even though the bottom fifth of American households earn poverty wages, their plight is overstated, since as years pass, those in the bottom fifth change. That is, low-wage earners do not always remain so. Yet even if poverty is not persistent for all households or individuals, life still requires the basics of food, clothing, housing, and medical care.

15. Halberstam, *The Reckoning*, p. 84.

16. Today, although Ford's automobile remains a centerpiece of the American way of life, the middle class created by the auto industry, thanks to the globalization of manufacturing, has come under ever more distress. With U.S. automakers currently asking for wage and benefit concessions of 50 percent or more, the middle-class standard of living of America's auto workers may become an opportunity of the past. For example, see Jeffrey McCracken, "A Middle Class Made by Detroit Is Now Threatened by Its Slump: Henry Ford's Gold-Plated Pay Belongs to an Older Era; Realities of Globalization," *Wall Street Journal*, November 14, 2005, p. A1.

17. See "Returns with Positive '1979 Income Concept' Income," tables 7 and 8, Internal Revenue Service, http://www.irs.gov/taxstats/index.html. Search for "1979 Income Concept" and click on "Individual Income Tax Rates and Tax Shares" to find these tables. See also Michael Strudler, Tom Petska, Lori Hentz, and Ryan Petska, "Analysis of the Distributions of Income, Taxes, and Payroll Taxes via Cross-Section and Panel Data, 1979–2004," available at http://www.irs.gov/taxstats/index.html. Click on "Products and Publications," then "American Statistical Association Conferences," and select 2006 papers.

18. J. Scott Moody, Wendy P. Warcholik, and Scott A. Hodge, *The Rising Cost of Complying with the Federal Income Tax*, Special Report Number 138, December 2005, Tax Foundation, available at http://www.taxfoundation.org. Search for "Report 138" to find the article. The estimated cost of tax compliance varies widely depending on who is making the estimate, but most estimates are on the order of hundreds of billions of dollars annually, several times what the federal government spends each year on education and homeland security combined. Because the bottom 50 percent of U.S. taxpayers pays less than 4 percent of total taxes, a flat tax of around 25 percent along with an exemption for the first $50,000 of income offers a low-cost alternative to our present Byzantine tax code.

Also, thanks to the exemption, a flat tax would be fairly progressive for incomes that are small multiples of its value. For example, for incomes of two, three, and four times the exemption, the tax rates would be one-half, two-thirds, and three-quarters of the flat-tax rate, or tax rates of about 12.5, 16.7, and 18.8 percent respectively for a flat tax of 25 percent.

19. For example, see Fred Kaplan, "They Scrapped the F-22!" *Slate*, July 21, 2009, available at http://www.slate.com/id/2223287.

20. If this sounds needlessly apocalyptic, see Naomi Klein, "Disaster Capitalism," *Harpers Magazine*, October 2007, pp. 47–58.

21. Most Americans report themselves as belonging to the middle class even though their incomes range widely, and for those who live within their means secure home ownership is still possible.

4. The New Liturgy

1. E. F. Schumacher, *A Guide for the Perplexed* (Harper & Row, New York, 1977), chap. 10.

2. Peter M. Senge, *The Fifth Discipline: The Art and Practice of the Learning Organization* (Doubleday, New York, 1990), p. 6.

3. Charles J. Sykes, *A Nation of Victims: The Decay of the American Character* (St. Martin's, New York, 1992), p. 254. Sykes cites and thanks Irving Kristol for establishing the distinction between "solutions" and "remedies." Whereas experts can provide solutions to convergent problems (for example, the design of modern aircraft), divergent problems (for example, abortion) can only be ameliorated through remedies provided by those affected.

4. "Dear Landlord," Schools Brief, *Economist*, February 9, 1991, pp. 75–76. The *Economist* website defines "rent-seeking" as "Cutting yourself a bigger slice of the cake rather than making the cake bigger" or "Trying to make more money without producing more for the customers." Examples include protection rackets, price fixing, and lobbying the government for special tax or regulatory privileges. See http://www.economist.com. Go to Research Tools at the bottom of the home page and click on "Economics A–Z" to find this and other definitions.

5. Beyond the way a particular vocation is practiced is the intent brought to the work. Are the client's interests put before the practitioner's income? The roles of the entrepreneur and the rent seeker become entangled when either health or accident insurance enters the picture, along with what economists call "moral hazard." In this case, the stakes are raised because a third-party payment is now possible. While insurance companies take on a moral hazard by dealing with

either the entrepreneur or the rent seeker, it is the responsibility of both to negotiate in good faith for their client, their client's insurance pool, and their own
interest of an equitable or fair income. Although such divisions may require a
Solomon-like wisdom, negotiations like these provide opportunities for exemplary behavior by all. See the *Economist* website given in note 4 for a definition of
"moral hazard."

6. "Our Screwed-Up Tax Code," *Fortune*, September 6, 1993, pp. 34–48. See also
   page 206, note 18.

7. The total cost and cost of efficiency are shown without units. These can be considered to be arbitrary for this illustration. For this curve, the constant has been set to
   one. The curve can be used to make universal arguments, since the shape-related
   values given here are independent of the constant. Also independent of the constant is the result given in chapter 2 that for the least-cost design, equal amounts
   of money should be spent on energy and efficiency over the lifetime of the house.

8. David A. Robinson, "Insulating a Solar House," in *Proceedings*, 1978 Annual
   Meeting, American Section of International Solar Energy Society, Denver, CO,
   Vol. 2.2, 1978, pp. 196–201.

9. An unappreciated amenity of energy-efficient housing is the enhanced comfort
   provided by a house that is properly sealed, insulated, and ventilated. Beyond
   this, because the low, flat curve is not symmetric, it costs less to err on the side of
   spending too much on efficiency, making investments in energy efficiency a substantive form of low-cost, low-risk insurance against future fuel price increases.

10. For another example of such savings, see Art Rolnick and Rob Grunewald, "Early
    Childhood Development: Economic Development with High Public Return," Fed-
    eral Reserve Bank of Minneapolis, 2003. This and related papers may be found
    at http://www.minneapolisfed.org. Click on "Early Childhood Development" and
    select the original 2003 paper. By focusing on development that improves the lot
    of children rather than that of business, sports, or entertainment, Rolnick and
    Grunewald show that the proper development of children produces vast public
    benefits. Properly prepared children not only reduce education costs by perform-
    ing better in school, but also have greater lifetime earnings, require less welfare
    assistance, and, most important, are far more likely to stay out of the criminal jus-
    tice system. In short, a properly educated child adds greatly to the economy and
    general welfare of the community. With an estimated return of over $8 for each
    dollar spent, the social and economic benefits of such investment in the early
    lives of our children cannot be dismissed. The savings potential of long-term
    investment in universals such as early childhood education and energy-efficient
    housing is enormous and constitutes a positive way forward in these challenging
    economic times.

11. Scott Adams regularly illustrates this in his comic *Dilbert*.

12. Richard P. Feynman, as told to Ralph Leighton, *What Do YOU Care What Other People Think? Further Adventures of a Curious Character* (Norton, New York, 1988).

13. Assuming a flight duration of one hour, the chance of a general aviation flight resulting in a fatal accident is approximately 1/100,000. Due to less strict regulations for pilot skill and experience, this accident rate is about 100 times greater than that for commercial aviation. See Scott McCartney, "Inside the Mind of a Weekend Pilot," The Middle Seat, *Wall Street Journal*, October 17, 2006, p. D1. For aviation safety data, see tables 2–9 and 2–14 at *National Transportation Statistics*, U.S. Bureau of Transportation Statistics. Available at http://www.bts.gov /publications/national_transportation_statistics.

14. For a personal and graphic description of the *Challenger* tragedy by a space shuttle astronaut, see Mike Mullane, *Riding Rockets: The Outrageous Tales of a Space Shuttle Astronaut* (Scribner, New York, 2006), pp. 220–33.

15. "Partnering: A Concept for Success" (The Associated General Contractors of America, Washington, DC, 1991).

5. The New Work

1. For example, consider these observations: "In the United States associations are established to promote the public safety, commerce, industry, morality, and religion. There is no end which the human will despairs of attaining through the combined power of individuals united into a society" (Vol. 1, p. 192). "Wherever at the head of some new undertaking you see the government in France, or a man of rank in England, in the United States you will be sure to find an association" (Vol. 2, p. 106). "Nothing, in my opinion, is more deserving of our attention than the intellectual and moral associations of America" (Vol. 2, p. 110). "In democratic countries the science of association is the mother of science; the progress of all the rest depends upon the progress it has made" (Vol. 2, p. 110). Alexis de Tocqueville, *Democracy in America*, Vols. 1 and 2 (Vintage Books, New York, 1990).

2. "Volunteering in America Research Highlights" is available at http://www .volunteeringinamerica.gov. Click on "Related Research," then "Volunteering in America Fact Sheet." See also "Facts and Figures about Charitable Organizations," http://www.independentsector.org. In the Research tab click on "Research Overview," then "Facts and Figures about Charitable Organizations."

3. Mary T. Quigley, "Volunteers Form Backbone of 125-Year-Old Catholic Charities," *Saint Paul Pioneer Press*, July 28, 1994, p. 7A. For current information, go to http://www.ccspm.org and click on "About Catholic Charities."

4. Peter F. Drucker, *The New Realities: In Government and Politics, in Economics and Business, in Society and World View* (Harper & Row, New York, 1989), p. 197. For current data on nonprofit revenues, see "Quick Facts and Figures," National Center for Charitable Statistics, http://www.nccs.urban.org. For U.S. gross domestic product, see National Income and Product Accounts Table, NIPA Table 1.1.5, Gross Domestic Product, Bureau of Economic Analysis, http://www.bea.gov.

5. Fred R. Bleakley, "How an Outdated Plant Was Made New," *Wall Street Journal*, October 21, 1994, p. B1. According to an Owens Corning press release of February 23, 2004, the plant described here was expanded and further upgraded in 2004 to improve still more its energy and environmental performance.

6. "The Final Frontier," Economics Focus, *Economist*, February 20, 1993, p. 63, shows the steady rise of U.S. service employment (the "final frontier") from 15 to 75 percent of total employment between 1850 and 1992, along with commensurate decreases in farm and industrial employment. For recent data on manufacturing productivity, see U.S. Bureau of Labor Statistics, http://www.bls.gov. To find employment percentage by sector, go to Employment Projections and click on Employment Projections Program (EPP) table 2.1, "Employment by Major Industry Sector." For analysis of the ongoing decrease in U.S. manufacturing employment, see "Factors Underlying the Decline in Manufacturing Employment Since 2000," Congressional Budget Office, December 23, 2008, http://www.cbo.gov. On the Publications tab, find "Special Collections" and click on "Labor." Reported here is that the ongoing decline in manufacturing labor "is associated with two interrelated developments: rapid gains in productivity (output per hour) in U.S. manufacturing and increased competition from foreign producers."

7. With ever-decreasing employment in the manufacturing sector, most new work will be found in the service sector of the economy. As discussed in chapter 3, this will require bringing a living wage as well as enhanced dignity to what is now condescendingly known as low-income labor.

8. Here it is useful to distinguish the low-income poor from those living in poverty. A poor single parent will turn off the TV and help their child with homework or read to them. They will know where to buy fresh food and how to find the public library, even though this may not be easy. A single parent living in poverty does and knows little of this. While both parents lack money, the parent living in poverty lacks agency—the capacity to act in their own best interests and, more importantly, in the best interests of their child.

9. Garland Wright, "Principles of Leadership," *The Guthrie Theater Program*, Summer 1992, p. 11.

10. Mike Steele, "Guthrie Builds Ensemble in Shakespeare Works," *Star Tribune*, June 24, 1990, p. 1F.

11. Garland Wright, "Celebrating a Shared Understanding," *The Guthrie Theater Program*, Fall 1990, p. 7.

12. For example, see Bruno Latour, "The Last Critique," *Harper's Magazine*, April 2004, pp. 15–20, and also his essay "Why Has Critique Run Out of Steam?" *Critical Inquiry*, Winter 2004. What I gather from Latour's dense thinking is that criticism should change its focus from disassembling everything in sight to finding new ways to fit life together. In terms of the metaphors of this book, he seems to be calling for those who practice the vocation of criticism to turn from the role of rent seeker to that of entrepreneur, to turn from the work of cashing in on the human condition to actually contributing to its transcendence.

13. The success of the history plays at the Guthrie Theater demonstrated not only what is possible when an ensemble finds its voice but also the difficulty of maintaining it when it has been achieved. Maintaining such a community is difficult and dicey work. For example, after its initial success, Wright's acting company became what he described as a "dysfunctional family" squabbling over plum roles and professional position within the acting company. To bring a new order to the group, Wright named "ongoing" and "associate" members, a move that greatly helped to recover the focus and energy of the ensemble and to restore its lost collegiality. Although the group went on to further good work, the goal of a resident acting company at the Guthrie left with Wright in 1995. What remains today are those ensemble members who continue to bring their talents to the many theaters around the Twin Cities. My twin towns continue to reverberate with Wright, his leadership, and his ensemble. Wright died of cancer in 1998 at age fifty-two. Tad Simons, "A Troubled Repertoire," *Twin Cities Reader*, July 28– August 5, 1993, pp. 14–19, and Mike Steele, "Acting in Repertory: It's Exhausting, Exhilarating," *Star Tribune*, January 8, 1995, p. 1F.

14. Václav Havel, World Theatre Day speech, March 27, 1994.

15. For a description of Reell Precision Manufacturing and thirteen similar well-run, privately held small companies, see Bo Burlingham, *Small Giants: Companies That Choose to Be Great Instead of Big* (Portfolio, New York, 2005). See also www .reell.com. Burlingham does not discuss how globalization will affect these companies. However, in 2004, Reell stumbled as it entered the commodity market with its sales of laptop computer hinges. By building domestic production capacity to produce a product that had the unfortunate success of becoming a commodity, they found it increasingly difficult to both make a profit and maintain their social principles. See also Bo Burlingham, "Paradise Lost," *Inc.com*, February 1, 2008, available at www.inc.com/magazine/20080201/paradise-lost.html.

16. These ideas are not new but were first proposed as Theory X (direction and control) and Theory Y (responsibility and trust) by Douglas McGregor in his

much-cited essay "The Human Side of Enterprise," *Management Review*, Vol. 46, 1957, pp. 22–28. This essay, with additional commentary on McGregor's ideas, appears in Gary Heil, Warren Bennis, and Deborah C. Stephens, *Douglas McGregor, Revisited* (Wiley, New York, 2000), pp. 129–44.

17. Every so often I meet someone whom I readily dislike. The disagreeable person is frequently a self-important fool with a witless sense of humor. Egad, that's me! These painful self-revelations occur when we meet people who outwardly have characteristics we hide in ourselves, characteristics we would rather keep out of our conscious minds. Yet, when we meet in the personality of another what Jungian psychologists call our personal shadow, what is hidden in our minds produces a visceral reaction in our bodies. By examining the disagreeable behaviors that we give to—or project onto—others, we can learn a great deal about what we dislike most about ourselves. Although such revelations may not be welcome, it is by integrating them into who we are that we develop our capacity not only to know ourselves, but to follow and lead as well.

    For an excellent reader on the shadow, see Connie Zweig and Jeremiah Abrams, eds., *Meeting the Shadow: The Hidden Power of the Dark Side of Human Nature* (Tarcher, Los Angeles, 1991). In chapter 7, William A. Miller discusses five ways of finding the shadow in daily life. See also William A. Miller, *Make Friends with Your Shadow* (Augsburg, Minneapolis, 1981), and Harry A. Wilmer, *Practical Jung* (Chiron, Wilmette, IL, 1987).

18. Parker J. Palmer, *Let Your Life Speak: Listening for the Voice of Vocation* (Jossey-Bass, San Francisco, 2000), chapter 5, "Leading from Within," pp. 73–94.

19. David A. Ogren, "Enemies," *Peace Review*, Vol. 10, March 1998, pp. 113–18.

20. Robert Bly, "The Long Bag We Drag behind Us," in Abrams and Zweig, *Meeting the Shadow*, pp. 6–12.

21. Harry A. Wilmer, *Practical Jung: Nuts and Bolts of Jungian Psychotherapy* (Chiron Publications, Wilmette, IL, 1987), p. 101.

22. Bruce W. Tuckman, "Developmental Sequence in Small Groups," *Psychological Bulletin*, Vol. 63, No. 6, 1965, pp. 384–99. Tuckman's optimism with the level of openness achieved in norming is tempered by both M. Scott Peck's experience and my own. Nevertheless, Tuckman's sequence remains relevant today. Peck has written extensively about this process; see main text and note 23.

23. M. Scott Peck discussed this process extensively in his book *The Different Drum* (Simon & Schuster, New York, 1987). He identifies the four stages of community building as Pseudocommunity, Chaos, Emptiness, and finally Community. The Forming, Storming, Norming, Performing model fails when group members fail to move beyond the comfort of norming, beyond what Peck calls "pseudo-

community," where all are friendly and none is vulnerable. Peck asserts that there are only two ways out of storming or chaos: the first is into norming or conventional organization, the second through emptiness. For Peck, emptiness requires the letting go of expectations, prejudices, ideologies, solutions, and the need to convert, fix, or control. My own experience of a weekend community-building exercise conducted using Peck's methodologies followed the pattern I described in the main text. While our weekend group came into "community," if presented with real work to do, we most likely would have returned to chaos and needed to start all over again. Thus, as Peck describes in his book, maintaining community requires continuous work and may include frequent returns to chaos and pseudo-community—returns to storming and norming.

24. Roger Fisher and William Ury, *Getting to Yes: Negotiating Agreement without Giving In* (Penguin Books, New York, 1983).

25. The work of the third sector is most frequently associated with the provision of services to the poor. Today, with the increasingly shameless accumulation of riches by the wealthy (compared to world standards, most all in America are rich), the work of the third sector necessarily needs to go beyond social services to the poor to the personal transformation of all people, rich, poor, or in-between. Signs of such personal transformation, beyond moderate living and increased savings, would be an increasing civic engagement by all people—organizing a neighborhood block party, recycling, teaching others to read, listening to kids, serving in public office—the list goes on.

26. John McKnight, director of Community Studies at Northwestern University, has written extensively about the value of building communities based on their capacities to care for themselves. For example, see John McKnight, *The Careless Society: Community and Its Counterfeits* (Basic Books, New York, 1995). McKnight's thesis is that professionalization has turned community service into a profitable and needed commodity. With this the community begins to doubt its own capacity to care as it becomes dependent on human services provided by others. For multiple stories of community programs that work, see John P. Kretzmann and John L. McKnight, *Building Communities from the Inside Out* (ACTA Publications, Chicago, 1993), a workbook on asset-based community building.

27. For discussions of citizen work, the new liturgy, in action, see John L. McKnight and Peter Block, *The Abundant Community: Awakening the Power of Families and Neighborhoods* (Berrett-Koehler, San Francisco, 2010), and Harry C. Boyte, *The Citizen Solution: How You Can Make a Difference* (Minnesota Historical Society Press, St. Paul, 2008).

6. From the Apple to the Cross

1. Robert W. Funk, Roy W. Hoover, and the Jesus Seminar, eds., *The Five Gospels: The Search for the Authentic Words of Jesus: New Translation and Commentary* (Macmillan, New York, 1993), p. 34. My ordained readers have suggested that by including this section on the Jesus Seminar, I have compromised my position as a layperson writing on the issues of today's church. The question I want to address is why I and many others have found the seminar's work so engaging. For me, whatever its methodological shortcomings might be, the seminar's work is attractive because it illuminates some of my lifelong questions of just how the Bible has been used to inform the faith. For a vigorous response to the work of the seminar and others, see Gregory A. Boyd, *Cynic Sage or Son of God? Recovering the Real Jesus in an Age of Revisionist Replies* (Victor Books, Wheaton, IL, 1995). Having begun with the teachings of Arius in 318 CE, the millennia-old controversy concerning the nature of Jesus remains unabated.

2. Funk et al., *The Five Gospels*, pp. 35–37. The authors present a variety of descriptions of their four-point scale. My language here is my interpretation of their intent.

3. Mark 10:25 and Luke 6:27.

4. Funk et al., *The Five Gospels*, pp. 25–34.

5. Matthew 16:15–19. This giving of authority to Peter appears only in the Gospel of Matthew and is thought to be a construction of the evangelist or later Christian storytellers. In Mark and Luke the dialogue ends with Peter's acknowledgment of Jesus as the Messiah.

6. Matthew 25:40.

7. This is not to diminish the good works of those many evangelicals who look forward to the second coming while still working to provide earthly deliverance, working to make the world a better place today. Earthly deliverance is not the same as personal salvation. My own response to the evangelist's question, "Are you saved?" is that I am a child of God, and that before I was, I was a child of God, and that after I am, I shall remain one still. For me, this is salvation enough. Of course, this all turns on the faith that God's grace is open to all, even to those who question it. Or as Garrison Keillor put it, "God does not condemn his children." Garrison Keillor, "News from Lake Wobegon," *Prairie Home Companion*, radio broadcast, June 17, 2006.

8. Luke 24:46–47.

9. Funk et al., *The Five Gospels*, p. 400.

10. 1 Corinthians 15:3. This scripture demonstrates the power of Paul in the formation of early Christian belief. First Corinthians was written around 55 CE, several

years before Mark, the earliest Gospel, and several decades before the later Gospels of Matthew and Luke. The nature of Jesus' saving action on the cross did not fall full-blown from the sky, but has come to us through the hands, minds, and spirits of many.

11. Luke 22:26.

12. Walter Wink describes the difference between dying for a cause and dying to a cause by viewing Jesus' death on the cross as marking either a *final* sacrifice or an *end* of sacrifice. The difference between *final* sacrifice and *end* of sacrifice is that the first view ends in atonement and marks the beginning of waiting for heaven, while the second ends in freedom and marks the beginning of a new age of peace and justice. Since the first view accommodated the powers of empire far better than the second, it became the dominant view. Walter Wink, *Engaging the Powers: Discernment and Resistance in a World of Domination*, The Powers, vol. 3 (Fortress Press, Minneapolis, 1992), pp. 153–54.

13. Uta Ranke-Heinemann, *Putting Away Childish Things: The Virgin Birth, the Empty Tomb, and Other Fairy Tales You Don't Need to Believe to Have a Living Faith*, trans. Peter Heinegg (HarperCollins, New York, 1995), p. 278.

14. Barbara G. Walker, *The Woman's Encyclopedia of Myths and Secrets* (HarperCollins, New York, 1983). See pages 77–79 and 663–65.

15. For example, see John Dominic Crossan, *Jesus: A Revolutionary Biography* (HarperCollins, New York, 1994), chapter 7.

16. Sociologist Robert Bellah has described the origins of this disconnect as a long-existing fundamental misunderstanding between belief and faith. While beliefs were used to maintain order among the people, those in charge remained free to think whatever they wished. Keeping the public peace therefore led to the application of "noble lies," misrepresentations of faith that continue to compromise the Christian movement yet today. See Harvey Cox, *The Future of Faith* (HarperOne, New York, 2009), pp. 219–21.

17. Marcus J. Borg, *Meeting Jesus Again for the First Time: The Historical Jesus and the Heart of Contemporary Faith* (HarperSanFrancisco, New York, 1994), pp. 128–33; and "Atonement," *Columbia Encyclopedia*, 5th ed., 1993.

18. W. H. C. Frend, *The Early Church* (Fortress Press, Minneapolis, 1991), pp. 123–24.

19. Frend, *The Early Church*, p.148.

20. For example, see Richard P. McBrien, *Catholicism*, new ed., completely rev. and updated (HarperSanFrancisco, San Francisco, 1994), pp. 275–331. On page 327 McBrien summarizes the actions of the church at the Council of Nicaea in this way: "For the first time, the Church moved officially from biblical to speculative categories to define its faith."

21. Karen Armstrong, *A History of God* (Ballantine, New York, 1993), pp. 123–24.

22. The United Methodist Church, *The Book of Discipline of the United Methodist Church* (The United Methodist Publishing House, Nashville, 2008), p. 61.

23. Elaine Pagels, *Adam, Eve, and the Serpent* (Random House, New York, 1988), pp. 125–26.

24. Pagels, *Adam, Eve, and the Serpent*, pp. 145–46.

25. An empire of church and state without turmoil is a false hope. For example, see Kevin Phillips, *American Theocracy: The Peril and Politics of Radical Religion, Oil, and Borrowed Money in the 21st Century* (Viking, New York, 2006), chap. 7. Reviewing his own work and that of others, Phillips shows that church-state combinations do not end well. By extending power and privilege to one another, both the church and the state grow in intolerance while civility and the common good suffer. Less than a century after the Council of Nicaea, the Roman Empire was in shambles. Phillips argues that the United States is not immune from such disorder and could just as well go the way of empires past.

26. 2 Corinthians 11:3.

27. "Serpent," *Random House Dictionary of the English Language, Unabridged*, 1971, p. 1303.

28. For example, see Walker, *The Woman's Encyclopedia of Myths and Secrets*, pp. 903–9.

29. William A. Miller, *Make Friends with Your Shadow: How to Accept and Use Positively the Negative Side of Your Personality* (Augsburg, Minneapolis, 1981), p. 44.

30. Terence E. Fretheim, "Rehabilitating the Serpent in Genesis 3," Luther Northwestern Theological Seminary Convocation, St. Paul, November 2, 1993.

31. Terence E. Fretheim, "Is Genesis 3 a Fall Story?" *Word and World*, Vol. 14, No. 2, Spring 1994, pp. 144–53.

32. For example, see Borg, *Meeting Jesus Again for the First Time*, p. 29, and Funk et al., *The Five Gospels*, pp. 136–37.

33. Luke 17:20–21.

34. The Greek word *basileia* used in the verse above may be translated just as well as either "kingdom" or "realm." More important is the centrality of this text to the ministry of Jesus.

35. For example, see Borg, *Meeting Jesus Again for the First Time*, chapter 4, and Crossan, *Jesus: A Revolutionary Biography*, chapter 5.

36. Mark 12:29–31. The first and second portions of the great commandment as taught by Jesus reflect his emphasis on Moses' teachings to the people (Deuteronomy 6:4–5) and God's teachings to Moses (Leviticus 19:18) as given in the Hebrew scripture. Jesus was a Jew teaching from the Hebrew Bible.

37. Borg, *Meeting Jesus Again for the First Time*, p. 50.

38. Drorah O'Donnell Setel, "Purity, Ritual," and Derek J. Tidball, "Social Sciences and the Bible," *The Oxford Companion to the Bible* (Oxford University Press, New York, 1993).

39. Borg, *Meeting Jesus Again for the First Time*, pp. 51–52.

40. Crossan, *Jesus: A Revolutionary Biography*, pp. 66–74.

41. Elaine Pagels, *The Gnostic Gospels* (Vintage, New York, 1989), p. 34.

42. Pagels, *The Gnostic Gospels*, p. 150.

43. Walter Brueggemann, *Texts Under Negotiation: The Bible and Postmodern Imagination* (Fortress Press, Minneapolis, 1993), pp. 19–20.

44. For more on the new liturgy and the future of the church, see Loren B. Mead, *The Once and Future Church: Reinventing the Congregation for a New Mission Frontier* (Alban Institute, Washington, 1991). For a hopeful look at the Christian movement past, present, and—most importantly—future, see Cox, *The Future of Faith*.

45. Besides *liturgy*, I co-opt a second term, *Docetism*, from the Christian lexicon. Broadly, Docetism can be regarded as the denial of humanity and is traditionally used to name the early Christian heresy that claimed that the crucified Jesus avoided suffering because he only seemed to be alive. For our work here, economic Docetism describes our disregard for the suffering of the poverty-level workers who produce the low-cost goods we so gratuitously consume.

7. The Chaos Paradigm

1. Proverbs 6:6–8.

2. Nigel R. Franks, "Army Ants: A Collective Intelligence," *American Scientist*, Vol. 77, March–April 1989, pp. 138–45.

3. Deborah M. Gordon, "The Development of Organization in an Ant Colony," *American Scientist*, Vol. 83, January–February 1995, pp. 50–57.

4. Alexis de Tocqueville, *Democracy in America* (Vintage Classics, New York, 1990), Vol. 1, p. 192.

5. M. Mitchell Waldrop, *Complexity: The Emerging Science at the Edge of Order and Chaos* (Simon and Schuster, New York, 1992), p. 241. Waldrop reports on a workshop presentation made at the Santa Fe Institute by Craig Reynolds. This algorithm was used to simulate the birds shown in the film *Batman Returns*. For an update of work on understanding bird flight by Reynolds and others, see Brian Hayes, "Flights of Fancy," *American Scientist*, Vol. 99, January–February 2011, pp. 10–14.

6. Marcus J. Borg, *The Heart of Christianity: Rediscovering a Life of Faith* (HarperSanFrancisco, New York, 2003), pp. 56–57.

7. Stuart A. Kauffman, *At Home in the Universe: The Search for Laws of Self-Organization and Complexity* (Oxford University Press, New York), 1995, chapter 4. Kauffman would describe the enhanced organization of the ant colony as "order for free." While local order is created, the larger natural order suffers. In Kauffman's words, local order is "paid for" by exporting disorder or heat to the larger environment. This is a reality of nature that many people, including environmentalists, would rather ignore. For any of us to be alive, and to feed, clothe, house, and transport ourselves, the environment must suffer. Just how and how much the environment must suffer because of our daily round is the question of the age.

8. For example, consider our failure to increase motor vehicle mileage standards or gasoline excise taxes in response to our ever-growing oil imports and trade deficit.

9. Philip P. Hallie, *Lest Innocent Blood Be Shed: The Story of the Village of Le Chambon, and How Goodness Happened There* (Harper & Row, New York, 1979).

10. Although the GDP per capita has tripled in the United States since World War II, our national happiness has remained unchanged. The future of our well-being depends far more on things such as good governance, robust communities, and public health than on further economic growth. Sharon Begley, "Wealth and Happiness Don't Necessarily Go Hand in Hand," Science Journal, *Wall Street Journal*, August 13, 2004, p. B1.

11. Bruce J. West and Michael Shlesinger, "The Noise in Natural Phenomena," *American Scientist*, Vol. 78, January–February 1990, pp. 40–45.

12. Mathematically the utility function is written as $U(f) = \log(f/f_0)$, where f_0 is the threshold value of f required for survival. Differentiation yields $\Delta U(f) = \Delta f/f$. Our present state of unsustainable exponential growth in material consumption springs from our seemingly relentless desire to constantly increase the material utility of our lives.

13. Although we now know that Bernoulli largely fails at predicting our happiness with the material, our unrelenting consumption shows us we are, nevertheless, driven by his utility function. Today can we satisfy our drive for ever more of the material by living with less while consciously scaling our experiences to live as if Bernoulli *were* correct? My thesis is we can and must. See "meals out" calculation in next section. See also Daniel Gilbert, *Stumbling on Happiness* (Knopf, New York, 2006), pp. 235–38.

14. Faye Flam, "Beating a Fractal Drum," Research News, *Science*, December 13, 1991, p. 1593.

15. Data appeared in John R. Dorfman, "Stock-Market Pros Speculate: Has Correction Run Its Course?" Heard on the Street, *Wall Street Journal*, July 19, 1996, p.

C1. A simple regression analysis showed that the cumulative number of declines was proportional to 1/size of decline$^{1.72}$. This fit explained over 99 percent of the variation between the number and size of the decline (log scale). For a cumulative random walk, the exponent would have been equal to one. The exponent of 1.72 shows the market is highly correlated with its most recent history, making market timing difficult if not impossible. For example, investment guru Peter Lynch reports that by remaining fully invested for the last four decades of the twentieth century, an investor would have earned 20 times more (11 percent versus 3 percent annual gain) than someone who was invested 92 percent of the time but missed out on the market's best forty months (Jeff D. Opdyke, "How to Tiptoe Back into the Stock Market," *Wall Street Journal*, November 5, 2002, p. D1). Over time, the market will predictably experience a constant stream of unpredictable bull and bear excursions, a few large, but most moderate to small. However, knowing when a small excursion will become a large one, either up or down, appears to be beyond analysis. Greed and fear seem to know no time scale.

16. Robert Pool, "Chaos Theory: How Big an Advance?" *Science*, July 7, 1989, pp. 26–28.

17. There is no simple or single definition of what complexity is. But as we have seen so far, it may describe the self-organization of ants into a colony, of boids into a flock on a computer screen, or of people into a common cause. It also may be used to describe the self-similarity of nature itself—a self-similarity that results in robust organisms from trees to vascular systems. Later, as we examine the motion of the planets, we will find that it also describes a future far more sensitive to where we are at the moment than previously imagined. Most basically, the science of complexity is the search for order in the presence of the unpredictable. For an excellent introduction to these ideas and more, see Melanie Mitchell, *Complexity: A Guided Tour* (Oxford, New York, 2009).

18. Robert J. Geller, David D. Jackson, Yan Y. Kagan, and Francesco Mulargia, "Earthquakes Cannot Be Predicted," *Science*, March 14, 1997, pp. 1616–17. Interestingly enough, Geller et al. close their argument by making an appeal to Bayesian statistics when they state, "Each failed attempt at prediction lowers the a priori probability for the next attempt." Describing Japan's recent devastating Tohoku earthquake, Geller said that even in a country as well studied as Japan, major quakes always "seem to be ones not expected." Quoted in Dennis Normile, "Devastating Earthquake Defied Expectations," *Science*, March 18, 2011, pp. 1375–76.

19. Gerald Jay Sussman and Jack Wisdom, "Chaotic Evolution of the Solar System," *Science*, July 3, 1992, pp. 56–62. See also Richard A. Kerr, "From Mercury to Pluto, Chaos Pervades the Solar System," *Science*, July 3, 1992, p. 33.

20. James Gleick, *Chaos: Making a New Science* (Viking, New York, 1987), p. 16.

21. Such a broad statement requires an equally broad response. Clearly we cannot influence the motion of the planets, other than by sending an ineffectually small amount of mass, a spacecraft, for example, from Earth to Mars. More important to our collective life today is the possibility of significant global climate change as described in chapter 8. In this case, the aggregate action of the world's people could dramatically change the self-organizing climate patterns that we call the weather. And this is a complex system that *does* present an array of options for assuring our life on the only planet we have.

Beyond these chaotic systems lie what Stuart Kauffman describes as evolutionary systems driven by Darwinian preadaptations, biological bits and pieces that when placed in the proper environment can themselves evolve into new organs—organs out of which new organisms may emerge. Kauffman's self-described "outrageous claim" is that such a process is "radically nonpredictable and ceaselessly creative" (page 130). Kauffman further points out that this sort of chaos lies beyond the deterministic chaos described in this chapter. While the motion of the planets is predictably unpredictable, in Kauffman's view evolution is not only unpredictable, but unpredictably unpredictable. In conclusion, Kauffman asks, "Is not this new view, a view based on an expanded science, God enough?" (page 283). Independent of nature's chaotic nature, the fact that we have emerged from the primordial soup of the big bang ought to be reason enough for even the most jaundiced to stand in awe. Stuart A. Kauffman, *Reinventing the Sacred: A New View of Science, Reason, and Religion* (Basic Books, New York, 2008), chaps. 10 and 19.

22. Gordon Solvut, "SE Asian Babies Healthy Despite Lack of Prenatal Care," *Minneapolis Star Tribune*, March 22, 1997, p. B1.

23. More recent data (2002–2004) show that although Asians and Pacific Islanders continue to have lower family incomes, greater poverty rates, and less prenatal care than whites, they still have lower infant mortality rates than any other group, including whites. "Monitoring Infant Mortality in Minneapolis and St. Paul," Research Brief, Minneapolis Department of Health and Family Support, September 2006. Available at http://www.ci.minneapolis.mn.us/dhfs/TCHS.pdf.

24. John McKnight has written extensively on the application of these ideas to community service systems. See John L. McKnight and Peter Block, *The Abundant Community: Awakening the Power of Families and Neighborhoods* (Berrett-Koehler, San Francisco, 2010), and John McKnight, "Why 'Servanthood' Is Bad," *Other Side*, January/February 1989, pp. 38–40.

25. Judith M. Bardwick, *Danger in the Comfort Zone: From Boardroom to Mailroom—How to Break the Entitlement Habit That's Killing American Business*

(American Management Association, New York, 1991). According to Bardwick, between the slack life of entitlement and the paralyzing life of fear experienced in many workplaces lies a level of uncertainty or anxiety that makes for an optimal work environment. Between entitlement and fear lies a satisfying personal and communal life at the edge of chaos, a place where in the midst of uncertainty, hope is maintained and lives grow.

26. "The Deserving Poor," *Economist*, April 25, 1987, p. 14. The remedy of education, marriage, and work has been a long-standing conservative tenet for the reduction of poverty in the United States, and I offer it here as a bookend to my earlier arguments for a living wage. If we are to get serious about poverty in the United States, we must provide not only a living wage but enough universals such as accessible health care, housing, and transportation, so that those who *do* finish school, *do* get married before creating a child, and *do* stay employed have both the personal and the communal assets required for a successful—that is, self-supporting—work life. Only by focusing on both improvident behavior as well as access to progressive circumstance will we begin to see a decline of poverty in America. These broad remedies ought to find support by conservatives and progressives alike.

27. Hal Lancaster, "Making the Break from Middle Manager to a Seat at the Top," Managing Your Career, *Wall Street Journal*, July 7, 1998, p. B1. Organizational consultant Al Parchem is reported as "surprised by the sheer number of traits needed to squeeze through to the top, and by the importance of humor, which enabled fast trackers to soften tough messages and relieve stress." Because of the self-similar nature of complex life, these characteristics, rather than being simply additive, are multiplicative. With the increasing need to have many desirable characteristics all at once, missing one characteristic out of ten, rather than reducing one's chance of success to just nine out of ten, may actually reduce it to near zero. As more skills and other resources are added, greater success is achieved. The multiplication of skills and resources in high skill/high resource individuals and organizations is the principal source for much of the growing inequality we see in the world today. Those who have, get. For example, see West and Shlesinger, "The Noise in Natural Phenomena."

28. Matthew Fox, *Original Blessing* (Bear Books, Santa Fe, 1983).

8. A Crisis to Pray For

1. Daniel Yergin, *The Prize: The Epic Quest for Oil, Money & Power* (Touchstone, New York, 1992), p. 567.

2. Jerry Taylor and Peter Van Doren, "Gasoline Prices in Perspective," Publication No. 6440, Cato Institute, Washington, DC, June 21, 2006. Available at http://www.cato.org. Click on Publications and search for "6440." Adjusted for inflation and purchasing power, the relative price of gasoline decreased steadily between 1950 and 2000 with only a few small exceptions in addition to its early 1980s excursion.

   Tables of historical gasoline prices may be found in the U.S. Energy Information Administration, Annual Energy Review. Go to http://www.eia.doe.gov/emeu/aer and click on "Petroleum."

3. Jeffrey Ball, "As Gasoline Prices Soar, Americans Resist Major Cuts in Consumption," *Wall Street Journal*, May 1, 2006, p. A1. Reported here is that spending on gasoline amounted to 3 percent of our personal-consumption spending in 2006, down from 5 percent in 1981. Rather than showing us that our oil supply was on the wane, the world's capacity to produce ever more oil in response to the price increases of the late 1970s and early 1980s demonstrated that the oil market was far more robust than fragile.

4. M. King Hubbert, "U.S. Energy Resources, A Review as of 1972," Committee on Interior and Insular Affairs, U.S. Senate, Serial No. 93-40 (92–75), Part 1 (U.S. Government Printing Office, Washington, DC, 1974), p. 65.

   In a recent application of the Hubbert methodology to world coal production, Tadeusz W. Patzec and Gregory D. Croft use oil production data to show why Hubbert's curves actually work. In appendix A, "Why Do Hubbert Cycles Exist?" Patzec and Croft show that a normal distribution curve of remarkable fidelity results when the production of individual oil fields is summed over all oil fields in a given production area. From this result and the central limit theorem of statistics, it can be concluded that each oil field's production is largely random and independent of the others. This remarkable nature of nature is shown for sixty-five separate North Sea and Norwegian Sea oil fields (Figures 21 and 22). The success of Hubbert's famous curve emerges from the sheer complexity and randomness of oil production, plus the fortuitous similarity between Hubbert's original logistic curve and the normal distribution. Tadeusz W. Patzec and Gregory D. Croft, "A Global Coal Production Forecast with Multi-Hubbert Cycle Analysis," *Energy*, Vol. 35, August 2010, pp. 3109–22. Available from ScienceDirect, http://www.sciencedirect.com.

5. As I proceed with this idea, I will continue to use the conventional notion of oil "production" but use "extraction" where it seems appropriate for the point being made.

6. The term *lower forty-eight* is used by the oil industry to mean the contiguous forty-eight states and does not include Alaska. Alaska production peaked in 1988

and will total about 15 billion barrels. Total lower-forty-eight production is now estimated to be about 190 billion barrels, in good agreement with estimates used by Hubbert. Although Alaska was a major oil discovery, it adds less than 10 percent to total U.S. oil production. At the current rate of U.S. consumption, about 20 million barrels per day, Alaska added only about two years' worth of supply. In other words, if the United States wanted to remain independent of imported oil, it would need to discover and place in production one Alaska every two years.

7. Yergin, *The Prize*, p. 567.

8. Yergin, *The Prize*, pp. 514–15, 520–23.

9. The five founding countries of OPEC were Iran, Iraq, Kuwait, Saudi Arabia, and Venezuela.

10. Yergin, *The Prize*, pp. 665–70.

11. Ronald A. Heifetz and Riley M. Sinder, "Political Leadership: Managing the Public's Problem Solving," in Robert B. Reich, ed., *The Power of Public Ideas* (Ballinger, Cambridge, MA, 1988), pp. 179–203. An excellent discussion of all three problem types. The authors summarize the work of the new liturgy this way: "But in situations where the group's values are unclear, the shapes of problems are indistinct, and solutions have yet to be fashioned, success requires shifting the primary locus of work back to the group" (p. 194).

12. It is useful to remember that the character of Cassandra was not wrong about the ploy of the Trojan horse and the final destruction of Troy; she was just not believed.

13. Growth equation assumes continuous compounding and is approximate.

14. Hubbert, "U.S. Energy Resources, A Review as of 1972," pp. 30–31. Curves of world oil production are shown in figures 5 and 6. The fidelity of an activity as complex as the discovery and production of oil to simple exponential curves shows that, like the stock market, complex behavior, even if it defies easy explanation, may be simply described.

15. Albert A. Bartlett, "Forgotten Fundamentals of the Energy Crisis," *American Journal of Physics*, Vol. 46, September 1978, pp. 876–88.

16. A student exercise demonstrating this may be constructed by sticking a row of six bamboo skewers (each about ten inches long and no more than ⅛ inch in diameter) into a block of foam board. Evenly space the skewers about one inch apart or less to get a good effect. Exponential growth may now be shown by placing Cheerios cereal over each skewer. By placing one Cheerio over the first skewer, two over the second, four over the third, and so on, a rising curve of Cheerios may be constructed. The rising curve shows the power of exponential growth and allows the experimenter to easily compare the number of Cheerios on any skewer

with the sum of all the Cheerios preceding it. In each case, the skewer will contain one more Cheerio than all the previous skewers put together. Viewed from the side, the rising columns of Cheerios trace out an exponential curve for which there is no limit until we run out of either Cheerios—or, in our case, oil. Fun math note: although there are many books that talk about Cheerios math for the elementary student, the exponential curve generated here can be used to demonstrate that both the integral and the differential of e^x are e^x. Cheerios calculus!

17. Hubbert, "U.S. Energy Resources, A Review as of 1972," p. 182.

18. Colin J. Campbell and Jean H. Laherrere, "The End of Cheap Oil," *Scientific American*, March 1998, p. 78. Others, such as the Cambridge Energy Research Associates (CERA), claim that more than three trillion barrels remain to be recovered (CERA press release, November 14, 2006). Within this range of one to three trillion barrels of oil remaining, two trillion barrels seems a reasonable upper estimate.

19. Richard A. Kerr, "Splitting the Difference between Oil Pessimists and Optimists," *Science*, November 20, 2009, p. 1048. See also Ibrahim Sami Nashawi, Adel Malallah, and Mohammed Al-Bisharah, "Forecasting World Crude Oil Production Using Multicyclic Hubbert Model," *Energy and Fuels*, Vol. 24, March 18, 2010, pp. 1788–1800. By applying multiple Hubbert curves to oil produced to date plus proven reserves of 1.2 trillion barrels yet to be produced, Ibrahim Sami Nashawi et al. have estimated, based on a country-by-country analysis, that world oil production will peak in 2014. The use of proven reserves is conservative and makes this a conservative calculation for peak oil production. It is important to note that the shape of the oil peak may be pronounced or not, but whether oil peaks or plateaus, it will nevertheless begin a steady decline within decades, if not years.

20. Current members of OPEC outside the Middle East include Algeria, Angola, Ecuador, Libya, Nigeria, and Venezuela. Although Venezuela has about as much oil as Iran, the vast majority of oil remaining in the world, about two-thirds, is in the Middle Eastern countries of Iran, Iraq, Kuwait, Saudi Arabia, and the United Arab Emirates.

21. Richard A. Kerr, "Peak Oil Production May Already Be Here: Outside of OPEC's vast resources, oil production has leveled off, and it's looking like it may never rise again," *Science*, March 25, 2011, pp. 1510–11. Kerr reports that some remain optimistic about non-OPEC production and concludes that "the next 5 years, assuming oil prices remain on the high side, should show who the realists are."

22. Yergin, *The Prize*. Yergin continues to hold this point of view. See Daniel Yergin, *The Quest: Energy, Security, and the Remaking of the Modern World* (Penguin Press, New York, 2011), chapter 11.

23. See note 4 and the work of Patzec and Croft cited there.

24. L. F. Ivanhoe and George G. Leckie, "Global Oil, Gas Fields, Sizes Tallied, Analyzed," *Oil and Gas Journal*, February 15, 1993, pp. 87–91. Percentage of oil fields is calculated based on a world total of 11,514 fields. This is equal to the world number shown by Ivanhoe and Leckie, a total of 41,164 fields, minus the number of very small and smaller fields shown for the U.S. lower forty-eight. Although the United States has 76 percent of the world's oil fields, the vast majority of them are very small and are subtracted here to better represent the United States in the world's oil distribution. The many small fields in the United States are largely a result of its extensive infrastructure of rural roads and electrification. In most parts of the world, such oil would never be recovered.

25. L. F. Ivanhoe and George G. Leckie, "Global Oil, Gas Fields, Sizes Tallied, Analyzed."

26. C. D. Masters, D. H. Root, E. D. Attanasi, "Resource Constraints in Petroleum Production Potential," *Science*, July 12, 1991, pp. 146–52.

27. L. F. Ivanhoe, "Updated Hubbert Curves Analyze World Oil Supply," *World Oil*, November 1996, pp. 91–94. Ivanhoe shows Hubbert curves for known discoveries and projected production and observes that "it is commonly overlooked by economists and the general public that oil must be discovered before it can be produced."

28. Actual question I was asked during the 1990s oil crisis.

29. "Tarred with the Same Brush," The Americas, *Economist*, August 7, 2010, pp. 35–36. Today, Canada's tar sands are the world's dirtiest source of oil, consuming large amounts of water, four barrels per barrel of oil produced, and generating over 80 percent more greenhouse gases than the production of an average barrel of U.S. oil. Oil prices for profitable production range from $60 to $85 per barrel or higher. The *Economist* concludes that the best hope for reduced pollution from this oil source is to either find alternative energy sources or cut consumption. In other words, the best use of Canada's tar sands oil is to leave it in the ground.

30. Philip H. Abelson, "Improved Fossil Energy Technology," *Science*, April 25, 1997, p. 511.

31. Here it is important to distinguish between oil reserves and resources. Reserves describe oil that can be economically recovered over a given period of time from known fields using known methods. Resources are an estimate of the total amount of oil that might be recovered over time. Reserves are conservative estimates based on current exploration and technology; resources are optimistic estimates based on speculation.

32. Roger N. Anderson, "Oil Production in the 21st Century," *Scientific American*, March 1998, p. 86.

33. Anderson, "Oil Production in the 21st Century," p. 90. Current production prices per barrel are from Daniel Yergin, quoted in Jonathan Fahey and Chris Kahn, "Yergin: Only Politics Can Threaten Energy Supplies," Associated Press, October 26, 2011.

34. Paraphrase of actual comment made to me during the 1990s oil crisis.

35. "Astonishing Trove of Oil Is Waiting in Caspian Sea," *Minneapolis Star Tribune*, June 15, 1997, p. A6.

36. Richard A. Kerr, "The Next Oil Crisis Looms Large—and Perhaps Close," *Science*, August 21, 1998, p. 1130.

37. Albert A. Bartlett, "An Analysis of U.S. and World Oil Production Patterns Using Hubbert-Style Curves," *Journal of Mathematical Geology*, Vol. 32, January 2000, pp. 1–17. Numbers very close to Bartlett's may also be obtained from L. F. Ivanhoe, "Future World Oil Supplies: There Is a Finite Limit," *World Oil*, October 1995, figure 3.

38. CERA press release, November 14, 2006. See also Ibrahim Sami Nashawi et al., "Forecasting World Crude Oil Production Using Multicyclic Hubbert Model," *Energy and Fuels*, Vol. 24, March 18, 2010, pp. 1788-1800. As described in note 19 above, by applying multiple Hubbert curves to all oil reserves both produced and yet to be produced, Nashawi et al. have estimated that world oil production will peak in 2014. Adding fifteen years to this conservative estimate would move their peak estimate to 2029, in reasonable agreement with the beginning of the plateau proposed by CERA. Although few deny that oil is finite, the range of opinions as to the actual shape and date of the peak remains large.

39. Increases in system efficiencies can produce more work from less energy, but for any fixed system or technology, half the energy still gets just half the work done. Depending on the application, improvements in energy efficiency and use can provide up to tenfold decreases in energy consumption. Yet, no matter how great the improvement, our need for energy cannot be reduced to zero.

40. However, as energy ultimately degrades to low-temperature heat, it may do more than one useful thing along the way. For example, the steam from a factory's coal-fired boiler may first be used to drive a steam turbine to generate electricity and then, at a lower temperature, to provide process heat for the factory's production line. Finally, after it has condensed to nothing but hot water, it may be used to heat the company's offices.

41. Thomas S. Kuhn, *The Structure of Scientific Revolutions* (University of Chicago Press, Chicago, 1970), p. 77.

42. Brian Halweil, "Grain Harvest Sets Record, but Supplies Still Tight," *Vital Signs 2009* (Worldwatch Institute, Washington, DC, 2009), pp. 12–13. The recent decade-long annual world grain yield of 3 metric tons per hectare reported here was converted to Calorie yield per square meter per day using a conversion fac-

tor of 3,500 Calories per kilogram of grain produced. The capital *C* in Calories is used to distinguish the nutritionist's Calorie from the physicist's calorie, which is 1,000 times smaller.

43. This is the maximum population for a basic diet consisting of staple grains only. Such diets, even with sufficient Calories, present many nutritional problems because they lack critical vitamins and minerals. Moreover, such diets would be devoid of animal products such as meat, milk, eggs, and cheese and would be largely unacceptable to most in the developed world.

   Today, roughly one-half, or three billion, of the earth's people live in absolute poverty on incomes of less than $2 per day. Of these billions, one billion go hungry each day, and more than two billion lack proper nutrition. See Christopher B. Barrett, "Measuring Food Insecurity," *Science*, February 12, 2010, pp. 825–28. One encouraging observation from this special issue of *Science* on food security is that the Green Revolution focused on wheat and rice and not on the critical food crops of Africa, such as sorghum and cassava. A perspective by Gebisa Ejeta supports the view that similar improvements in African agriculture, along with enhanced institutional support, could produce equally good results. Gebisa Ejeta, "African Green Revolution Needn't Be a Mirage," *Science*, February 12, 2010, pp. 831–32. Without vast increases in world agricultural productivity along with improved governance and reduced poverty, it is unlikely we will be able to adequately feed the world's current population of 6.5 billion, much less the 9 billion this special issue of *Science* expects the earth to provide for in 2050.

44. The outlook for natural gas has changed considerably in the last decade. During the 1990s, production matched discoveries, and proven reserves remained fixed at about 170 trillion cubic feet, or about eight years' production at the current rate. In the late 1990s, discoveries began to exceed production, and proven reserves began a net growth rate of about 4 percent a year. This remarkable increase resulted from the application of two existing technologies, horizontal drilling and hydraulic fracturing (fracing or fracking), to newly discovered deposits of deep shale gas. By making it possible to drill down miles and then to turn horizontally another mile or so into shale deposits a few hundred feet thick, such technology has dramatically altered the outlook for natural gas production in the United States. Yet, beyond this success, the process remains controversial, because for many the drilling and fracing process may be permanently damaging water aquifers drilled though to get to the much deeper shale deposits. Nevertheless, it is thought that such deposits could maintain present U.S. gas production for decades to come. Richard A. Kerr, "Natural Gas from Shale Bursts onto the Scene," *Science*, June 25, 2010, pp. 1624–26.

   For general information about the production and use of oil and gas in the United States, see U.S. Energy Information Administration, http://www.eia.gov.

Under the Sources & Uses tab, click on either "Petroleum & Other Liquids" or "Natural Gas," then on either the Petroleum or Natural Gas Explained boxes shown for these fuels. Finally, click on the Data and Statistics tab for detailed numbers. This website changes frequently, so some searching may be required.

45. Keith R. Briffa and Timothy J. Osborn, "Seeing the Wood from the Trees," *Science*, May 7, 1999, pp. 926–27. Authors compare several proxies for northern-hemisphere temperature extending from about 1000 CE to the present. Data show a cooling of about 0.3 degree Fahrenheit ending around 1850, and then, beginning after 1900, a warming of somewhat more than 1 degree Fahrenheit to the present. This *Science* perspective was written by scientists from the Climate Research Unit at the University of East Anglia, Norwich, UK. For a further discussion of their research methodology, see Moises Velasquez-Manoff, "Climategate, Global Warming, and the Tree Rings Divergence Problem," *Christian Science Monitor*, December 14, 2009, http://www.csmonitor.com/Environment /Bright-Green/2009/1215/Climategate-global-warming-and-the-tree-rings -divergence-problem.

46. Kendrick Taylor, "Rapid Climate Change," *American Scientist*, Vol. 87, July–August 1999, pp. 320–27.

47. Wallace S. Broecker, "Thermohaline Circulation, the Achilles Heel of Our Climate System: Will Man-Made CO_2 Upset the Current Balance?" *Science*, November 28, 1997, p. 1588, note 13. The flow rate of the great conveyor is about 15 million cubic meters per second.

48. Richard A. Kerr, "Warming's Unpleasant Surprise: Shivering in the Greenhouse?" *Science*, July 10, 1998, pp. 156–58.

49. The effect of salt on the density of water can be readily demonstrated in your own kitchen by observing how an egg sinks in freshwater, but floats with the addition of salt. Just as the egg floats in your kitchen, the great conveyor sinks in the North Atlantic. Archimedes would be proud.

50. Wallace S. Broecker, "Thermohaline Circulation, the Achilles Heel of Our Climate System: Will Man-Made CO_2 Upset the Current Balance?" *Science*, November 28, 1997, pp. 1582–88.

51. The great conveyor model is but one of several ideas proposed to explain the well-documented phenomenon of rapid climate change. I use it here to illustrate how nonlinear effects can affect the planet and our lives on it. Other ideas hold that rapid climate changes are driven by changes in the atmosphere and originate in the tropics rather than in North Atlantic. See R. B. Alley et al., "Abrupt Climate Change," *Science*, March 28, 2003, pp. 2005–9, and W. S. Broecker, "Does the Trigger for Abrupt Climate Change Reside in the Ocean or in the Atmosphere?" *Science*, June 6, 2003, pp. 1519–22. Alley and colleagues conclude their paper

with this recommendation: "The persistence of some uncertainty regarding future abrupt climate changes argues in favor of actions to improve resiliency and adaptability in economies and ecosystems." Wallace S. Broecker makes a similar plea in a letter to *Science*, "Future Global Warming Scenarios," *Science*, April 16, 2004, p. 388. More directly Broecker states, "Exaggerated scenarios serve only to intensify the existing polarization over global warming. What is needed is not more words but rather a means to shut down CO_2 emissions to the atmosphere." Uncertain situations demand a variety of remedies applied by a variety of people, including all of us.

52. For example, whatever the source of rapid climate change, it must behave in a way that produces threshold behavior. That is, it must behave in a nonlinear way in which, unlike the example of the spring, cause and effect are not proportional. In such "stick and slip" systems, plots of cause versus effect, rather than tracing a single line, trace some sort of open loop. Known as a hysteresis loop, systems with such behavior are not readily reversible without the application of an enhanced force or cause. In this analysis, a crisis to pray for is one with little or no hysteresis. That is, a crisis to pray for is one that may be gradually reversed through the gradual application of remedies to the problem.

53. This metaphor belongs to Wallace Broecker ("The climate system is an angry beast, and we are poking it with sticks"), and I thank him for it. I like it and use it here because it is imaginative and graphic. My only quibble with Broecker is that my beast is not as angry as it is indifferent. It is our work to move beyond our own indifference and to stop poking the beast.

54. If we are to act on global climate change, we must in the end become Bayesian in our thinking. As discussed in chapter 2, Bayesian statistics begins with an estimated probability and calculates whether or not the chance of something being true, or in our case happening, is getting either smaller or larger as time goes by. While standard statistics tells us where we are at the moment, Bayesian statistics tells us how far we have come. And while standard statistics is made subjective at the end by the decision to stop and act, Bayesian statistics is made subjective at the beginning by guessing where we are when we start. For one-time experiments such as global warming Bayesian thinking simply works better. Rather than guessing about when to stop measuring and start acting, Bayesian thinking informs us about whether we are actually gaining or losing ground in our understanding.

For example, while we know a great deal more about global climate today than just a decade ago, have we really learned enough about global climate change to discern today's human-induced global warming from natural fluctuation? For me this question is made moot by today's understanding that the earth's climate emerges from a complex, self-organizing system that has a mind of its own. With built-in multiple triggers for climate change, today's climate could just as well become colder (due to a slowing down of the great conveyor in the North Atlantic) as warmer (due to a persistent El Niño in the tropical Pacific) within the present generation. Still, although we are gaining ground in understanding the chaotic nature of our self-organizing climate, it seems from my armchair perspective that we are losing ground in understanding what to do about it. For me, Bayesian thinking requires a response that is as robust as possible given such uncertainty. Today, Reverend Bayes would probably tell us it's time to stop dithering and start acting on the only remedy to emerge so far—the reduction of greenhouse gases.

9. The Poised Century

1. Discovering what it is of our natural, social, and spiritual abundance that brings well-being to our lives is a highly personal quest requiring a lifetime of discernment. Much of this work will involve recapturing our lost public life and the social capital of our communities. Volunteering, serving in public office, rallying for a good cause, organizing a neighborhood block party, gathering friends for a potluck dinner, participating in a spiritual community—all of these build social capital. For example, see Robert D. Putnam, *Bowling Alone: The Collapse and Revival of American Community* (Simon & Schuster, New York, 2000), pp. 287–95.

2. Just how this mix of calories and protein is achieved is controversial, since competing interests make different recommendations. Industrial countries currently consume about 7.5 ounces of meat per day per person. With meat providing about 7 grams of protein per ounce, people living in the industrial world get, on average, nearly all their protein from meat. By way of comparison, those who advocate for meatless diets cite research showing that if one eats an adequate number of minimally processed nonmeat calories, one will get sufficient protein, and that getting too little protein is in fact difficult. Considering the high inputs of water, feed grain, and antibiotics required for meat production and the benefits of a more moderate diet, our present level of meat consumption in America is hard to justify. For nutrition data, see *The New York Public Library Desk Reference*, 1989, pp. 621–43. For world meat production, see Danielle Nierenberg, "Happier Meals: Rethinking the Global Meat Industry," Worldwatch Paper 171, Worldwatch Institute, September 2005, pp. 7–18. For a discussion of diet and protein, see John Robbins, *Diet for a New America* (H. J. Kramer, Tiburon, CA, 1998), pp. 170–88.

3. This example is of course made possible by the low-cost offshore labor of others. The low cost of my shirt and pants is made possible by exporting their full social cost to the working poor around the world. We need look no farther than to the labels in our own closets to see an international bazaar of low-cost labor—a sobering example of globalization within our reach every morning. As I said in chapter 3, my life is made richer by the labors of the poor. This is neither a moral nor a sustainable way to live. This example further turns on the acceptance of modest fashion. No Wall Street banker would be caught dead in my office clothes, and many teens insist on the same designer labels all their friends wear.

4. Garrett Hardin, "The Tragedy of the Commons," *Science*, December 13, 1968, pp. 1243–48. Hardin gets taken to task by many for being too pessimistic about life in the commons and for his recommendation that "mutual coercion" is required for such arrangements to work. Although Hardin might overstate his case with a call for coercion, the present ruin occurring in the world's oceans as they run out of fish shows that ruin of the commons is real. Hardin's argument that freedom in the commons brings ruin to all is fundamentally correct. The bone of contention should not be that Hardin's fundamental assertion is wrong, but that the idea of freedom itself, particularly freedom in America, must be reconsidered.

   Writing thirty years after his original essay, Hardin said that his "weightiest" omission in writing his original paper was to leave the modifier "unmanaged" out of his description of the commons. Hardin himself struggled with the concept, and after a half dozen revisions continued to revise his thoughts even on the way to the meeting where his essay was first presented. It was in this final edit, with the help of family and friends, that Hardin came to the language that global disaster can best be avoided through "mutual coercion, mutually agreed upon." Garrett Hardin, "Extensions of 'The Tragedy of the Commons,'" *Science*, May 1, 1998, pp. 682–83.

   Most arguments that dismiss Hardin's work seem to focus more on his ideas of "freedom" than management. Hardin's work points to the need to return the work of the people to the people, that is, points to what in this book I call the new liturgy. Hardin tells us that freedom without obligation, though popular, is but a chimera.

5. Elinor Ostrom's Nobel Prize–winning work demonstrated that many commons can be successfully governed through collective action that springs from the freedom of individuals to self-organize into communities of like-minded people. In these communities members live within autonomous arrangements of covenants and sanctions that serve to sustain both their commons and their lives in it. Elinor Ostrom, *Governing the Commons: The Evolution of Institutions for Collective*

Action (Cambridge University Press, New York, 1990). A list of detailed variables that have been found to lead to self-organization in the commons can be found in Elinor Ostrom, "A General Framework for Analyzing Sustainability of Social-Ecological Systems," *Science*, July 24, 2009, pp. 419–22. Ostrom's short list of ten variables (a subset of thirty-four) includes understanding the size, productivity, and value of the commons; the presence of community resources such as entrepreneurial leadership, shared community values, and trust; and, perhaps most important, the capacity of the community to act autonomously.

6. Claiming the opportunities of America's many commons requires the efforts of all. Such work will be led by the self-directed organizations described in chapter 7, with many taking the form of the nonprofit or third-sector organizations as discussed in chapter 5. As Tocqueville told us in chapter 7, "[In the United States] there is no end which the human will despairs of attaining through the combined power of individuals united into a society."

    In a time of unprecedented accumulation of material wealth and growing inequality, the capacity to organize into groups for the common good is America's most essential asset. This is our national abundance, and it ought to be the basis of our national leadership. For many examples of community organizing in the Twin Cities today, see Harry C. Boyte, *The Citizen Solution: How You Can Make a Difference* (Minnesota Historical Society Press, St. Paul, 2008).

7. For example, see Sarah Susanka, *The Not So Big House* (Taunton Press, Newtown, CT, 1998). This was Susanka's first book on rethinking the scale and design of U.S. housing. Others in The Not So Big House series have followed, all worthwhile. In particular, see Sarah Susanka, *The Not So Big Life* (Random House, New York, 2007).

8. Indeed, the bottom half of America's household income does follow such a fractal distribution. A log-log plot of household income shares for 2008 (Table H-2, page 201, note 9) produces a straight line for incomes in the first four quintiles. These income data are census-based and include government transfers such as social security and public assistance. The plot shows that from the first through the fourth quintiles, incomes follow a power law and are arranged in a self-similar or fractal order. These first four quintiles account for 50 percent of the nation's household income. The fifth and last quintile, the top 20 percent of households, receives the remaining 50 percent of the nation's income. Even more, of this 50 percent, the top 5 percent of households receives 43 percent, or 21.5 percent of America's total income. Plotted on same log-log paper as the first four quintiles, the incomes for the top 5 percent and next 15 percent of households show a marked upward departure from the straight line of the first four. The non-linearity of my log-log plot for incomes above the fourth quintile is thought to come from the greater compensation that top earners receive today

as well as from their enhanced capacity to generate capital gains and dividends from investment.

Bringing equity, or fairness, to such income inequality remains a challenge in today's world. One approach would be to straighten such fractal plots of income versus rank through increased taxation of those in the fifth quintile. To achieve this, incomes in the top 5 percent would need to be taxed at a rate of 65 percent, with the next 15 percent taxed at 21 percent. "Tax the rich" has a popular ring today thanks to the outsized incomes of the top earners. As an alternative to enhanced taxation, such curve straightening could also be accomplished by offering to the wealthy the opportunity to fund a variety of organizations supporting the arts, education, research, or venture capital, with the payoff being the accomplishment and the social recognition that come with such generosity.

9. If you doubt the importance of this work, just imagine what our daily life would be like if all of America's low-income workers called in sick for a few weeks. Without clerks or cashiers, our economy would grind to a halt. Without housekeepers and custodians, the place would be a mess. And without farm workers and cooks, we would all be hungry to boot.

10. Today, a negative income tax is provided by the Earned Income Tax Credit established by Congress in 1975. Although it provides a tax refund for most who file for it, wouldn't it be simpler and more affirming to pay people a living wage in the first place?

11. It can be argued that buying a house is itself a good investment. Although real estate can be a good investment, a larger house also has larger attendant costs, such as heating and cooling, maintenance, insurance, and taxes, to say nothing about the costs of decorating and furnishing a larger space, all of which reduce the buyer's ability to save. Many have discovered the easy-to-create, but hard-to-live-with, condition of being "house poor." Although it is frequently stated that our houses are our largest investment, retirement income proportional to one's lifestyle requires actual plus imputed savings equal to at least three to five times the value of one's house (imputed savings are the savings equivalent required to provide defined benefit income such as social security). Such retirement security requires a lifetime of prudent savings that begins with the ability to discern between what one can afford to buy in contrast to what one can afford to own. Because it will limit your ability to save, always question any Realtor or banker who tells you to buy the biggest house you can afford.

12. Although our belief in constant growth remains unabated, it has certainly not gone unchallenged. Kenneth Boulding, past president of the American Economic Association, put it this way: "Only madmen and economists believe in perpetual exponential growth." Quoted in Garrett Hardin, *Living within Limits: Ecology,*

Economics, and Population Taboos (Oxford University Press, New York, 1993), p. 191. For additional quotes on economic growth, ranging from its necessity to its folly, see sidebar on page 190.

13. In Minnesota, while population and boat registrations have increased in the past two decades, actual boat use has remained stable. In a recent statewide survey, the most frequently cited reason for reduced participation in outdoor recreation was "I don't have enough time." Although survey participants reported lakes and rivers as more crowded, it is believed that this perception rises from the growing number of larger and more powerful boats, as well as more boat riding than fishing. Minnesota Department of Natural Resources presentation, St. Paul, January 23, 2006.

    My own urban dockside and launch-ramp conversations confirm these data, as other sailors ask us about the easy pleasure of sailing our dinghy on a nearby city lake and then speak of their own lack of time for getting out on more distant waters with their own larger boats.

14. I thank the late M. Scott Peck for this paradox. Public lecture, Minneapolis, April 9, 1988.

15. Huston Smith, *The Religions of Man* (Harper & Row, New York, 1986), p. 126.

16. The eight right actions of Buddha's Eightfold Path are right knowledge, right aspiration, right speech, right behavior, right livelihood, right effort, right mindfulness, and right absorption. See Smith, *The Religions of Man*, pp. 147–66.

17. E. F. Schumacher, in *Small Is Beautiful*, compares what he calls Buddhist economics with modern economics this way: "The former, in short, tries to maximize human satisfactions by the optimal pattern of consumption, while the latter tries to maximize consumption by the optimal pattern of productive effort." E. F. Schumacher, *Small Is Beautiful: Economics As If People Mattered* (Harper & Row, New York, 1989), p. 61.

18. Here I am hoist with my own petard. Stock indexing is not something that we can all do, because if everyone did, there would be no average to average to. If everyone indexed, an index would become impossible to calculate, and the whole thing would mathematically, if not literally, blow up. In practice, however, the system does work, since only about 20 percent of the market is indexed. Even though the stock market consistently demonstrates a powerful force of regression to the mean, most investors believe that the market can be beat and is theirs to profit from. Over the short term many do profit, but just as many don't. Yet because most all who "play the market" profit at some time, and sometimes handsomely, the incentive to continue such investing remains irresistible. On the average, everyone does about the same, except that those who index do it with less work, and most important, less expense.

Beyond this we must distinguish between savings and investment. If we are going to move from an exponentially growing economy to a steady-state or low-growth economy, the way we save for retirement will need to change. No longer will we be able to depend on the perpetual growth of the economy and the stock market for retirement savings. The most we could expect from a steady-state market would be prices that keep up with inflation and grow in value due to earnings reinvestment. For an economy of limited growth in a finite world, prudent retirement planning will require vastly enhanced savings, broad diversification, and reduced expectations.

19. In this case, the company's expectations are an example of the tragedy of the commons in time. Here the workers' time is used to the benefit of the business while the social commons of the worker's family and community suffer. Such use of the commons in time is rampant in our current economy; from increased expectations for unpaid work to endless telephone trees, to interminable waits on computer help lines, to "some assembly required" consumer products, the gratuitous use of the worker's and customer's time has become ubiquitous.

20. This, of course, assumes that one partner can earn a family income working forty hours per week. Although we claim to value the family in the United States, many aspects of our economy give just the opposite message.

21. Ivan Illich, *Tools for Conviviality* (Heyday Books, Berkeley, 1973). Most fundamentally this is called the remedy of agency. While conservatives call it personal responsibility and progressives frame it as claiming one's power, both groups are calling for all of us to claim our agency or capacity to act. If we are to make it through the poised century, we will clearly need leadership based on the development of personal agency, based on returning the work of citizenship to the people of the nation and our acceptance of that work, or based on what I call the new liturgy, the work of the people. For multiple examples of agency in action, see Boyte, *The Citizen Solution*. See also the remedies of chapter 10.

22. Sidewalks are particularly convivial when they are used to walk to a convivial school in a convivial neighborhood. My belief is that the single most effective remedy we could offer our most vulnerable schools and neighborhoods is that all children through the sixth grade would live within a safe walk or bike ride from a neighborhood school. Success at this would be a measure of many great accomplishments, of which the greatest would be the development of convivial neighborhoods and the education of convivial citizens.

23. Walter Brueggemann, *Texts Under Negotiation: The Bible and Postmodern Imagination* (Fortress Press, Minneapolis, 1993), p. 20.

24. Even on a camping trip in the wild, a cup of hot coffee requires the destructive burning of dry wood.

25.   When electrical power is used to heat a house directly, even if it is used with 100
      percent efficiency as with an electric space heater, the overall efficiency is still
      no more than that of the power plant. Since most power plants have an overall
      efficiency of about 40 percent, directly burning fuel in an efficient home furnace
      is still a better choice for a simple combustion heating system. However, even a 90
      percent efficient furnace, because of its high flame temperature, has a so-called
      second-law efficiency of only 10 percent. That is, compared to an ideal second-
      law heating system, a furnace produces only 10 percent of the energy available
      from the high temperature of the furnace flame. This low efficiency can be sub-
      stantially increased through the use of a heat pump system that delivers not only
      the energy required to power it, but also additional heat extracted from the envi-
      ronment surrounding the house. Ideally, such a system can reduce the overall
      amount of electricity required to heat a house by a factor of three or more. For
      further analysis and examples, see *Efficient Use of Energy*, American Institute of
      Physics Conference Proceedings No. 25, series editor Hugh C. Wolfe, American
      Institute of Physics, New York, 1975.

      Again, as with solar heating systems, capital costs for heat pumps are high,
      so they too need to be compared with the costs of conservation. Because internal
      heat gains from occupying a well-insulated space lower the outside temperature
      for which heating is required, they also reduce heating demand and, in the case
      of air-to-air heat pumps, system efficiency as well. Due to such interactions, heat
      pump design requires a careful analysis to make sure that capital expenses are
      properly allocated between providing and conserving energy. This is yet another
      example of Buddha economics and the tyranny of time and the low, flat curve (see
      chapter 4).

      High second-law efficiencies are particularly achievable for manufacturing
      businesses that require both electrical power and process heat. By using a fuel's
      high-temperature heat to generate electricity and then using the resulting low-
      temperature "waste" heat as process heat, second-law efficiencies may be greatly
      enhanced.

10. Sing a New Song

1.   Although this idea has been offered by many, it still remains outside the realm
     of policymakers and the public. A country with a growing GDWB is growing its
     greatest asset, its people.

2.   Producing a pound of feedlot beef requires seven pounds of grain, about three
     times that required to produce a pound of chicken. Lester R. Brown, Gary Gard-

ner, and Brian Halweil, "Beyond Malthus: Sixteen Dimensions of the Population Problem," Worldwatch Paper 143, Worldwatch Institute, September 1998, pp. 55–57. Beef ought to be consumed for what it is, a high-input indulgence. Having said this, my favorite summer indulgence is still a grilled rib eye steak, fresh sweet corn, and a Beefeater martini. But please make the rib eye grass fed, and serve me the corn.

3. Rebecca Smith, "U.S. Foresees Thinner Cushion of Coal," *Wall Street Journal*, June 8, 2010. See also James A. Luppens et al., "Assessment of Coal Geology, Resources, and Reserves in the Gillett Coalfield, Powder River Basin, Wyoming," U.S. Geological Survey Open-File Report 2008-1202, 2008.

4. Tadeusz W. Patzec and Gregory D. Croft, "A Global Coal Production Forecast with Multi-Hubbert Cycle Analysis," *Energy*, Vol. 35, August 2010, pp. 3109–22. Available from ScienceDirect, http://www.sciencedirect.com.

5. Richard A. Kerr, "Natural Gas from Shale Bursts onto the Scene," *Science*, June 25, 2010, pp. 1624–26. See page 227, note 44, for further discussion of this fuel's potential and problems.

6. It should be noted that although hydrogen gets attention bordering on ballyhoo, it is not a primary energy resource, but rather a manufactured fuel (produced by the electrolysis of water using wind-generated electricity, for example). Because hydrogen is a carrier of energy that requires energy to produce, it is not an energy resource but, like electricity, a means for energy transmission. Since our greatest challenge today is to develop new energy resources, it is premature to develop hydrogen, or "the hydrogen economy," until further experience with alternative energy resources and their applications demonstrate that using hydrogen as a primary fuel is really worth it. Far better than using hydrogen as an extraordinarily low-density primary fuel would be using it as a chemical feedstock, along with carbon from the atmosphere, to produce high-density liquid fuels for transportation. The easiest and best way to transport and use hydrogen is to hook it up with some recycled carbon.

7. Robert Hargraves and Ralph Moir, "Liquid Fluoride Thorium Reactors," *American Scientist*, July–August 2010. In this review Hargraves and Moir make a compelling case for thorium as a nuclear fuel.

8. To understand the absolutely monumental amount of new science that went into America's wartime nuclear program, see Richard Rhodes, *The Making of the Atomic Bomb* (Simon & Schuster, New York, 1986).

9. The term *U-233* means that this form of uranium has a total of 233 protons and neutrons in its nucleus. Because U-233 has 92 protons (this is what makes it uranium) it has 233 minus 92 or 141 neutrons. Atoms that have the same number of protons but differ in their number of neutrons are called isotopes of that atom.

Thus U-233 is an isotope of uranium that has 92 protons and 141 neutrons. Naturally occurring uranium contains two isotopes, U-238 mixed with 0.7 percent of U-235. The discovery that U-235 could be split through neutron absorption to yield nuclear energy marked a turning point in the years just before World War II and gave the nations of the world the capacity to build weapons of previously unimaginable power.

An atom is fertile if it can be converted to a fissionable atom by neutron absorption. A fissionable atom is one that can be split into two smaller atoms, fission products, again by neutron absorption. Because the total mass of the resulting fission products is less than the total mass of the original atom, the conservation of mass and energy requires the fission products to carry off the missing mass in the form of kinetic energy. This energy is materialized in the form of enormous amounts of heat.

By now you may have asked yourself about the source of neutrons required to transform thorium into U-233. Interestingly enough, they come from the fission of the U-233 itself! As U-233 splits into two smaller atoms, it produces lots of heat and a few neutrons, enough not only to keep the fission reaction going, but also to breed new U-233 from plain ordinary thorium. This leads to the final question: where do the very first neutrons come from that make the very first U-233? These neutrons must come from an external source and could be supplied by current uranium reactor waste, existing stores of weapons materials, or even a compact particle accelerator or "atom smasher."

10. The transmutation of thorium to U-233 follows the same fertile-to-fissile process as the transmutation of U-238 to plutonium, with the important difference that thorium leads to a superior power reactor fuel, whereas uranium leads to an effective bomb material. The choice between these material facts ought not to be taken lightly. Although nuclear weapons may keep the peace for some, the international development of energy from thorium would bring abundance and peace to many more.

11. Over a period of nearly five years, ending in 1969, researchers at the Oak Ridge National Laboratory successfully demonstrated the fundamental working principles of using thorium as a nuclear reactor fuel. Hargraves and Moir, "Liquid Fluoride Thorium Reactors."

12. Although it is not impossible to build a nuclear weapon using U-233, it is far more difficult than other options that are available to the determined terrorist. Most important is that the worldwide adoption of thorium and U-233 for electrical power generation would leave just a single use for natural uranium, the fabrication of nuclear weapons. The delegitimization of uranium as a nuclear fuel would be a powerful tool for containing nuclear proliferation.

13. Since a very large amount of energy can be got from just a small amount of mass, little mass is required to power even a large, 1000-megawatt power plant for an entire year. Indeed, Einstein's famous equation, $E = mc^2$, shows us that such a power plant needs to convert just twelve ounces of mass to energy annually. Given this, a ton of fuel produces, but for twelve ounces, a ton of waste.

14. Although thorium is slightly radioactive, its alpha-particle radiation is readily shielded by a few inches of air or a single sheet of aluminum foil. An annual pickup load of thorium going through your town clearly trumps a daily trainload of coal.

15. Currently a variety of ambient and high-temperature methods are being examined for the production of these basic feedstocks. See Kevin Bullis, "Solar-Power Breakthrough," *MIT Technology Review*, July 31, 2008, available at http://www .technologyreview.com/energy/21155; Kevin Bullis, "Making Gasoline from Carbon Dioxide," *MIT Technology Review*, April 25, 2007, available at http://www .technologyreview.com/energy/18582; and William C. Chueh et al., "High-Flux Solar-Driven Thermochemical Dissociation of CO_2 and H_2O Using Nonstoichiometric Ceria," *Science*, December 24, 2010, pp. 1797–1800. For news on the work of Chueh et al., see "New Reactor Paves the Way for Efficiently Producing Fuel from Sunlight," Caltech press release, January 19, 2011.

16. This relationship assumes that the lifetime energy cost goes as the inverse of the cost of efficiency.

17. Further research is likely to show that the costs and benefits of going forward with thorium are too attractive not to be pursued by private capital. Such recapitalization of the power industry will produce major dislocations in the coal mining and nuclear fuel fabrication businesses. In fact, with a sufficient infusion of private capital, an effective thorium program could displace both of these industries within a few decades. Economist Joseph Schumpeter spoke of "gales of creative destruction" that blow through economies as one technology replaces another. Such is the nature of the innovation demanded by today's circumstances. While the American coal industry winds down over the next decade or two, those whose business it is to fabricate nuclear fuel rods could turn their attention to providing starter fuel for thorium reactors or to getting into the thorium reactor business themselves.

All of this depends on bringing the development of the molten-salt thorium reactor to the forefront of American energy research. While molten-salt technology remains on the Generation IV International Forum short list as a technology worthy of consideration, such considerations are so uncertain and distant as to be virtually meaningless in terms of the problems at hand. With Oak Ridge National Laboratory—where a gratifyingly successful molten-salt

thorium reactor was demonstrated in the 1960s—now named as the lead organization for the examination of new nuclear options for America, it is simply
time to give thorium a good second look.

For a complete list of the six reactor designs that constitute the Generation
IV short list, see "Nuclear's Next Generation," *Economist*, December 10, 2009. To
develop the Generation IV uranium designs described here before fully developing what amounts to a Generation II thorium design is to miss an opportunity to show the American public that safe, low-waste, and cost-effective nuclear
power is far more than wishful thinking. Have we not now come far enough in
our understanding of what the public demands of nuclear power to reconsider
what was so long ago abandoned in the expediency of war? The issues of the day
are far too pressing to develop advanced uranium options while what could well
be a far superior technology languishes.

Finally, this will require Wall Street to return from its recent excursion into
impenetrable fantasy products to its noble purpose of capital formation. There is
plenty of money in America to make this happen. All that is required are investors who value the future and communal and the long-range opportunities they
offer for the creation of real wealth.

18. It is important to distinguish between the vocation practiced and the work done.
    Depending on one's disposition to the common good, people of any vocation may
    practice that vocation as either rent seekers or entrepreneurs. In reality, most of
    us are some of each. The healing physician or the problem-solving lawyer must
    still receive some compensation for their work, even if it is just a chicken for sup-
    per. One way to distinguish the difference between our own actions as either rent
    seekers or entrepreneurs is to examine the compassion, our capacity to suffer
    with the other, that we bring to our work.

19. Federal spending for 2010 included $745 billion in cash paid to social security
    recipients and $393 billion in defense contract opportunities open to the private
    sector. Find tables for each department at the Office of Management and Budget
    at http://www.whitehouse.gov/omb/overview.

20. Steven D. Levitt and Stephen J. Dubner, *Freakonomics: A Rogue Economist
    Explores the Hidden Side of Everything* (William Morrow, New York, 2005), p. 12.

21. Peter H. Lindert, *Growing Public: Social Spending and Economic Growth Since
    the Eighteenth Century* (Cambridge University Press, New York, 2004).

22. Brian K. Bucks et al., "Changes in U.S. Family Finances from 2004 to 2007: Evi-
    dence from the Survey of Consumer Finances," *Federal Reserve Bulletin*, February
    2009, available at http://www.federalreserve.gov/pubs/bulletin/2009.

INDEX

abortion, 53

Adam and Eve, 99–102

addiction to more, 3–15; bringing
meaning to suffering, 8–10;
choices that serve the immediate
and personal, 7–8, 9–10, 25–26,
198n6; and hard work of laziness,
7–8, 11, 12, 198n7; inventions
that hold promise of free energy,
3–6, 197n1; new products
and meaningless illusions of
choice, 14–15, 199n17; suffering
and recovery, 10–11; wealth/
possessions and happiness, 13–14,
45–46, 179, 199nn13–14, 218n10;
and the work of discernment, 6–8,
11, 14–15. *See also* material goods
and consumption

agency, personal, 235n21

agrarian communities, pre-industrial,
39, 204n5

agricultural sector: employment/
workforce, 204n6, 210n6;
productivity, 69, 204n6, 227n43;
and world food security, 148,
203n23, 227n43

alchemy. *See* new alchemy

Alley, R. B., 228–29n51

Anselm of Canterbury, St., 96

ant colonies, 113–15, 116, 218n7

antidepressants, 11

Apostles' Creed, 86

Arian controversy, 97

Aslett, Don, 200n5

Associated General Contractors of
America, 65

associations, formation of, 68, 115,
209n1

atonement theologies, 92, 93, 95–99

Attanasi, E. D., 142

Attis, myth of, 94

Augustine of Hippo, 97–99, 102

self-organization (*continued*)
  commons/the common good, 159,
    231–32n5, 232n6; environmental
    consequences of bringing order
    to a local environment, 116–17,
    218n7; metaphor of the ant
    colony, 113–15, 116, 218n7;
    metaphors and paradigms, 116;
    metaphors of local order and
    leaderless organizations, 116–19;
    metaphors of local order under
    the direction of common rules,
    113–16; and threefold work of the
    servant leader, 117–19
servant leadership, 36, 67–84; and
    community problem solving,
    78–82; the courage required,
    76; and group dialogue, 80–82;
    and Jesus' teachings, 92–93; and
    the new liturgy, 71–75, 169; and
    participation, 74; and personal
    responsibility in one's community,
    84; and power, 78–79; and self-
    organization, 117–19; and the
    shadow, 75–77; and success/
    failure, 73–74; and the third
    sector (nonprofit sector), 67–84,
    169; the work of, 72–76, 78–79,
    80–82, 92, 117–19. *See also*
    nonprofit sector (third sector)
service workers, 40–42, 44–45, 181,
    210n7; and economic docetism,
    217n45; and a living minimum
    wage, 44, 161–62, 210n7; and
    social cost of entropy, 160–62,
    233n9. *See also* low-wage workers
shadow: and followership, 76–77;
    Jungian, 212n17; and servant
    leadership, 75–77
Shaw, George Bernard, 51, 85
shopping malls, 168
sidewalks, 168, 235n22
Sinder, Riley M., 223n11
singing the national anthem, 176–77

skills and equality, conventional
    wisdom about, 42
Slater, Philip, 3
Smith, Adam, 40, 45, 59, 164, 189
social capital, 25, 31–32, 230n1; and
    child rearing, 32; and crime,
    31–32, 201–2n15, 203n25; and
    income inequality, 25, 31–32,
    201–2n15, 203n25
solar energy, 17, 119, 185–86, 199n1,
    199–200n2, 236n25
solar system, 125–27
Sommers, Sumner, 3–4, 20, 197n1
Soros, George, 154
Southeast Asian community of the
    Twin Cities, 127–28, 220n23
space shuttle *Challenger*, 61–62
"The Star-Spangled Banner," 176–77
stock market: and Buddha economics,
    165, 234–35n18; scaleless, fractal
    behavior in, 122–23, 218–19n15
The Structure of Scientific Revolutions
    (Kuhn), 146
substitutionary atonement, 92, 93,
    95–99
success, personal characteristics
    necessary for, 221n27
suffering: addictions and recovery, 10–
    11; avoidance through therapies
    and drugs, 11; bringing meaning
    to, 8–10; and hard work of
    laziness, 7–8, 198n7; and meaning
    of Jesus' death on the cross, 91–93
superconductors, 198n4
Sussman, Gerald, 125
Sykes, Charles J., 207n3

tax code, U.S., 44, 163, 169, 206–7n18,
    232–33n8; attractiveness of a
    flat-tax system, 44, 206–7n18;
    and conservative frames of
    thinking that favor the immediate
    and personal, 198n6; entropy
    taxes, 163; estimated costs of tax

11833128R00152

Made in the USA
Charleston, SC
23 March 2012